D0438410

LIVING BIOGRAPHIES OF
Famous Novelists

LIVING BIOGRAPHIES OF
FAMOUS
NOVELISTS

By HENRY THOMAS AND
DANA LEE THOMAS

Illustrations by
GORDON ROSS

BOOK LEAGUE OF AMERICA

New York

PUBLISHED BY THE BLAKISTON COMPANY, PHILADELPHIA
DISTRIBUTED BY BOOK LEAGUE OF AMERICA

COPYRIGHT, 1943
BY GARDEN CITY PUBLISHING CO., INC.

PRINTED IN THE UNITED STATES OF AMERICA

Contents

CONTENTS

Introduction

WHEN THE MINOR POET, Walter Scott, entered upon his career as a major novelist, he was ashamed of his new role. "I shall not own *Waverley,*" he wrote. "I am not sure it would be considered quite decorous for me, as a Clerk of the Courts, to write novels." Fiction was in his day regarded as a stepchild of the Muses. And a rather unlovely stepchild—the ugly duckling of the literary family. "It is neither fish nor flesh nor red herring," wrote the editor of the *Edinburgh Review*. "It has no moral value, because it is too entertaining."

Today, however, fiction has come into its own. For it has given us masterpieces which rank with the noblest types of literature. The modern novel even on its lower levels is a magic carpet which transports us into blessed forgetfulness—a vital tonic for these days. On its higher levels it is an exposition of philosophic thought presented in dramatic form. At its best it is a prose reincarnation of the ancient epic poem. "Every great novel," said Emerson, "is a debtor to Homer." Like the poems of Homer, the novel at its highest is not only an epitome of philosophy as applied to life; it is a form of literature which includes all the other forms—

poetry, drama, history, biography, science, sociology, politics, adventure, religion and art. The great novel today—and this is true of the great novel of any other day—is an interpretative picture of Man. An *inclusive* picture of his body, his mind, his soul.

And it is something in addition to all this. It is a revealing picture of *one man*—the novelist. The best part of the story of any novel is the story of the novelist.

In telling the story of each of the novelists included in this book, it has been our purpose to depict not only the *outer man*, as seen through the facts of his life, but also the *inner man*, as seen through the thoughts of his mind. And it has been our delight to discover that every great novelist, when viewed from this double angle, is himself the hero of a great novel.

H. T.
D. L. T.

BOCCACCIO

Important Works by Boccaccio

Filocolo   *Amorosa Visione*
Filostrato   *Decameron*
Teseide   *Ameto*
Fiammetta   *Corbaccio*
                              Life of Dante

Giovanni Boccaccio

1313–1375

THEY called him "Giovanni the Tranquil," because of his ability to maintain his cheerful good humor in the face of misfortune. And he was blessed with the rare power to transfer his cheerfulness to others. Finding himself in a society of women bored with the monotony of life, he set himself to the task of amusing them out of their boredom. And he found that there was nothing in the world more amusing than a good love story. A woman's greatest joy, he noticed, was to play with the fires of passion. But if she was afraid of burning her fingers, she took an almost equal joy in reading about others who had played with these fires. This "loving by proxy," he observed, produced almost all the thrills but presented none of the dangers of love at first hand. "What the adventurous women do, their less adventurous sisters love to imagine themselves to be doing." And thus Boccaccio, in his effort to feed the imagination of his less adventurous sisters, became the inventor of the modern novel.

Boccaccio's novels in miniature are as picturesque, in their infinite variety, as an Italian landscape. Moonlight moods of silver laughter, meadows of serene beauty, headlong brooks of dashing humor, sudden twists of the road and revelations of unexpected splendors, storms of jealous rage, passing clouds of momentary sadness, and the all-embracing sun of universal good-fellowship—these are the elements out of which he creates his stories. His is a wide-awake world bathed in the glory of the midday sun. A medieval landscape teeming with well-rounded and full-blooded figures—men and women who talk so naturally and who love so lustily that we can still see and hear and enjoy them across the centuries that separate their world from ours. Boccaccio reproduced so faithful a mirror of life that a critic once remarked of him: "When God created Giovanni, He doubled creation."

II

GIOVANNI BOCCACCIO, the natural son of a Florentine merchant, was born in the religious age of Dante (1313). Educated in the mysticism of the church, he soon gave it up for the realism of life. His formal schooling was perfunctory. A mere taste of the classics, and then he was apprenticed—at the age of ten—to a Parisian businessman. A few years later he became a commercial traveler for his father. But he had an insatiable love for reading and a hearty disinclination for peddling. "The young scamp," complained his father, "buys more books than he sells goods." A student by instinct, he acquired a knowledge of literature superior to that of most of the university graduates of his day. And he familiarized himself not only with literature but with life. He had become equally proficient in writing verses and in making love. He was passionately fond of the society of books, and just as passionately fond of the society of women. As for the Boccaccio business, "let my father attend to it—he has a goldstream in his veins, but I have red blood."

His father, disappointed in his effort to turn his son into a businessman, was now determined to turn him into a lawyer. He sent him to the University of Naples. Here Giovanni began to apply himself diligently—to everything but his legal studies. Receiving an adequate allowance from his father, he set out to familiarize himself with all the unfamiliar fruits of knowledge. Especially the *forbidden* fruits. The more serious young men of his day, under the influence of Dante, were delving into the mysteries of Hell and Purgatory and Heaven. Boccaccio added to this curriculum of the three divine mysteries a fourth—to him the more interesting because it was the more human—the mystery of the earth. Dante and Petrarch had directed the attention of the world to the spiritual loves of Beatrice and Laura. Boccaccio turned his eyes—and his heart—to the material love of Maria, the natural daughter of King Robert of Sicily. He was twenty-eight years old when he became entangled in this love affair. Maria was already married; but in the easy virtue of Boccaccio's world a legal husband was but a minor obstacle to an illegal lover. He gave her the poetical name, *Fiammetta* (Little Flame), and he allowed himself recklessly to be warmed at the stolen fire of her affection. But he more than repaid her for her favors. He wrote a novel named after her, and he immortalized her as one of the leading characters in his *Decameron*.

A devotee of the here and now, he was yet—true child of his age—profoundly interested in the hereafter. He wrote a biography of Dante. But the book was a failure. Boccaccio was too deeply immersed in the *human* comedy to understand Dante's *Divine* Comedy. He was spiritually too blind to get a clear picture of the man he was trying to describe. He admired Dante's poetry, but he was indifferent to his theology. In his effort to reproduce the fire of Dante's religion, he succeeded merely in raising a smoke-screen of hazy mysticism. He referred to theology as "the poetry of God." But since he was skeptical about the existence of God, he had his doubts about the reality of His poetry. Boccaccio's *Life of Dante* strikes a beautiful note in Italian literature. But it is an *indistinct* note. It is an attempted glorification of the medieval belief written by a man who was at heart a disbeliever.

Following his *Life of Dante,* Boccaccio made several other literary attempts—and continued to strike an indistinct note. The style of his day was heavy and artificial and ornate. But Boccaccio was simple and unaffected and sincere. When he tried to put on airs, like his contemporaries, he failed. The pretentious prose and the bombastic poetry of his day sounded strange in his laughter-loving mouth. He wrote a long and learned romantic novel, *Filocolo,* which meanders like a long and sluggish river between banks of heavy clay. It is utterly devoid of any charm. Boccaccio had not as yet learned to write, as he talked, in a wholesome and natural style. He was too prone to tangle himself up into the intricacies of pedantic phraseology such as the following, "People in the aurora of life who have set the sails of their roving minds to the winds which float from the golden fanning feathers of the young son of Cytherea"—when all he wanted to say was, "Young people in love." In *Filocolo* the evening never comes quietly, but descends with a blare of trumpets and a flare of the setting sun as "the eager horses of Apollo, hot from their diurnal stress, plunge their steaming bodies into the oceanic waters of the West." The characters in this story are monstrosities who never speak to us in a natural voice but always shout at us through a megaphone. They cannot ask for a drink of water without delivering a long and flowery oration about their thirst. Boccaccio's language is still garish and unwieldy. He imitates his inferior predecessors instead of expressing his own superior self. He prefers the awkward Greek or Latin compound to the simple Italian equivalent. In *Filocolo,* the clumsy prototype of the modern novel, Boccaccio reveals himself as a first-rate classical scholar but a second-rate romantic poet.

Yet *Filocolo,* for all its clumsiness, was a financial success. The world was ready for fiction. Boccaccio had struck a new note in literature, and the public found it to its taste. Encouraged by the popularity of his prose romance, he now attempted a romance in verse. This book, the *Teseide,* an epic poem modeled roughly after Virgil's *Aeneid,* was as successful—and as lifeless—as *Filocolo.* It was a book of heroes written by a man who himself was a disbeliever in heroics. The *Teseide* is a magnificent but dead panorama—an ancient and beautiful pageant turned to stone.

There is no movement in it, and no life. It has all the fine in-gredients of a poem—except poetry. The literary ability is there, but the spark of enthusiasm is lacking.

Little by little, however, Boccaccio was learning to write with his heart as well as with his head. His next book, the *Filostrato,* came a little closer to the life of Boccaccio's day. In this book Boccaccio tells the story of Troilus and Cressida; and here for the first time he gives us two characters who have ancient names but modern minds. Their love is a healthy and earthly passion, stripped of all the rhetorical bombast and sickly mysticism that petrified the feelings of Boccaccio's earlier characters. Boccaccio has now returned from his excursions into literature. He has settled down to study life. He has shifted his gaze from marble statues to living people. People whom he knows most intimately and likes best. Having groped in the dark for a number of years, Boccaccio is now at last finding himself. We are here beginning to get glimpses of the gay satirist, the good-natured philosopher who has learned to laugh *with* men instead of laughing *at* them. He jabs them with his pungent wit; and then, fearful that he may have hurt them, he caresses them with his gentle humor. As we steer our course toward an appreciation of the genius of Boccaccio, we feel that in *Filostrato* we are approaching closer to the land. We already see a few scattered leaves and branches floating toward us from the magical groves of his later genius. We hear the voice of the real Boccaccio, the future creator of the *Decameron,* speaking to us in the following apostrophe to love: "Oh to think of the sad misers who find fault with lovers and who insist that it is better to make money than to make love! Let them ask themselves whether the hoardings of a lifetime have ever brought them as much pleasure as a single moment of love. They will answer, 'yes,' and they will not be telling the truth. They will laugh at love and call it a 'painful madness.' But while they gather their money, they allow the real essence of joy to slip from their fingers. Their money may be gone in an hour; but love, once tasted, is a joy forever. May God bring the misers to grief;

and may the money they have scraped together be given to lovers!"

Boccaccio the scholar is gradually becoming transformed into Giovanni the poet. He is getting ready to renounce his allegiance to Apollo, the God of Learning, and to adopt the religion of Venus, the Goddess of Love. In his next book, *Amorosa Visione,* we see a further step in this direction. This book, though inspired by Dante's poem, is yet a distinct departure from the master's "abstract mirror of a visionary heaven." On the contrary, it is a very concrete mirror of a realistic earth. Dante rises from the flesh to the spirit. Boccaccio descends from the spirit to the flesh. And in this descent, he becomes less unintelligibly sublime but more understandingly human. Boccaccio's women of the world are more interesting, because they are less perfect, than Dante's angels of Paradise. While Dante's angels arouse our admiration, Boccaccio's women incite our compassion. "How like ourselves they are, and therefore how lovable!" Boccaccio proclaims a new gospel—the gospel of human love. "Love is no longer a sin, but a joy."

Boccaccio is learning to depict "the eternal feminine" in all her wayward and sinful charm. He disperses the halo of sentimental chivalry with which the women of his generation have been surrounded, and he reveals to us not only the innocent speeches of their lips but the not quite so innocent thoughts of their minds. In the following sonnet—translated by Dante Gabriel Rossetti—we get one of the first true-to-life pictures of the Italian woman in the fourteenth century:

By a clear well, within a little field
Full of green grass and flowers of every hue,
Sat three young girls, relating (as I knew)
Their loves. And each had twined a bough to shield
Her lovely face; and the green leaves did yield
The golden hair their shadow; while the two
Sweet colors mingled, both blown lightly through
With a soft wind that ever stirred and stilled.

[8]

After a little while one of them said
(I heard her), "Think! If, ere the next hour struck,
Each of our lovers should come here today,
Think you that we should fly or be afraid?"
To whom the others answered, "From such luck
A girl would be a fool to run away."

This frank avowal of a natural emotion marks the opening chord in the realistic symphony—many critics would call it the realistic *cacophony*—of modern literature.

Boccaccio strikes another and even clearer note of realistic frankness in his *Corbaccio*. The poet has been jilted by a merry widow. His first impulse is to stab himself with his dagger. But he is too much in love with life, and so he decides upon the wiser plan to stab his faithless lady with the dagger of his wit. The idea of the story is somewhat vulgar, but the satire is good. Boccaccio is getting closer and closer to the spirit of the *Decameron*.

III

IN THE *Decameron*, Boccaccio finds himself at last perfectly at home. The world of the *Decameron* is *his* world. The characters in these stories—like the characters in real life—have stopped analyzing themselves and have begun to enjoy themselves. They not only *think* freely, but they *act* freely. Their outlook on life is as frank as it is frivolous. Professing no mission to cure the evils of the world, they are content to shut their eyes to these evils. They subscribe to but a single commandment—*live and let live*. On the one hand, they have no desire to sacrifice themselves for others; but on the other hand, they have no desire to sacrifice others for themselves. They have shed their medieval fanaticism, and along with it they have also shed their medieval intolerance. They are moved by no crusading spirit. They ask neither to convert nor to be converted. They are equally unconcerned either with the past or with the future. They are ready to trade the memories of yesterday and the promises of tomorrow for the pleasures of today. Their attitude is well depicted in one of their favorite stories. When Diogenes met Alexander, he tried to upbraid him for the foolishness of his ambition. "After you have conquered Athens," said the philosopher, "what then?"

"I will conquer Persia."

"And after Persia?"

"I will conquer Egypt."

"And after Egypt?"

"I will conquer the world."

"And after you have conquered the world?"

"I will take it easy and enjoy myself."

"Then why," asked Diogenes, "can't you take it easy and enjoy yourself now?"

The characters in the *Decameron* are all bent upon taking it easy and enjoying themselves now. They have no sense of public responsibility. When the plague breaks out in Florence (1348), they do not feel obliged to stay in the city and to help the victims. They find it pleasanter, and safer, to move into the country where they can spend their days in eating and drinking and flirting and telling spicy tales to one another. *"Horas non numero nisi serenas,* I am concerned only with the serene hours of life."

This is the sort of life—superficial, thoughtless, sophisticated, serene, unstirred by any depths of devotion or of hatred—that we find so delightfully pictured in the *Decameron* of Giovanni the Tranquil. For several centuries the world had been overwhelmed with the sense of original sin and with the fear of future punishment. People had forgotten the cleansing stimulus of laughter. Boccaccio taught them how to laugh.

His stories in the *Decameron* are really twice-told tales. They are not of Boccaccio's invention. Like the stories of the *Arabian Nights,* they are the products of many countries and of many brains. But Boccaccio took them in their crude and illiterate outline and whittled them into shape and put the breath of life into them.

The *Decameron* is not merely a random collection of discon-

nected stories. It is an organic unit built upon a logical framework. There are ten leading characters in the book—seven ladies
and three gentlemen who have taken refuge from the horrors
of the plague in a "carnival of the imagination." In order to
while away their time over a period of ten days, each of the
refugees narrates one story on each of the ten days. Thus there
are ten stories for every day, or a hundred stories in all. Each
daily group of ten stories is more or less similar in plot. The
stories we hear on the second day, for example, are all concerned
with people who have suffered misfortune but who have finally
met with success. On the third day we are diverted with the adventures of unscrupulous rascals whose knavery has brought
them an unjustified but none the less enjoyable reward. The
fourth day is devoted to tales with an unhappy ending. The sixth
day is a day of anecdotes. Every anecdote turns upon a clever
answer. Somebody who is about to be outwitted manages, by
means of a caustic bit of repartee, to outwit his opponent. The
seventh day brings us a gallery of women who trick their husbands—men who are so ungallant to their wives that they deserve
to be tricked. And so on and on.

Whatever the subject of the individual stories, the entire book
is a cascade of laughter. Even the sad tales leave no bitterness in
their wake. Boccaccio's sorrow is but a shadow in a brilliant
landscape. Without the contrast of pain, his joy would be colorless. Voltaire is said to have laughed in order to conceal his tears.
Boccaccio may be said to have shed an occasional tear in order
to season his laughter.

Boccaccio is a satirist, but he is not a cynic. He ridicules people,
but he does not lash them. He raises against them a laughter that
is so good-natured, so gentle and so contagious that they themselves are constrained to laugh together with him. He pokes fun
at folly and gains the affection of the fools. "You play, my
friends, such a ridiculous role in life." And then, with a good-
natured shrug of the shoulders, "But don't we all?"

IV

MOST OF THE TALES in the *Decameron* are very brief. Today we would call them "short short stories." They develop a situation in a few words, and then they come to an abrupt end with a sudden twist of surprise. Such is the story of the avaricious Ermino Grimaldi, who said to a witty friend of his—"I want a new painting in my house. I wish you would suggest, for a subject, something which I have never seen." And his friend promptly replied, "Paint Liberality." Another story of this type is the adventure of the king at the house of the lady he is trying to seduce. The king, in his eagerness to possess this lady, has sent her husband off to the Crusades and has invited himself to dine at her house. The lady, unable to disobey the command of the king yet unwilling to submit to his advances, prepares a sumptuous banquet consisting of a large number of chickens, each one of them dressed and cooked in a different manner. When the king notices that he is being served with nothing but chickens, he is struck with amazement. "Madame, is there no other food in this country?"

"There is, my lord. But women, like chickens, however differently they may be dressed, are everywhere the same."

The king took the hint, and without further ado returned to his own wife.

At times in this type of story Boccaccio varies the surprise by climaxing it with a still greater surprise. This trick, which has been popularized by O. Henry, supplies the ending with a double snap of the whip. One of the best examples of this type in the *Decameron* is the story of Abraham the Jew. Abraham is such an honest man that his friend, Jeannot de Chivigni, is anxious to convert him to Christianity. The Jew, however, lends a deaf ear to his friend's entreaties. He maintains that he esteems no religion like his own, that he has been born in it, and that in it he intends to live and die. Notwithstanding this stubbornness, Jeannot persists in his efforts until the Jew finally consents to become a Christian. "But before doing so," Abraham declares, "I have a mind to go to Rome, to see the Pope, and to consider his ways a little, and those of the other Cardinals; and if they appear to me in such a light that I may be able to comprehend through them that your religion is better than mine, I will then do as you ask. Otherwise I will continue a Jew as I am."

When Jeannot heard this, he was much troubled. "I have lost all my labor," he said to himself. "For should Abraham go to Rome and see all the wickedness of the clergy, he would not only refuse to become a Christian, but, were he a Christian, he would insist upon becoming a Jew."

And so he tried to dissuade his friend from going to Rome. The Jew, however, was adamant in his resolution. Taking horse, he went to Rome and began to study the ways of the clergy. And, to his amazement, he found that "they were given to all sorts of lewdness . . . that they were generally more solicitous about their bellies than anything else . . . He found them to be such lovers of money that they would barter not only the blood of people in general, but even the blood of Christians . . . These, and other things which I shall pass over, gave great offense to the Jew, who was a sober and modest person. And now that he had seen enough, he returned home. . . ."

This would seem to be the logical end of the tale. But Boccaccio, with his tongue in his cheek, winds up with a final surprise that transforms a merely competent story into a masterpiece. When Abraham returns from Rome, he tells his friend that he has decided to become a Christian after all. "For," he argues, "since the clergy are trying so hard to overthrow the Christian religion, and since it is growing so rapidly in spite of all their efforts to discredit it, I can easily see that the Spirit of God protects it as being the most true and holy of all the religions."

Giovanni the Tranquil can be tolerant not only of people's beliefs, but of their weaknesses as well. His general attitude toward the "harmless little transgressions" of life is, "Good luck to those who can get away with them." Take and give pleasure whenever you can. There is no disgrace in enjoying yourself, provided you share your enjoyment with others. When his characters are caught in their most embarrassing moments, they are never ashamed of themselves. They realize, like good sports, that the joke is on them, and they are ready to pass the good time on to those who have caught them. Boccaccio is the Poet Laureate of Laughter. He is unwilling to depict sorrow because he is unable to inflict it. He is too genial and too gentle to hurt anybody. In an age noted for its bigotry and its hatred, Boccaccio stands out as a man without any prejudice or malevolence of any kind. Race, class, creed, nation—these words had for him but a single meaning, a small unit of men within the larger brotherhood of mankind. He was an indifferent citizen of his country because he was an ardent citizen of the world. He admitted all sorts of people, from all sorts of places, into the circle of his universal good fellowship. He respected the Frenchman no less than the Italian, the Jew no less than the Gentile. One of the finest things in the *Decameron*—indeed, one of the pure gems in all literature—is Boccaccio's story of the *Three Rings*. These three rings are symbolical of the three religions—the Jewish, the Christian and the Mohammedan. "Once upon a time," writes Boccaccio, "there was a great and rich man who possessed a ring of exceeding beauty and value . . . Desirous that this ring should continue forever in his family, he declared in his will that to whichsoever of his sons he should give this ring, him he designed for his heir, to be acknowledged and respected as the head of the family." In due time—continues Boccaccio—the rich man died, and his son inherited the precious ring. For many generations thereafter, the ring passed down from father to son until it finally came into the possession of a man who had three sons, "all virtuous and dutiful to their father, and all equally beloved by him." The father, anxious to bequeath to each of his three sons an equally precious gift, secretly got a jeweler to model two other rings after the original. When the jeweler returned the three rings, they were so much alike in their value and their beauty that even the father couldn't tell the original from the others. At his death he gave one of the rings to each of his three sons. Whereupon they began to quarrel amongst themselves, each of them claiming that he was the possessor of the one true ring. "To law then they went, which of them should succeed, and the case is not decided to this day." And "thus"—concludes Boccaccio— "it has happened with regard to the three religions given us by God the Father . . . Every one believes he is the true heir of God . . . But which of us is in the right is uncertain in like manner as of the rings."

And so, since none of us can be certain of the exclusive partiality of God, it behooves all of us to make certain of the inclusive partnership of man. "Nations of the world, unite in the exercise of good will!"

V

IN HIS EARLY LIFE Boccaccio had played with the world. In his later years he took a serious part in its affairs. He gave a course of lectures on Dante, he traveled to various states on a series of diplomatic missions, and he almost entered holy orders as an atonement for the "crime" he had committed in the writing of the *Decameron*. He was dissuaded, however, from taking this step; and instead of ending his life as a frowning saint, he died, as he had lived, a friendly sinner.

In the charming company of the world's friendly sinners, of the men and the women who love and forgive and who hope to be loved and forgiven, Giovanni the Tranquil holds a not unimportant place.

RABELAIS

Important Works by Rabelais

Pantagruel   *Gargantua*

François Rabelais

1495–1553

It is a curious fact that the greatest writers, the men who can speak so eloquently about others, are generally reticent about themselves. We know as little of the life of Rabelais as we know of the life of Shakespeare. Both of them were so interested in recording their thoughts that they forgot to tell us about their persons. The whole story of Rabelais can be related in a few hundred words.

François Rabelais owed his frank and healthy coarseness to the peasant blood that flowed in his veins. His more immediate ancestors had graduated from the peasantry into the bourgeoisie. His father, Antoine Rabelais, was a well-to-do landowner and lawyer of Chinon, the town in which Joan of Arc had launched upon her memorable career half a century earlier. François was born in 1495. His childhood and his adolescent years are shrouded in obscurity. We catch our first clear glimpse of him at the age of twenty-six—"a tall, fine and jovial figure of a man, very handsome, with a strong forehead, prominent and forceful cheek-bones, and magnificent eyes." His knowledge is amazing. "It is doubtful whether any other head of that period could have carried so copious a store of information." It is not known just where he received his training. It *is* known, however, that in 1520 he joined the order of St. Francis at the convent of Puy-St. Martin.

Nobody knows why Rabelais entered this order. His convivial character seemed so unsuited to the life of humility and poverty enjoined upon the Franciscan friars. Perhaps he took this step to please some of his friends who had joined the Franciscans before him. Friendship was one of the consuming passions of his life. It gave Rabelais the greatest pleasure to give pleasure to others.

Moreover, life in the monastery was not without its compensations for a man of learning. It offered him the leisure to study and to write, and it removed from his shoulders the burden of financial worry. If he happened to be adventurous as well as studious, the Church enabled him to travel as a missionary in its sacred or as an agent in its secular business.

The monastery, in short, was not an altogether uncongenial place for a man who loved learning and who also loved life. The routine obligations of the monastic life were neither too long nor too exacting. At the convent of Puy-St. Martin, Rabelais was able to pursue his literary hobby to his heart's content. The town of Fontenay, in which this convent was situated, had become the center of an intellectual circle of humanists—that is, men who tried to apply "the sublime culture of the past to the human needs of the present." Inspired by their spiritual godfather, Desiderius Erasmus, the circle met at the garden of the magistrate, André Tiraqueau, where they sipped their wine in the shade of the laurels and discussed poetry and politics, music and religion, art and metaphysics and morality and law.

Rabelais joined this circle and, young as he was, came soon to be recognized as its intellectual leader. At the moment there was a tempest of controversy raging in the quiet little teapot of their informal discussions. The quarrel had arisen over the question of women and marriage. Tiraqueau, who had married a little girl of eleven, had written for her guidance a book on the duties of a wife toward her husband. He regarded all women as irresponsible children, and he treated them accordingly. His book, appealing as it did to the conservatives who insisted upon keeping their womenfolk "in their proper place," had enjoyed an enthusiastic reception and a wide sale. Tiraqueau was acclaimed as the greatest anti-feminist of his day.

But in the literary circle of Fontenay there were a number of young men who took vigorous exception to Tiraqueau's views. One of these "rebellious" young men published a book in which he espoused the cause of the "somewhat feebler but far more fascinating" sex. Whereupon the enraged Tiraqueau issued another and larger book—a manual on the duties of women and on the privileges of men. A woman must always obey her husband, and a man must never indulge his wife. No man, he said, should ever marry a woman who is too homely or too pretty. If she is too homely, she is unlikely to give pleasure to her own husband. If she is too pretty, she is likely to give pleasure to other husbands. Don't allow your wife to consider herself your equal. On the other hand, don't allow your equal to become your wife. Keep your wife ever at a discreet distance—neither near enough to bewitch you, nor far enough to bewitch other men. Treat her at all times with a kindly severity. Feed her on a slender diet of caresses interspersed with the spice of occasional threats.

When this book came out, the intellectual circle of Fontenay flew into a battle of tongues. Everybody took sides. And Rabelais, strangely enough, took the side of the conservative Tiraqueau. Though unimpressed by the arguments of the magistrate, he was always ready to aim the shafts of his own satire against the follies of the fair sex. He had no great fondness for women as a class.

Nor for men as a class—though he liked them as individuals. He felt a friendly contempt for the "stupid and malevolent" human family. He pitied his "fellow contemptibles" and laughed with them and studied them and then painted them to the life in his *Pantagruel* and *Gargantua*. The lawyers, the doctors, the merchants, the artists, the academicians—all those professional and business men that he met in the garden of Tiraqueau became the models for his innumerable and inimitable character sketches. With a facility equaled by Shakespeare alone, he got under the skins of his characters and probed down to their very hearts. He knew all sorts of people from every walk of life. He had learned the ways of the peasants at Chinon. He spoke their dialect, analyzed their emotions, understood their thoughts. He had acquired an intimate insight into the lives of the Franciscans. His familiarity with the magistrates at Fontenay had given him a practical foundation in the study of politics. And now he took another step in his program "to survey the entire circular horizon of manners and men." He left the Franciscan order and joined the Benedictines. He did this for three reasons: first, because this transfer to a more educated body of clergymen would enable him to pursue his studies with greater facility; second, because Geoffrey d'Estissac, the head of the Benedictine abbey to which Rabelais had been transferred, was one of the most cultured men in the kingdom; and third, because d'Estissac offered him a position as his traveling secretary—"a God-given opportunity to widen his experience of the world."

He took a trip over Italy. To a man of his vivid imagination, this trip was like a visit to Fairyland. Rome, that stimulating combination of Pagan beauty and Christian piety, was a city of a thousand enchantments. With his usual exuberance of language, Rabelais called it "the capital of the world." Within the short period that he stayed in the city he learned to know it as intimately as if he had lived there all his life. "No man's house is more familiar to its owner," he wrote after his return from Italy, "than Rome, with all its streets and alleys, is to me."

In the company of his abbot, Rabelais traveled to several other European countries. And wherever he went, he made it his business to study the people and their princes in their various "attitudes, activities and tempers." He had an opportunity to observe them at peace and at war. For then, as ever in human history, the aggressors were trying to despoil the possessors. The kings of France and of Spain were devastating the provinces of northern Italy; the Sultan of Turkey was besieging Vienna; the soldiers of Germany were trampling over Rome. And so it went, in a continual whirlpool of madness and murder. Rabelais watched this shameful spectacle of man's inhumanity to man, and decided to attack it with laughter rather than with rage. In the thirty-third chapter of *Pantagruel*, he exposes the stupidity of aggressive warfare by reducing it to a burlesque. Duke Picrochole (Bitterbile) is anxious to enhance his glory and to enrich his purse. He believes in the ridiculous notion that a country can be prosperous only at the expense of other countries. Accordingly he plans to attack his neighbors under the generalship of his three cronies-in-crime—Sir Smalltrash, Count Swashbuckle, and Lord Lousylocks. He calls these three generals to a council, and together they outline a campaign that is designed to cover their own country with glory and the neighboring country with corpses. "But there was present at that council an old gentleman well experienced in the wars . . . named Echephron (Mr. Sobersense) who, hearing the plans of the campaign, said: 'I do greatly suspect that all this enterprise will be like the tale of the pitcher full of milk wherewith a shoemaker made himself rich in conceit; but when the pitcher was broken, he had not whereupon to dine . . . What do you pretend by these large conquests? You will only break your pitcher.' . . . 'Oh,' said Count Swashbuckle, 'here is a fine simpleton! Come, let us hide ourselves in the corner of a chimney, and there spend our life among the ladies, knitting and spinning and threading pearls. He that nothing ventures finds neither horse nor mule.' . . . 'But he who ventures too much,' rejoined Mr. Sobersense, 'loses both horse and mule.' "

Here, in a nutshell, is the whole idea of aggressive militarism. Rabelais knew, as every wise man in every age knows, that there is no such thing as ultimate triumph for the aggressor—that his initial victories are but the prelude to his final defeat.

But Rabelais was not deeply concerned with the question of

peace and war. Indeed, he was not deeply concerned with any political or social questions. He was essentially not a satirist but a humorist. He felt most happy, he said, when he could "sit down, rest, and make merry" over the apparently meaningless human comedy. He was always in the best of spirits. The growl of the cynic never intruded into his laughter. He enjoyed too healthy a digestion ever to wax indignant at the stupidities of his fellows. His outlook upon life was at all times detached. He appeared like a superior creature sent down from another planet to bring back a report on the amusing farce that was being enacted upon the earth.

An insatiable reporter of life, he tried always to observe it from a new angle. Having completed his assignment as a Benedictine monk, he now entered a new assignment as a student of medicine. He was thirty-two when he began his medical studies at the University of Montpellier. Three years later he received his doctor's degree, whereupon he settled down to the important business of his life—the purging of human ills with medicine and laughter. He began to write his prescriptions and his *Pantagruel;* and five years later he gave his masterpiece—under an assumed name—to the world.

II

THE STORY OF *Pantagruel* cannot be pigeonholed under any classification. It is an astonishing mixture of madness and morals, coarseness and beauty, irreverence and devotion, metaphysical nonsense and philosophical wisdom, irrational prattling and poetical grandeur. It is as plotless as life, and as full of surprises. Throughout the book there are twists of ideas and turns of style that only the Lord and Rabelais could have ever conceived. He takes you along a pleasant road and then unexpectedly confronts you with an impassable mountain. As you stop, astounded and disappointed at his trickery, he suddenly opens a tunnel in the mountain and whirls you along through caverns of subterranean beauty such as you have never imagined even in your dreams. And then, just as you emerge into the sunlight, he overwhelms you with a deluge of filth that well-nigh takes your breath away. You are about to give him up in disgust when he cleanses and invigorates you with a magical bath of morning dew and you are ready to go on with him to the enchantment of the next landscape. Such is the effect, or rather the succession of effects, that Rabelais produces upon the mind of his reader. He is the Proteus of the literary world, the magician of a million moods and fancies.

Rabelais has no respect for literary structure. Technically considered, the story of Gargantua, Pantagruel and Panurge is an illogical muddle of nonsense. The first book describes the birth, childhood and education of Gargantua, the father of Pantagruel—how he came to Paris and stole the bells of Notre Dame in order to hang them around his horse's neck, how his grandfather won a victory over Bitterbile through the assistance of Brother John, and how he rewarded the monk by building for him the Abbey of Theleme, which became the home of the new religious order of Do-as-you-like. The only rule of this order, Rabelais informs us, was to observe no rule at all. There was to be no clock in the abbey to remind anyone of time or duty. Instead of submitting to the three vows of chastity, poverty and obedience, the monks and the nuns of this abbey were permitted to marry, to accumulate riches and to take the law into their own hands. The doors of this abbey were to be forever closed against "bigots, hypocrites, attorneys, judges, magistrates, bankers, lechers, liars, cowards, swindlers and thieves." On the other hand, this place was to be a congenial retreat for men who loved pleasure and women who loved to please—"gay, witty, frolicsome, cheerful, spruce, jocund, lively, jovial, handsome, worthy, courteous and gentle blades, and delicious, charming, mirthful, lovely, magnetic, sprightly, personable, precious, ripe, young, choice, dear, alluring, capricious, clever, sweet and ravishing ladies."

Such are the men and the women—we have quoted but a

handful of the Rabelaisian adjectives—who are to make up the personnel of the new order of Do-as-you-like. And their lives are to be spent in feasting rather than in fasting, in taking and in giving pleasure, in the peaceful contentment of a full belly and a merry heart. Feed their desire, and you kill their greed. "For it is the nature of man to be greedy after those things that are denied him."

With this farcical picture of the Abbey of Theleme the first book of *Pantagruel* comes to an end.

The second book deals with the birth and the education of Gargantua's son, Pantagruel, and of his meeting with Panurge, that ingenious doctor of deceit who suffered from a chronic starvation of the purse—"a sharper, drinker, roysterer, adulterer, and far and away the most debased and dissolute scoundrel in Paris; otherwise and in all things else, the finest fellow in the world." And then, having formally introduced his hero, the author takes us by the hand—or is it by the nose?—and leads us across the horizons of nowhere into the gardens of nonsense. "And may you fall into sulphur, fire, and the bottomless pit," Rabelais warns us, "if you do not firmly believe everything that I shall tell you in this present chronicle"—how Panurge escapes out of the hands of the Turks, how he prevails upon six hundred thousand and fourteen dogs to besprinkle a lady who has refused his advances, how Pantagruel in a most unusual manner begets fifty-three thousand little men and an equal number of little women, how he wins a great victory over the giants, and how Epistemon, whose head has been cut off, comes back to life and brings to the world the latest news from Hell. And so the second book comes to an end with a "good night to you, gentlemen, and think not so much upon my faults that you forget your own."

The third book of this "farcical fantasy and flimflam foolery" is, from the structural point of view, even less logical than the first two books. Beginning with a picture of the philosopher Diogenes who rolls his tub over the space of a hundred and three consecutive verbs—not even Shakespeare possessed a more amazing facility for language—Rabelais then goes on to transport us into Utopia. This "never-never-land" contains nine billion inhabitants who are bent upon conquering the entire world—"not, however, by force of arms but by unburdening the people of their worries, by teaching them how to live peacefully and well, by giving them good laws, and by using them with all possible affability, courtesy, gentleness and love." And now, having brought us to this land of the heart's desire and having prepared the wings of our expectation for flights into further adventures, the author puts a sudden stop to his narrative and devotes an entire book to a discussion of marriage. The motive for the discussion is this: Panurge would like to marry, but he hesitates to do so because of his fear that his wife may prove unfaithful to him. With this perplexity in his mind, he launches into a thirty-four-chapter investigation as to whether or not women are true to their husbands. He consults a great number of people—including a prophetess, a poet, a deaf mute, an astrologer, a theologian, a physician and a clown—and he leaves them all a much wordier but none the wiser man. From the clown, however, he receives a practical suggestion—to repair with his problem to the oracle who knows the answer to everything.

And this brings us to the fourth and the fifth books—the journey to the oracle. This journey blazes a trail of adventure and laughter all over the earth, above it and underneath. When at last Pantagruel and Panurge arrive at the end of their search, they learn from the oracle that the only answer to their question is the one word—*Drink*. Drink deeply of life, of beauty, of pleasure, of knowledge, of truth. "All this," as Panurge points out, "is lovely." But it leaves him just as wise on the subject of marriage as he was before his visit to the oracle.

And thus the tangled thread of sublime nonsense, beginning nowhere and leading nowhere, comes to a sudden break.

So much for the illogical plot of the story. As for the details, they are handled with an equally illogical carelessness. In some of the passages Gargantua is a giant; in some of the others, he is a man of ordinary stature. Panurge is at times a wise and courageous and honest man, and at other times a scoundrel, a coward and a fool. The action of the story whirls along as madly and as merrily as the world itself. In the first book Gargantua lives in the legendary country of Utopia. In the second book he is whisked, "without any reason or season," into Rabelais' native country of the Touraine. In the twenty-third chapter of the second book Gargantua disappears from the story, having been translated into the land of the fairies. And then, in the thirty-fifth chapter of the third book, he walks right back into the middle of the page as if nothing had happened to him. These are but a few of the many inconsistencies in the book. Rabelais was never burdened with the bugaboo of little minds. He was too busy creating a masterpiece to bother with the tinkering of the ordinary craftsman in literature. The best artists are sometimes the worst artisans. Thank the Lord for that!

III

EXTERNALLY, as we have seen, the work of Rabelais is a crazy, ramshackle, meandering, senseless and planless contraption. But let us open the door again and look more closely at some of the astonishing treasures within. What shall we examine first? The view is so fantastic, so rich, so varied, so dazzling, so alive that the mind is intoxicated and hardly can decide as to what to select. The only way to evaluate Rabelais is to read him from beginning to end. To sample the unique flavor of his work, however, we may take any page almost at random. Let us do this and taste him, not at his "saltiest best," but at his superb average.

Observe, for example, how he satirizes the meaningless pomposity of the judges' decisions in the law courts. The Lord Kissbreach and the Lord Suckfist have become entangled in a dispute in the presence of Pantagruel. Here is Pantagruel's judgment after he has heard both sides:

"Having seen, heard, calculated and well considered of the

difference between the Lords of Kissbreach and Suckfist, the court saith unto them, that in regard of the sudden quaking, shivering and hoariness of the flickermouse, bravely declining from the estival solstice, the attempt by private means the surprisal of toyish trifles in those who are a little unwell for having taken a draught too much, through the lewd demeanor and vexation of the beetles that inhabit the diarodal climate of a hypocritical ape on horseback, bending a crossbow backwards, the plaintive truly had just cause to calfet, or with oakum to stop the chinks of the galleon which the good woman blew up with wind, having one foot shod and the other bare, reimbursing and restoring to him, low and stiff in his conscience, as many bladdernuts and wild pistaches as there is of hair in eighteen cows, with as much for the embroiderer, and so much for that. He is likewise declared innocent of the case privileged from the knapdardies, into the danger whereof it was thought he had incurred . . ." And so on and on for several more paragraphs, at the end of which gibberish the judge orders the plantiff to pay the defendant a fine "about the middle of August in May."

And if the reader complains that he can't make head or tail out of this, the author confesses with a waggish smile, "Neither can I."

Rabelais had a healthy contempt for the legal profession. "Our laws," he said, "are like cobwebs; the silly little flies are stopped, caught and destroyed therein, but the stronger ones break them, and force and carry them whichsoever way they please." The trouble with most of the lawyers, he said, is that they have "too many words on their tongues and too little wisdom in their heads."

The same, declares Rabelais, is true of most of the philosophers, especially "the metaphysicians who describe in scholarly phrases, and measure in scientific terms, the things that do not exist." One of these metaphysicians, Rabelais tells us, wrote a learned dissertation on the question, *whether a chimera buzzing in a vacuum could devour second intentions.* Others preoccupied themselves with such problems as, *whether a Platonic Idea, bounding to the right under the orifice of Chaos, could drive away the atoms of Democritus; or whether the hibernal frigidity of the antipodes, passing in an orthagonal line through the homogeneous solidity of the center, could by a gentle antiperistasis warm the superficial connexity of our heels.* "A plague upon these windbags who stifle an idea to death under a blanket of words"—these pseudo-scholars who learn more and more about less and less, until they know everything about nothing—these blind teachers of the blind who flounder around in a dark room looking for a black cat that isn't there.

From all such stupidity the good Rabelais delivers us. He brings us face to face not with vapory ideas but with solid facts. And he enables us to experience these facts with all our living senses.

But he touches our senses with the flashlight of reason. His superabundant imagination dances over his pages in a cataract of wisdom and beauty. He is one of the world's supreme masters in the interpretation of truth through the medium of fiction. His book is full of illuminating anecdotes and stimulating tales. Some of these anecdotes and tales may bring the blush of disapproval to the ears, but all of them bring the glow of understanding to the heart. All life to Rabelais is an anecdote, a divine joke with a pungent ending. Without the dramatic pungency—that is, without the shock of surprise—no life is worth the living and no story is worth the reading. Rabelais is the perfect dramatist. In his stories you must always expect the unexpected. You will find this sudden bolt-out-of-the-blue in the adventure of the man who married a dumb wife, in the anecdote about François Villon and King Edward of England, in the story of the porter who paid for the smoke on his bread with the sound of his money, in the five remedies adopted by Panurge for the subduing of his carnal appetites, and in that most amusing gem of them all—the tale of Hans Carvel's ring. Too indelicate perhaps for the direct simplicity of our modern English, these stories sound perfectly decorous in the subtle nuances of the sixteenth century French. Rabelais knew how to season even his spiciest wine with the aroma of common sense.

IV

THE FINAL YEARS of Rabelais' life were, unlike his stories, seasoned with spice but not always with common sense. He lectured on medicine and was one of the first to introduce dissection into the study of anatomy. He invented a surgical instrument called the *glottotomon* (tongue cutter). For a while he lived in the Abbey of St. Maur, where he deported himself as "a right monk, if ever there were any since the monking world monked a monkery." But then he got mixed up in politics and went to prison. Released after a short term, he acted as a publisher's adviser and for a while even tried the stage as an outlet for his exuberant energy.

He then returned to the monastery, entered the priesthood, renewed his vow of chastity, broke it and became a father in the flesh as well as in the spirit, repented of his weakness and then repented of his repentance, and finally fell asleep (April 9, 1553), rich in adventures but not in years.

And thus lived and laughed and died the gayest satirist of them all.

CERVANTES

Important Works by Cervantes

Galatea   Novelas Exemplares
Don Quixote   Persiles y Sigismunda
                       Numerous plays and poems

Miguel de Cervantes

1547–1616

WE ARE INDEBTED to Cervantes for two of the most interesting stories in the history of literature. The first of these stories is the strange life of Don Quixote. The second is the even stranger life of Cervantes.

There has been a regrettable tendency, on the part of Cervantes' biographers, to ignore the more unpalatable aspects of his career. There is no reason, however, why we cannot admire his work and at the same time tell the truth about his life. It is no disparagement of the rose bush to admit that it grows out of the common soil. The food of beauty is compounded of moisture and mud. The art of Cervantes was the product of his suffering. If the life of Cervantes had not been so bitter, the story of Don Quixote would not have been so sublime.

Miguel de Cervantes Saavedra was a contemporary of Shakespeare. Born in the university town of Alcala de Henares, he absorbed but little of its cultural atmosphere in his early life. For his father was a quack doctor who traveled from town to town and who made a living by cupping and cutting the poor devils who offered themselves as his patients. Little Miguel, who accompanied his father on his travels, learned very little out of books but a great deal out of life. Though he never went to college, he grew up into a sophisticated young gentleman of the period. At a rather early age he had a duel. Shortly thereafter he was mixed up in a rather dishonorable love affair with a Maid of Honor. He was rapidly gathering and storing away the material that he was to use later on in his books.

At the age of 23 we find him in Rome—probably an exile because of his youthful indiscretions. He worked in that city for about a year, and then his restlessness drove him on to enlist in the army.

He fought in the Battle of Lepanto, where he came near to losing his left hand from the blow of a scimitar. As a result of this wound, which disabled him for life, he was nicknamed "the Cripple of Lepanto." To the end of his days he took greater pride in his ordinary talent as a soldier than he did in his extraordinary genius as a writer.

On his way home from the war he fell into the hands of Moorish pirates. They sold him into slavery, and it was five years before he was ransomed.

And now, having served both as a soldier and as a slave, he tried his luck as a poet. He succeeded in turning out some of the most atrocious doggerel in the history of Spanish literature.

Still restless, he turned to the drama. He wrote between thirty and forty plays. An erupting volcano of energy. But he spurted forth ashes instead of lava. His dramas were, if anything, even worse than his poetry.

Finally he attempted a pastoral romance. This was the most dismal failure of them all. Cervantes, it seemed, was not destined to be a writer.

Unsuccessful in his bid for fame, he settled down to find happiness. He married a woman who was eighteen years younger than himself. In spite of her youth, however, she was unable to satisfy his vagrant fancy. Within a year after his marriage to this woman he became the father of a child by another woman.

For a time he tried to support his family—legal as well as

natural—by means of the pen. And then in 1588—he was 41 at the time—he turned to a "more sensible" source of income. He became a business agent for the Great Armada. But again he was unlucky. The Armada was defeated, and Cervantes lost his job.

He secured another job as a tax-collector in Granada. Whether through dishonesty or through neglect, there was a serious shortage of funds. Cervantes was arrested and sentenced to a term in prison.

When he was set free, he turned once more to literature for a living. He became what may be termed as a "professional backscratcher in verse." That is, he wrote laudatory metrical introductions to all sorts of books dealing with all sorts of subjects—from epic poems to treatises on obstetrics. These introductions were, as a rule, no better than the books. The great dramatist, Lope de Vega, writes (in a letter dated August 14, 1604) that there is no poet in Spain "tan malo como Cervantes," so bad as Cervantes. Even Cervantes himself admits this. "I am," he remarks with facetious bitterness, "more experienced in reverses than in verses."

And this brings us to his 58th year, the end of the average span of human life. Cervantes is a shattered, disappointed and disgusted old man. He is a failure in everything, and especially in literature. He is now, to quote his own description, a man "of silver beard, although not twenty years ago it was golden, large moustache, small mouth, teeth not important," since he has "but six of them, and those in bad condition and even more badly arranged, because the teeth on the top do not correspond with those on the bottom." He further informs us that he is "of a complexion rather white than brown, somewhat heavy-shouldered and not very nimble on his feet." A rather unprepossessing picture. The picture of a derelict who appears ready to shuffle his way into eternal oblivion.

II

AND THEN, without any blare of trumpets, he suddenly leaped into glory. An outburst of flame from the setting sun. The man who in his youth had written some of the world's worst poems was inspired in his old age to write one of the world's greatest novels. Cervantes had been working on *Don Quixote* for a long time. Parts of it had been written in a prison cell. All of it had been planned and composed amidst the squalor of poverty and the bitterness of despair. *Don Quixote* is in a literal sense a garden that grew out of the mud. It is wisdom born of suffering—the revelation of a gentle soul tortured in a sensitive body.

Yet this novel, though universally acknowledged as one of the world's masterpieces, is far from being a perfect book. It is full of glaring faults. It suffers, as many of its critics have observed, from "the besetting sin of the Spanish narrator, prolixity." The book is too long and too disjointed. The flowers of Cervantes' wit are scattered over too spacious a landscape. It is necessary to travel over many a dreary pathway in order to reach the isolated spots of beauty. *Don Quixote* might have been twice as good if it were half as long.

Moreover, the story is too often inaccurate, both in structure and in style. Apparently Cervantes never corrected his work. And he never re-read it in the process of the writing. Again and again, when he started a new chapter, he contradicted what he had written at the end of the last chapter. Like Joshua in the Old Testament, he blots out the passage of time on one occasion and compels the sun to stand still for several hours. Don Quixote and Sancho Panza have been invited into the duke's house for supper *at nightfall*. After they have eaten several courses and indulged in a lengthy conversation that must have lasted till well after midnight, Cervantes informs us that *"it was now beginning to draw towards evening."* On another occasion Cervantes tells us that a thief has stolen Sancho Panza's donkey, and then he puts Sancho Panza upon this stolen donkey no less than seven times. The book is full of similar inaccuracies.

Let us, however, take Cervantes' faults in the same spirit in which he himself took them. When he wrote the second part of *Don Quixote,* he called the attention of his readers to the imperfections of the first part and laughed them off. "Lord, what bunglers we mortals be!" He made no apology for his mistakes, and no effort to correct them. He wouldn't think of polishing up his story, any more than he would think of primping up his hero. It is the ridiculous wart on the face and the blundering absurdity in the phrase that make the man and the book so lovable and alive. Some works of art are too perfect to be human. The story of Don Quixote, however, is too human to be perfect.

Don Quixote is the story of a gentle madman told by a gentle cynic. It is a good-natured burlesque on the follies of mankind. There is satire in this book, but no bitterness. We laugh as we see our own foolishness mirrored in the foolishness of Don Quixote, and our own grossness mirrored in the grossness of Sancho Panza. At one moment we feel more closely related to the knight, whose valor is greater than his discretion; and at the next moment to the squire, whose discretion is greater than his valor. Again and again, as we see the one fighting with his sword and the other battling with his tongue, we are constrained to say, "There, thanks to the genius of Cervantes, goes a perfect image of myself."

For all of us, as Cervantes knew, have our days of the sword and our days of the tongue. Every human creature of us is a combination of Don Quixote and Sancho Panza. There are times when we trust in the strength of our arms, and other times when we rely upon the nimbleness of our legs. One moment, wise in our folly, we tilt at windmills with the Don. Another moment, foolish in our wisdom, we side with his Squire, "who today avoids the fight to sleep above the ground tonight." But wise or foolish, we are all of us aiming forever blindly at the selfsame goal—to make life more livable for someone in distress.

III

AND NOW let us for a few thrilling moments saddle our horses and ride to meet Don Quixote, the Gentleman of the Doleful Countenance, as he sallies forth upon Rozinante, the Steed of the Skinny Shanks, in quest of noble adventure. Don Quixote is a long and lanky bachelor of fifty, whose purse is empty of cash but whose brain is full of fancies. Having read a great many books about knight-errantry, he has decided to become a knight-errant himself. He arrays himself in a coat of mail which is as old and as rusty as his body and in a helmet which is tied with so many knots that he cannot untie them at night, and he steals out of his house on a bright morning in July. "His wit being wholly extinguished," he mistakes windmills for giants, curates for pirates, barbers for enchanters, hovels for castles, jailbirds for gentlemen, and barmaids for queens. In his effort to resist the oppressors and to aid the oppressed, he generally manages to be repaid with kicks and cuffs from oppressors and oppressed alike.

But the greater his troubles, the deeper his madness. He dedicates his life to the "rescue" of a country wench who does not even know of his existence. He calls her his "fair Lady Dulcinea," and he enlists the services of Sancho Panza as his faithful squire.

Sancho Panza is as stupid as his master is mad—although at times, as we shall see, Sancho Panza utters words that are barbed with the wisdom of Solomon. Mounted upon his donkey, he follows his master into all sorts of crazy situations in the hope that Don Quixote will repay him in the end by making him the governor of an island.

And thus we find them one morning, battered and weary and ridiculous and undismayed, preparing to plunge into one of their characteristic adventures. "Don Quixote, lifting his eyes, saw . . . about twelve men in a company on foot, inserted like beadstones in a great chain of iron, that was tied about their necks, and every one had manacles besides on his hands. There came to conduct them two on horseback and two others afoot; the horse-men had firelock pieces; those that came afoot, darts and swords. And as soon as Sancho saw them, he said: 'This is a chain of galley slaves, people forced by the king to go to the galleys.' 'How! people forced?' demanded Don Quixote. 'Is it possible that the king will force anybody?' 'I say not so,' answered Sancho, 'but that it is people which are condemned, for their offenses, to serve the king in the galleys perforce.' 'Howsoever it be,' replied Don Quixote, 'this folk, although it be conducted, go perforce and not willingly . . . Then, if that be so, here falls in justly the execution of my function, to wit, the dissolving of violences and outrages, and the succoring of the afflicted and needful.' "

By this time the chain of slaves has arrived, and Don Quixote asks the first one why he has been condemned to the galleys. "For being in love," replies the slave. "How so?" inquires Don Quixote. "I loved a basket of linen so ardently," explains the slave, "that I embraced it and tried to elope with it."

Don Quixote requests another of the slaves to give him the reason for his capture.

"Because I lacked ten ducats," replies the convict. "If I had possessed those ten ducats, I would have so anointed with them the notary's pen, and whetted my lawyer's wit so well, that I might today see myself in the midst of the market of Toledo instead of thus trailing like a greyhound at the end of a chain."

A third convict informs Don Quixote that he is condemned for a "serious crime." He has committed the unpardonable crime of confessing to a theft. If he had been able to hold his tongue, he laments, he would now be a free man.

Patiently Don Quixote listens to the story of every one of the convicts and then decides that these men, although criminals in the eyes of the law, are nevertheless people in distress. Their ill fortune is due to the accidental fact that they have been caught. He informs them that he deems it his duty, as a knight-errant, "to favor and assist the needful."

Suiting his crazy action to his silly words, Don Quixote makes a sudden attack upon the guards. The latter, taken by surprise, run off in a panic and allow the prisoners to break loose from their chains. Don Quixote, elated over his victory, orders the rescued slaves to take up their chains and to carry them as a trophy to his "lady love, the fair Dulcinea."

In answer to this extraordinary request, the escaped convicts belabor Don Quixote and Sancho Panza with a shower of stones.

The slaves then disappear, each in a different direction. "The donkey and the horse, Sancho and Don Quixote, remained alone. The donkey stood pensive, with his head hanging downwards, shaking now and then his ears, thinking that the storm of stones was not yet past, but that they still whistled around his head; the horse lay overthrown by his master, who was likewise struck down by another blow of a stone; Sancho stood crouching in fear of the bullets of the Holy Brotherhood (the Spanish police); and Don Quixote lay stretched out on the ground, lamenting to see himself so misused by those very men to whom he had done so much good."

Don Quixote and Sancho Panza are finally compelled to hide themselves in the mountains in order to escape the wrath of the Holy Brotherhood. Here the Knight of the Doleful Countenance proposes to do penance, like the cavaliers of old.

"Do penance for what?" asks the astonished Sancho.

"For nothing in particular," replies Don Quixote. Anybody can be foolish for a good reason. The trick is to be foolish for no reason at all. The cavaliers of old have tortured themselves because their ladies have proved themselves false. Don Quixote desires to torture himself because he finds it pleasant to suffer pain.

And so he takes off his clothes and begins to beat his head against the rocks. He commands Sancho Panza to "observe well my painful penance" and to bring a report of this penance to the fair Dulcinea.

Upon the completion of the penance, Don Quixote plunges into another series of crazy adventures. This series culminates in a desperate duel with a wine-skin which Don Quixote has mistaken for an enchanted giant.

And thus he goes on from madness to madness until at last the curate of his native village, who has undertaken a search for this "beloved lunatic," surprises him in the midst of his ridiculous adventures and carries him home in a cage.

As he and his squire are brought into the village, Sancho Panza's wife runs to her husband with an anxious question on her lips. "Is your donkey well?"

"Better than I am," replies Sancho Panza.

"Thank God!" she murmurs fervently.

And this brings us to the end of the first part.

IV

IT WAS IN 1605 that Cervantes gave this joyous book (the first part of *Don Quixote*) to the world. But his own life remained as bitter as ever. Pursued even now by his poverty, he was compelled as before to live among the dregs. Together with his daughter and his sister, he took an apartment in a house of questionable reputation. It has even been hinted that he encouraged his daughter to enter upon the "oldest profession in the world" and that he lived on the resulting income. And then, on June 27, 1605, came the lowest depth of his misadventures. A libertine of noble rank was found dying in the apartment occupied by Cervantes and his relatives. They were all arrested for murder. Fortunately they succeeded in establishing their innocence.

For the next ten years, while the world was chuckling over *Don Quixote*, Cervantes wrote very little. A number of mediocre poems, a handful of plays that never saw the stage, and a collection of fair-to-middling short stories—these comprised the sum total of his literary output for the entire decade. These, and the second part of his great novel.

V

THE second part of *Don Quixote* is in some respects even more interesting than the first part. It is a mixture of raving nonsense and sober wisdom. Don Quixote speaks at times like a maniac, at other times like a sage; and, thanks to the genius of Cervantes, these inconsistent utterances are welded into the consistency of a living character.

The leading character in the second part, however, is not Don Quixote but Sancho Panza. The sanity of this rascal has become even more absurd than the insanity of his master. He still loves to "caress his food and kiss his bottle," but he is no longer the carefree fool of the first part. He is now an *ambitious* fool. He is anxious to make money and to arrange a magnificent marriage for his daughter. "It is a dangerous thing for a buxom young girl to remain single. A daughter is safer unluckily wedded than unlawfully bedded."

He therefore keeps exacting from Don Quixote the island that the latter has promised him as a reward for his services. He is quite certain of his ability to make a competent governor; for, as he remarks of himself, "I know a little about everything"— and precious little about anything.

Indeed, it would seem as if Sancho Panza had gone to school between the beginning of the book and the end. In the first part of the book, he is as ignorant as he is wholesome. In the second part, however, he becomes "a leaking bushel" of proverbs. They come spilling out of his mouth—there are several hundred of them—on every occasion, with many a rhyme but with very little reason.

And so they go on, the squire and his master, upon their mettlesome and prattlesome course. Don Quixote is convinced that an enchanter stands between him and his exploits; and Sancho Panza succeeds in convincing him further that even his lady Dulcinea has been enchanted. From a beautiful damsel, the squire informs him, Dulcinea has been changed into an ugly country wench.

Don Quixote is determined to disenchant his lady. He hears, from one of the wags who are trying to make sport of him, that the man responsible for Dulcinea's plight is Sancho Panza. In order that Dulcinea may be released from her spell, Don Quixote is told, Sancho Panza must punish himself with "3300 lashes upon his valiant bottom."

"I fail to see the connection," complains Sancho, "between the blows upon my bottom and the happiness of Lady Dulcinea." He changes his mind, however, when his master proposes to pay him handsomely for the whipping. "Very well," he agrees, "I will do as you say and disenchant the lady." And so, accompanied by Don Quixote, he repairs to the forest, removes his clothing, conceals himself behind a clump of bushes with a heavy whip in his hand, and begins to lash—the bushes. With every stroke he utters a terrible groan; and Don Quixote, who stands on the other side of the thicket and who therefore is unable to witness the whipping, is convulsed with pity at the "self-inflicted torture of his noble squire."

Sancho Panza concludes the flagellation with a volley of proverbs, and then they go on to the next adventure.

This adventure brings them to a duke's castle. The duke, having heard of their ridiculous antics, eggs them on to a series of antics that are even more ridiculous. This man, observes Cervantes, is perhaps the most foolish character in the story, since he "finds so much pleasure in mocking other fools." He incites Don Quixote into a battle with "bewitched" cats; he ensnares him into a burlesque love affair with one of the duchess' ladies in waiting; and he subjects him to indignities and blusterings and blows on every side. While he thus "entertains" Don Quixote, he "sets up" Sancho Panza as the "Governor of the Island of Barataria." This "island" is in reality a village on the mainland; but Sancho Panza is too much of a simpleton to understand the difference. He is "served" with a pompous mockery which puffs him up with the arrogance of a king. He is overwhelmed with platters of the costliest food, seasoned with the most appetizing spices, and flanked by decanters of the most aromatic wines. His eager belly cries out for the fray, but the court physician warns him not to touch anything upon the table. "There are spies in the island who are bent upon poisoning the Governor's food and drink."

Poor Sancho! Though unable to enjoy the pleasures of his exalted rank, he is compelled to assume its responsibilities. He is placed upon the judgment seat to settle the disputes of his subjects. And suddenly, with all his ignorance, he becomes a very Daniel for justice. For ten days he rules the island "with a full heart and an empty stomach," and then he decides to withdraw from his royal honors. This he does all the more readily because he hears that the island is threatened with an invasion. "Better a live jack," he concludes, "than a dead king." All he asks for his services as Governor of the island is a handful of oats for his donkey and half a cheese and a loaf of bread for himself.

He returns to Don Quixote, ready to offer his services for his master's further adventures. But the adventures of the amiable madman are almost at an end. His friends have tried, by every possible means, to disenchant him from his madness. And at last they have hit upon a workable plan. They have induced him to fight a duel with Samuel Carrasco, an old friend of his who has concealed his identity under the disguise of a knight-errant. The punishment for a conquered knight, Don Quixote is told, is to submit himself to the will of the conqueror. Carrasco easily defeats Don Quixote and thereupon orders him to return home and never again to court the dangers of knight-errantry.

Yet even now the erratic Don is not quite finished. Having renounced his profession as an adventurous knight, he plans to take up the equally crazy profession of an amorous shepherd. A fatal illness, however, saves him from this final madness.

As the last day approaches, Don Quixote regains his sanity. "I possess now a free and clear judgment, no longer overshadowed with the misty cloud of ignorance which the continual reading and plodding on books of chivalry has overcast me withal . . . I have been very foolish in my life, but I shall try to be somewhat wiser in my death."

VI

CERVANTES had begun the second part of *Don Quixote* in a rather lazy and undecided state of mind. And he might never have finished it were it not for the rivalry of an impostor. This impostor, writing under the pseudonym of *Avellaneda,* had produced a spurious sequel to *Don Quixote*. Enraged at the audacity of this man, Cervantes hurried with the completion of his genuine sequel and gave it to the world in 1615.

It was well that he made haste, for the following year brought the completion of his own life. Two lovable madmen-philosophers—Don Quixote and Cervantes. Both of them had been "blest with the good fortune to live in folly and to die in wisdom."

DEFOE

Important Works by Defoe

Essay on Projects
The True-Born Englishman
Hymn to the Pillory
The Apparition of Mrs. Veal
Robinson Crusoe
Serious Reflections
The Dumb Philosopher

Duncan Campbell
Memoirs of a Cavalier
Captain Singleton
Moll Flanders
The Journal of the
   Plague Year
The History of Colonel Jack

Daniel Defoe

1661–1731

"THIS MAN," observed a contemporary of Daniel Defoe, "has been mothered by quicksilver and fathered by the Devil." And, indeed, the author of *Robinson Crusoe* was one of the most restless men of his generation, and his restlessness was not always in accord with the footsteps of the angels. Throughout his life he tried to serve two masters—God and Gold; and in his divided allegiance he was able to serve neither of them with sufficient devotion. Trained for the ministry, he went into business. In his varied career as a businessman he sold staples and stockings, wine and oysters, bricks and tiles and houses and ideas. He dabbled in politics, languished in prison and stood in the pillory. He visited the houses of the mighty—generally through the back door—and he consorted with rebels and outcasts. He defied the princes as a Dissenter and he served them as a spy. He made several fortunes and died in hiding—a fugitive from his creditors. And he wrote over three hundred books of which only three—*Robinson Crusoe, Moll Flanders* and *A Journal of the Plague Year*—are read at the present day. He was, in short, a composite of nearly every human activity, whether good or bad—a living landscape of winds and rocks and rivers and shadows and flowers—with the sunlight of genius transforming a commonplace patchwork into a thing of beauty.

But let us look more closely at this variegated patchwork of personality known as Daniel Defoe.

II

As a youngster he was known as Daniel Foe, son of the tallow-chandler, James Foe. It was not till after his fortieth year that he began to sign his name as D. Foe, then as Defoe and finally as Daniel Defoe. And then, to suit his station to his name, he bought a coat of arms and devised a fictitious genealogy to prove that he was of noble descent.

But his father had no suspicion of any nobility on his part. He brought up his children in "the wholesome tradition of the middle-class Englishman." He was a Dissenter from the Church of England, and he inspired his family with the spirit of discontent. From earliest childhood Daniel was trained to be a restless wanderer and an observant critic of life.

Scarcely had Daniel emerged from infancy when two horrible tragedies descended upon London—the Great Plague of 1665 and the Great Fire of 1666. The Foe family came out of these two tragedies unscathed but scared. "Life is a constant escape from danger."

And a constant endeavor to fortify yourself *against* danger. The danger of death, and the danger of poverty. The plague and the fire had brought starvation to thousands of homes. The Foes must never allow themselves to be confronted with *this* tragedy. "Fight against destitution, my son; fight against it all your life."

And James Foe himself fought against it, and succeeded tolerably well. He gave up his chandlery for a butchery, and found it more profitable to serve meat than to bring light. He could now afford to think of a good education for his children. He sent Daniel to a private academy. "I want you to be a minister," he said. "And if not a minister, I want you to be a merchant. But in any event, I want you to be a successful gentleman."

Following his father's advice, Daniel decided upon a business career. The road to success would be too difficult for a minister of the Dissenting Church. And so, at the age of twenty, we find him visiting the shops of London, a commission dealer in hosiery —an energetic young fellow full of ideas but empty of cash. On the side, he dealt in "liquor and tobacco, cloths and oysters and pipes and snuff." Everything was grist to the mill of his financial ambition.

He was a young man of vigorous talents and positive ideas. But he rarely lived up to his ideas. He advised against early marriage—and married at twenty-four. This, however, was a shrewd rather than a rash step. For his wife brought him a dowry of £3,700 (about $18,500).

He next advised his friends to keep out of politics—and got himself mixed up in it. He joined the Monmouth rebellion against the crown, and nearly paid with his life for his folly.

For a time he was cured of his rebellion, but not of his recklessness. He invested heavily in merchant ships, bought a town house and a country house, took a "flier" in every bold scheme that came to his notice—"there is more danger in overtrading than in want of trade"—and found himself, in his early thirties, a bankrupt to the sum of £17,000 ($85,000).

And then came a stormy period of lawsuits and counter lawsuits, accusations of perjury and extortion and fraud, and a final desperate effort to recoup his losses with his pen. He began to market a new commodity—thought. He wrote a number of poems and pamphlets, and found that they were but a poor insurance for a man with a growing family. And so he went back to business. He managed a state lottery, served as accountant in the revenue department, and became—strange employment for a bankrupt!—an expert adviser in the reform of British coinage.

But he found his progress as a government employe too slow for his restless ambition. He was anxious to start out once more for himself. Scraping together a few hundred pounds from his friends—he had a glib tongue as well as a facile pen—he opened a brick-and-tile factory, and found it successful beyond his dreams. He bought a coach and a new house, and within a few years he paid off the greater part of his debts.

And best of all, he found time for his writing. Having dragged himself to literature as a painful vocation, he now resorted to it as a pleasant avocation. He wrote scores of pamphlets on every sort of subject, from the building of roads to the emancipation of women; tirades against the unjust laws of England—"these are all cobweb laws, in which the small flies are catched, and the great ones break through"—and a satirical poem, *The True-Born Englishman,* in which he castigated the cruelty of the British natives against the alien, especially the Dutch, immigrants.

As a result of his poem, Defoe won not only a measure of fame but the favor of the King. For William III was himself a Dutchman. This "greatest and best of Princes"—we are quoting Defoe's words—rewarded him beyond his "capacity of deserving." The son of the chandler had become, at the age of forty-one, the adviser of the King.

Defoe was justly proud of his achievement. But he was unaware of the pitfalls that lay ahead of him.

III

DEFOE'S TROUBLES were due in some measure to a strange contradiction in his character. This Dissenter son of a tradesman was a paradox of material ambition and moral integrity. His ambition at times overrode his integrity, but at other times his integrity overruled his ambition. Though not always above double dealing with his business associates, he never stooped to double dealing with his own Puritanical faith. This stubborn Puritanical faith led him again and again to court disaster in the midst of his prosperity. In the political field he often sold his pen, but in the field of religion he never sold his conscience. On the contrary, he kept himself constantly in hot water through his courageous advocacy of the unpopular cause of the Dissenters in the face of a hostile Parliament. One of his pamphlets in behalf of the Dissenters proved so irritating to the reactionary Parliament that a warrant was issued for his arrest. Defoe went into hiding and a reward of £50 was offered to anyone who would find him. "He is a middle-sized man, about forty years old, of a brown complexion, and dark-brown coloured hair, but wears a wig; a hooked nose, a sharp chin, grey eyes, and a large mole near his mouth . . ."

He was discovered and (on July 9, 1703) sentenced "to stand three times in the pillory, to pay a fine of three hundred marks, and to lie in prison during the pleasure of Queen Anne"—Defoe's patron King was now dead, having been killed by a fall from his horse.

The public exposure upon the pillory, designed as a humiliation for Defoe, turned out to be a triumph. For the populace, instead of belaboring him—as was customary—with rotten eggs and with stinking fish, hailed him with cheers. Here was a man who had dared to say his say! His trip from the pillory to the jail was like the march of a conquering hero.

But when the doors of the prison were closed behind him, his admirers promptly forgot his existence. For several months he remained shut up in his cell at "the pleasure of Queen Anne"—a High Churchwoman who hated the Dissenters—while his brick factory went to ruin and his family came close to the verge of starvation. And he might have remained in his cell to the end of his days but for the astuteness of the new Secretary of State, Robert Harley. This statesman-politician, though unfriendly to Defoe's *religious* principles, was crafty enough to take advantage of Defoe's *political* principles. Or, to be more exact, he took advantage of Defoe's *lack* of political principles. He had noted that the pen of this facile pamphleteer could turn the most extraordinary political somersaults. Now it would praise the Whigs and now the Tories. Himself a Tory, Harley was anxious to win the favor of the more moderate Whigs. He therefore made a bargain with Defoe—he offered him his freedom in return for his literary services.

Defoe accepted the offer and became the mouthpiece of the government. With the financial help of his patron, he started a weekly paper—*The Review*. Defoe insisted that it was a periodical "independent of prejudice or party," but the readers knew better. The words of *The Review* were the words of Defoe, but the voice was the voice of Harley.

And, truth to tell, he found it no great difficulty to imitate the voice of Harley. For while Harley was a liberal Tory, Defoe was a liberal Whig. And liberalism, under whatever name and in whatever camp, had everywhere the selfsame complexion. Defoe felt, and perhaps not unjustly, that he was serving the cause of his country in his effort to bring the cooler heads of the two parties to a common ground of mutual understanding.

All this meant hard work, plenty of abuse, and little pay. Defoe wrote every word of every issue of the *Review,* for Harley wouldn't trust anyone else with so delicate a task. Yet with all his delicate finesse, Defoe kept constantly antagonizing the hot-headed extremists in both camps. His life as an editor was a continual battle against invectives and accusations and threats. And poverty. Harley was a man who paid with abstract promises rather than with concrete cash. Again and again he put Defoe— "I now must feed, alas, a family of seven children"—to the humiliation of begging for the money that was long overdue. It was Harley's business to keep his slave constantly loyal through his constant uncertainty as to the future.

With this purpose in view, Harley kept entangling Defoe more and more into the web of the government's secret machinations. He turned him, in short, into a spy—a *confidential agent,* he euphemistically called it. Defoe's duty, as the government's agent, was to travel over the country—under the assumed name of Alexander Goldsmith—to talk to the people, to pry into their affairs, and to find out what they thought of their Queen and her Secretary of State.

It was in the summer of 1704 that Defoe set out on his "secret intelligence" journey. And he found this journey—he confessed —much to his liking. A born reporter, he loved to associate with people, to observe their habits, to study their characters, to analyze their thoughts. He turned out to be a friendly adviser to the people rather than an inquisitive spy. And, from the stand-point of the government, it was just as well. For Defoe managed to *convince* instead of trying to *convict* the critics of the crown.

His services were especially valuable in the cementing of the Union between England and Scotland. Upon his first arrival in Scotland, he was greeted with a shower of stones. That night his house was attacked by an infuriated crowd of Anglophobes. "Down with the spies!" they shouted. "No union with the Eng-lish!" Defoe barely managed to escape through a back door. Little by little, however, he won the ears and the hearts of the Scottish leaders. And finally he was able to write to Harley: "I have now I hope the satisfaction of seeing the fruit of all this . . . labour-ing, fighting, mobbing . . . viz, the Union . . . While I write this, the guns are firing from the Castle (to celebrate this Union) . . . Methinks I may say: Now let me depart from hence for my eyes have seen the conclusion . . ."

But Harley wouldn't let him depart. Defoe was too valuable a slave to be so quickly released. "Keep his hand to the plow and feed him on empty hopes." He sent Defoe a check for £100— just enough to feed his family but not enough to set him up in any substantial business.

And Defoe continued to serve his master and to plan for a more hopeful future. A happier life not only for himself but for the world. He went on with his activity as an intelligence agent for Harley, but he supplemented this work with the selling of English table-cloths in Scotland and with the writing of several pamphlets for the reconstruction of society. He advocated, in 1709, the establishment of a League of Nations and of a World

Court. The aggressive Louis XIV had just suffered a humiliating defeat at the hands of the British army. "It is now," wrote Defoe, "within the power of England and her allies for ever to prevent any more war in Europe. It is within their power to make themselves arbiters of all the differences and disputes that ever can happen in Europe, whether between kingdom and kingdom, or between sovereign and subjects. A congress of this alliance may be made a Court of Appeals for all the injured and oppressed . . . Here the small states shall be protected against the terror of their powerful neighbours, the great shall no more oppress the small, or the mighty devour the weak . . . This confederacy [of unaggressive nations] may, if they please, preserve the power of banishing war . . . to the end of the world."

But the isolationists of the eighteenth century paid as little attention to Daniel Defoe as the isolationists of the twentieth century paid to Woodrow Wilson.

IV

FOR A NUMBER OF YEARS we lose track of Defoe. The wheel of political fortune has turned against Harley. From the heights of his power he has been hurled into prison. And with him he has carried along a number of his supporters, including Defoe. This last term in jail has cured Defoe of his interest in politics. "As the preacher said, that all was vanity and vexation of the spirit, so I of these [politicians]: all is a mere show and an abominable hypocrisy, of every party, in every age, under every government; when they are *out,* they fight to get *in;* when *in,* to prevent being *out* . . . Every party, and almost every person that we have an account of, have . . . been guilty, more or less, of the general charge—that their interest governs their principle."

Defoe's own dabbling in politics had advanced neither his interest nor his principle. Sick in body and disgusted in mind, he finally tore himself away from his diplomatic slavery and disappeared into the mist.

And then, on the verge of sixty, he appeared once more and the bigwigs of London nodded their heads in a condescension of pity. "What a sad comedown!" The adviser of princes had become a story teller for kitchen wenches. The author of dissertations on politics had descended to reporting the adventures of a shipwrecked sailor. Few of his contemporaries realized that Daniel Defoe, in stooping to write *Robinson Crusoe,* had risen to immortal fame.

V

DEFOE had found himself at last. He was not a businessman, not a pamphleteer, not a politician, but a writer of fiction. His whole life had been a groping toward this end. His assumption of all the contradictory characters—the manufacturer, the peddler, the Dissenter, the compromiser, the conservative, the rebel, the comrade, the spy—these were but a subconscious endeavor to understand from the inside the various activities of the human show. "If you want to describe your brother's sin, you must put yourself under your brother's skin."

Defoe had played all sorts of men, and now he became the interpreter of mankind. The last decade of his life was an amazing activity of creation. As his body grew weaker, his mind became more energetic. Novel after novel came to shape under the nimble shuttle of his fancy. *The King of the Pirates, The Adventures of Duncan Campbell, Memoirs of a Cavalier, Captain Singleton, Colonel Jack, Moll Flanders, Roxana, A Journal of the Plague Year, The History of the Devil.* "How can so old a man get out so many new books?"

And still find time for his business ventures? For Defoe, though cured of his politics, was never cured of his recklessness. To the end of his days he kept running after the pot of gold at the end of the rainbow. Whatever he made on his novels, he lost in his careless investments. And in these ill-advised investments he involved some of his closest friends and relatives—including his own daughter, Hannah.

Finally, to recoup the losses of his business failures, he wrote a *Complete Guide to Business Success*. This guide was—in Defoe's words—"calculated for the instruction of our . . . tradesmen, and especially of young beginners."

Defoe was an expert in giving advice—but not in following it. At the age of sixty-five we find him involved in a lawsuit in which he is branded—most likely without justice—as a "swindler." And four years later we cannot find him at all. He has gone into hiding from his creditors. The only clew to his whereabouts is a letter received by his son-in-law, Henry Baker (August 12, 1730). It is signed "Your unhappy, D.F.," and it is dated "About two miles from Greenwich, Kent." The letter tells of the plight of an old man weighed down by "a load of insupportable sorrows," neglected by his family, broken hearted at "the inhuman dealing of my own son"—the son had probably refused him the money for another wild speculation—suffering "under a weight of very heavy illness," and distracted because he cannot have the comfort of a last embrace from his daughter and her husband. For "just to come and look at you, and return immediately, 'tis a burden too heavy." And as for their coming to see him, this is out of the question. For his hiding place must not be revealed to anyone, not even to those most dear to him.

And then the letter ends upon a note of resignation. "I am so near my journey's end, and am hastening to the place where the weary are at rest, and where the wicked cease to trouble. Be it that the passage is rough, and the day stormy, by what way soever He please to bring me to the end of it, I desire to finish life with this temper of soul in all cases: *Te Deum Laudamus . . .*"

And thus, entrusting his soul into the hand of God, the shipwrecked sailor set out alone and unfriended toward the unknown island in the dark.

SWIFT

Important Works by Swift

The Battle of the Books	*Directions to Servants*
The Tale of a Tub	*Polite Conversation*
Gulliver's Travels	Numerous satires
Children of the Poor	in verse

Jonathan Swift

1667–1745

THE STORY OF JONATHAN SWIFT is the tragedy of a giant chained by Lilliputians. But it is also the comedy of a cynic who knew how to laugh at his chains. He had too strong an intellect in too feeble a body—a combination which turns a man either into a dull preacher or a brilliant wag. Jonathan Swift was both.

The superiority of his intellect became manifest when he was three years old. At that age he was already able to read the Scriptures by himself. And the infirmity of his body became manifest at about the same time. From earliest childhood he was afflicted with recurrent spells of nauseating dizziness.

His entire life, indeed, was a medley of contradictions. And these contradictions began with his birth. Though of English parentage, he was born in Ireland and lived there for the greater part of his career. And in his character he showed this two-fold influence of his ancestry and his environment—he grew up with an English mind and with an Irish heart.

At six months he lost his father, and at twelve months he was kidnaped by his wet-nurse. Having heard of the death of an uncle who had left her a legacy in England, she boarded a ship for England without any notice to her mistress—and she took along with her on shipboard her mistress' baby. It was not until three years later that Jonathan was returned to his mother. The child had developed a great love for the Bible and an impish fondness for the playing of pranks.

At six he entered the Kilkenny Grammar School, and at fourteen he matriculated at Trinity College, Dublin. Here he showed "a passion for reading, but an aversion for discipline." He barely managed to get his bachelor's degree, but he was suspended from his master's degree for his "unnecessary insolence to the Junior Dean." He returned home in disgrace.

Yet he managed, in spite of his "unnecessary insolence," to secure a job as secretary to Sir William Temple—a mediocre writer, a close adviser to the King of England and, so went the malicious but probably unreliable gossip, the "natural" father of Jonathan himself. The position carried with it a salary of twenty pounds a year and a place at the second table, with the servants.

And so, richer in pocket but poorer in pride, the brilliant young secretary settled down to copying out the thoughts of his mediocre old master. And in his spare moments—there were not many of them—he jotted down his own thoughts, mostly in verse.

But in these scanty spare moments of his apprenticeship, young Jonathan found another diversion—the teaching of a little girl by the name of Hester, or Stella, Johnson. This fascinating child of eight was a member of Sir William's household. Her position in this household, as well as her origin, seemed to be shrouded in mystery. Legally baptized as the daughter of Sir William's housekeeper and of Edward Johnson, his bailiff, she had taken the fancy of Sir William and was treated as one of the family. Rumor had it—and this time perhaps with justification—that Stella, too, was a "natural" child of Sir William. At any rate, Sir William not only promised her a legacy at his death but undertook to bring her up as a lady under the tutelage of Jonathan Swift.

Young Swift enjoyed the tutoring of Stella. And as for Stella, she was all adoration for this tall and not unhandsome taskmaster with the caustic tongue and the gentle smile.

This pleasant relationship between pupil and teacher lasted, on and off, for nine years. And then there came a change of occupation for Jonathan Swift. He was ordained chaplain at Dublin Castle. The young curate was pleased with the spiritual honor but displeased with the material position. Having determined upon an ecclesiastical career, he was anxious to rise to the top of the Church of England instead of being merely a twig upon its Irish offshoot.

Yet an important position in the Church of England, the one thing that he most ardently desired, was the one thing that his superiors most vigorously denied him. For this "mad parson"—as they called him—had too unpredictable a mind and too unconventional a pen for a leader of the orthodox faith. There was no telling what bombshell he might throw at what moment into the beliefs of his fellow churchmen. Already, it was generally known, he had written—although he had not as yet dared to publish—a devastating satire about certain of the religious practices in Europe. He called his satire *A Tale of a Tub*—a title which, as he explained in the preface, he took from a custom among seamen. When they meet a whale, he said, they fling out an empty tub to divert him from attacking the ship. In the same way he throws out his tale to divert the infidels from attacking the church.

And then he goes on to show how Christianity has deviated from the religion of Christ. He illustrates his point with an allegory about a father who has left three coats of equal worth to his three sons—Peter (the Catholic Church), Martin (the Church of England), and Jack (the Calvinist Church). "These coats," the father said, "will last you fresh and sound as long as you live . . . Now wear them and brush them often . . . Further," counseled the father, "I have commanded in my will that you live together in one house like brethren, for then you will be sure to thrive, and not otherwise."

The three brothers took their coats—continues Swift—and

promptly forgot their father's will. Each of them began to re-model his coat, over and over again, in accordance with the shifting fashion of the day.

Finally Peter, having embroidered his coat with shoulder pads and gold laces and whatnots until it was no longer recognizable as the coat originally given him by his father, assumed that he alone was the owner of the one true coat. Furthermore, he declared that he alone was the owner of his father's house and promptly kicked his two brothers out into the cold.

Whereupon, writes Swift, the two dispossessed brothers re-examined their father's will (the Bible) and attempted to restore their coats to their sensible original simplicity.

In this attempt, concludes Swift, Martin succeeded tolerably well. He pulled out all the unnecessary embroidery from the coat, taking care to leave only those decorations which served either to strengthen or to conceal a defect. As for Jack, however, he was so anxious to simplify his coat that he cut it up into a rag. And when people came to look or to laugh at it—but the rest of the story is too coarse for the modern palate.

It was several years after its completion that *A Tale of the Tub* was published—anonymously. Though intended as a parable to show the author's preference for the Church of England, it failed to win the approbation of the Anglican bishops and archbishops. They laughed at Swift's satire over the defects of the other churches, and they fumed over his allusions to the defects of his own church. This young chaplain, they decided, was far too clever for his own good. He was a man to be humored—and to be watched.

II

ONE DAY, when Swift was an old man, he glanced at a few pages of his *Tale* and murmured, "Good God, what a genius I had when I wrote that book!" This was his misfortune. His genius was too great for the understanding of his contemporaries. The little minds were afraid of the big mind. Deliberately they kept him chained down to one obscure position after another. From Dublin Castle to a country parish in Laracor. From the church in Laracor back to St. Patrick's Cathedral in Dublin. But no bishopric for him in England, or even Ireland. A deanery was the best that they ever dared to offer him. He had received a doctorate in divinity, had won the friendship of the most influential men in England, had dined with the Prime Minister and played cards with the Secretary of the Treasury—but all in vain. Whenever he applied for an important position in the Church, he was met with a polite refusal. His pen was too deeply steeped in fire and brimstone. On one occasion he even sent an appeal directly to the Queen—with the same negative result. Dean Swift remained the most famous nonentity of his day.

Yet through it all he remained outwardly cheerful. His days, save for the all-too-frequent attacks of his dizziness, were filled with epigrams and laughter. He loved people individually, though he hated them in the lump. A tall, vigorous, swarthy, center-of-the-stage type of man, with piercing blue eyes, dark bushy eyebrows and a booming voice. The tales that he could tell! And the language that he could use, especially in male company! And so gallant with the ladies!—in spite of the rumors of his constitutional defects.

A man outwardly cheerful, and inwardly seething with rage. Conscious of his superiority to the leaders of the day, he must needs play the lackey in their presence. Having come to London on a mission in behalf of the Irish people (and of his own advancement), he met the two foremost statesmen of England (Bolingbroke and Harley), tried his best to climb into their favor —"in London a man must climb on all fours"—and remained their favorite clown.

But a clown without pay. Like Defoe, he wrote political pamphlets for Harley. But unlike Defoe, he refused to receive compensation for his work. On one occasion, as Harley shook hands with him, he managed to slip into Swift's palm a note for fifty pounds. The outraged pamphleteer threw the note in Harley's face, stalked out of the room, and refused to see Harley again until the latter came to his house to offer a personal apology.

What Swift wanted for his work was not pay but preferment. And this he was never able to get—either from Harley or from anyone else.

Yet his stay in England, though a political failure, was an intellectual triumph. He became the outstanding figure in the coffee houses, where the keenest wits of London congregated for their daily duel of tongues. The "mad parson" was by far the most skillful, if not always the most stubtle, of the duelists. His cuts were deep and sharp and decisive. There was no salve of sympathy in his words when he really wanted to hurt. "No man," writes one of his biographers, Bertram Newman, "ever had more wit and less humor than Swift."

His was a curious kind of wit, a gruff and relentless tearing away of the hypocrisy that covered the ugliness of life, a cynical *reductio ad absurdum*—a reduction of the pomposity of the fanciful to the absurdity of the real. His sardonic wit would crop out in his friendly as well as in his unfriendly acts. Always he did the astonishing thing—utterly unexpected because utterly logical. "One evening," writes the poet, Alexander Pope, "Gay [the author of *The Beggar's Opera*] and I went to see Jonathan Swift—you know how intimately we were all acquainted. On our coming in, 'Hey-day, gentlemen,' says the doctor, 'what's the meaning of this visit? How come you to leave all the great lords, that you are so fond of, to come hither to see a poor dean?'

" 'Because we would rather see you than any of them.'

" 'Ay, any one that did not know you so well as I do might believe you. But, since you are come, I must get some supper for you, I suppose?'

" 'No, doctor, we have supped already.'

" 'Supped already! that's impossible; why, 'tis not eight o'clock yet.'

" 'Indeed we have.'

" 'That's very strange: but if you had not supped, I must have got something for you. Let me see, what should I have had? A couple of lobsters? Ay, that would have done very well—two shillings; tarts—a shilling. But you will drink a glass of wine with me, though you supped so much before your usual time, only to spare my pocket?'

" 'No; we had rather talk with you than drink with you.'

" 'But if you had supped with me, as in all reason you ought to have done, you must have drank with me. A bottle of wine— two shillings. Two and two is four, and one is five; just two-and-sixpence apiece. There, Pope, there's half a crown for you; and there's another for you, sir; for I won't save anything by you, I am determined.'

"And in spite of everything we could say to the contrary," concludes Pope, "he actually obliged us to take the money."

Such was the anomaly of Dean Swift—sardonic, gentle, vivacious, morose—a writer applauded for his genius, a preacher despised for his frankness, a celebrity who was everywhere quoted and nowhere understood. He returned from England loaded with honors and denied a job. A titan chained down in a world of pygmies.

But before he left his English pygmies, he had his sport with them. He punctured the balloon of their pretentiousness in the person of John Partridge. This Partridge, by trade a cobbler, tried to set himself up as a prophet. He published an astrological almanac in which he made annual predictions of things to come. In order to expose the stupidity of these predictions, Swift published—under the pen name of Isaac Bickerstaff—a rival almanac which contained a list of his own prophecies. "My first prophecy," he wrote, "relates to Partridge the Almanac-Maker. I have consulted the star of his nativity . . . and find he will infallibly die upon the 29th of March next, about eleven at night, of a raging fever . . ."

March 29th passed, and Partridge protested that he was still alive. But "Isaac Bickerstaff" stuck to his guns. He published a minute and circumstantial *Account of the death of Mr. Par-*

tridge, the Almanac-Maker, upon the 29th instant. Mr. Partridge once more protested that he was *not* dead. Whereupon "Mr. Bickerstaff" gravely announced that John Partridge was not only a corpse but a liar.

And thus the faker was faked, and remained "a dead man and a liar" to the end of his days.

III

SWIFT was a strange man; and one of the strangest things about him was his relationship toward Stella and Vanessa. Stella, as we have seen, was the little girl he had tutored while serving as secretary to Sir William Temple. When she grew up, she became to him something less than a lover, yet something more than a friend. As for Vanessa—her real name was Esther Vanhomrigh—he met her on one of his visits to London and became tenderly attached to her. And she—in spite of the fact that he was old enough to be her father—fell passionately in love with him.

And now began one of the most peculiar triangles in the history of romance. Swift devoted himself to both, yet surrendered himself to neither. When he was in England, he kept up an intimate correspondence with Stella; and when he was in Ireland, he kept up an equally intimate correspondence with Vanessa. And finally, when he settled down in Dublin as the Dean of St. Patrick's, he found himself pleasantly though embarrassingly burdened with the presence of both his devotees in the same vicinity. Stella lived in a house not far from St. Patrick's—frequently, when Swift was away, she came to live in his own apartment. And Vanessa took a house in a suburb of Dublin on the pretense that she had inherited some real estate in that locality and that she must now attend to the matter in person.

Stella and Vanessa never met. Yet each of them knew of the other's existence, and both of them harried Swift with their jealousy. Of the two women, Vanessa was the more impetuous.

"I was born with violent passions," she confessed to Swift in one of her letters, "and they all terminate in one—that unexpressible passion I have for you . . . Pray shew some tenderness for me, or I shall lose my senses . . ." And finally she broke under the strain of her emotions. On May 1, 1723, she made her will—in which she deliberately omitted Swift's name—and on June 1, 1723, she died—"without the services of God or priest," and "with a scrap of the *Tale of a Tub* in her hands."

Stella, no less sensitive but far more sensible than Vanessa, survived her by five years. On the whole she served as a steadying influence upon her "mad parson." A woman of solid character and of sober judgment, she was "more inclined to confirm a wrong opinion than to oppose it. The excuse she commonly gave"—we are quoting the words of Joseph Addison—"was that it prevented noise and saved time." Though she disliked her role as owner of only half of Swift's affections, she contented herself with an occasional pointed stab at "my dear's double dealing." On the whole she realized that Swift was an unusual man who must be handled with unusual tact.

And so she lived her tactful life as his "ministress rather than his mistress"—there is no evidence to prove, as some of his contemporaries hinted, that they were ever married. And when she finally died, she left a permanent void in the heart of the sad old dean. From now on Swift's outward conduct, like his inward thought, was that of an embittered man. "I detest the world," he wrote to one of his friends, "because I am growing wholly unfit for it."

IV

IT BECAME A RITUAL with Dean Swift on his birthdays to read the Biblical chapter in which Job curses the day he was born. More and more he was learning to despise mankind—and to serve his fellow men. He was especially anxious to lighten the burdens of the Irish. He lashed them with his tongue, and he caressed them with his hand. The suffering of Ireland had become the overmastering anxiety of his old age. And the alleviation of this suffering had become his overmastering ambition. On one occasion, when the English government had proposed an oppressive measure against the Irish people, he castigated the injustice in a series of letters so trenchant that the government found it necessary to drop the proposal. These letters, which he signed "M. B. Drapier, the owner of a shop of Irish stuffs," won for Swift the "eternal gratitude" of the Irish—and became to him an "eternal source of annoyance." For he didn't like the adulation of the people. He had helped them, he said, not because of his love for *them*, but because of his hatred against *slavery*. He knew the fickleness of the mob. They were ready to applaud him for his daring in their behalf. But would they raise a finger to save him from the consequences of his daring? To illustrate this point, he told an amusing story. A Spanish Jew, followed by an excited crowd of schoolboys, was being led to the stake. Fearing that they would be cheated out of their sport in the event of his recantation, the youngsters kept clapping him on the back and shouting, "*Sta firme, Moyse* (Moses, continue steadfast)."

And Swift continued steadfast in spite of the foolish youngsters and the savage inquisitors of the world. He had a compassionate contempt for the Yahoos of the human race, with their perjuries and their passions and their stupidities and their swindles and their wars. He was amazed at man's inhumanity to man. He had lost all faith in human reason. And he declared this bankruptcy of his human faith in a pamphlet whose devastating logic stands, even among Swift's writings, in a class by itself. The title of this pamphlet is *A Modest Proposal for Preventing the children of Poor People from being a Burthen to their Parents or Country, and for making them beneficial to the Publick*. What—he asks—is the good of all the suggestions offered for the relief of the "dire poverty and the griping want" of the Irish peasants? Why waste any more time trying to teach the absentee landlords "to have at least one degree of mercy towards their tenants?" Away with such "vain, idle, visionary thoughts!" He, the author of the

Modest Proposal, had a totally new and practical plan—a plan "which, I hope, will not be liable to the least objection."

And here, in brief, is the plan:

"I have been assured by a very knowing American of my acquaintance in London, that a young healthy child well nursed is at a year old a most delicious, nourishing, and wholesome food, whether stewed, roasted, baked, or boiled, and I make no doubt that it will equally serve in a fricassee, or a ragout."

Let the Irish peasants, therefore, raise children for the table of their English landlords. "A child will make two dishes at an entertainment for friends, and when the family dines alone, the fore and hind quarter will make a reasonable dish, and seasoned with a little pepper or salt will be very good boiled on the fourth day, especially in winter . . .

"I grant this food will be somewhat dear, and therefore very proper for landlords who, as they have already devoured most of the parents, seem to have the best title to the children . . .

"I have computed the charge of nursing a beggar's child . . . to be about two shillings *per annum* . . . and I believe no gentleman would repine to give ten shillings for the carcass of a good fat child . . . Thus the Squire will grow popular among his tenants, and the mother will have eight shillings net profit and be fit for work till she produces another child."

And then, with a final twist of his satirical lash—"Those who are more thrifty . . . may flay the carcass; the skin of which, artificially dressed, will make admirable gloves for ladies, and summer boots for fine gentlemen."

The landed gentry read the pamphlet, expressed their disgust at the author's barbarity, and went on with their "civilized" business of slowly starving their Irish tenants to death.

As for the "barbarian," he went about in a "perfect rage and resentment," snarling at everybody, and giving alms to a stream of beggars who came daily to his door.

He hated beggars; and the world, he said, was full of them. They were to be found among the rich as well as among the poor.

[73]

"The rich beg for a kingdom; the poor, for a crust of bread."
Swift detested the gigantic beggars ever so much more than the
little ones. The bigger they are, he tells us in *Gulliver's Travels*,
the greater the torture they inflict upon the eyes and the nose.
As for himself, he had no use for begging because he had no use
for money. In this respect, he said, he tried to model himself after
the image of the Almighty. "We can tell how little the Almighty
thinks of money by considering those upon whom He is pleased
to bestow it."

And thus the "mad parson" jested and scolded his way into
old age, appearing to everybody to be standing on his head because he alone stood on his feet in a topsy-turvy world.

V

SWIFT had now reached the years of disillusioned wisdom, and
he decided to incorporate this wisdom into the imaginary Travels
of Lemuel Gulliver. On August 8, 1726, he sent the manuscript
of *Gulliver's Travels* to the publisher, Benjamin Motte. And together with the manuscript he sent a letter, signed "Richard
Sympson," in which he described himself as a cousin of Lemuel
Gulliver. "Mr. Gulliver entrusted me some years ago with this
copy of his Travels . . . I have shown them to several persons
of great judgment and distinction; and although some parts may
be thought in one or two places to be a little satirical, it is agreed
they will give no offense . . ." Mr. "Sympson" then went on to
offer the manuscript for £200, with the stipulation that if the
sale of the book did not warrant this advance, he would refund
the balance to the publisher.

The book was published in the fall of 1726, and the first edition was exhausted in a week. Everybody laughed over Gulliver's
bitter attack against the stupidity of the yahoo-man race, because
everybody thought that it was not himself but his neighbor who
was meant to be the object of the attack. And Swift became more
bitter than ever. He had failed in his purpose. "I wanted to vex

the world, not to divert it." *Gulliver's Travels* was the story of a sane man adventuring over the inanities and the vanities of an insane world. If only the world, instead of being *amused* by its sane men, would allow itself to be *ruled* by them! Then there would be less greed and more graciousness, less private property and more common fellowship, less cruelty and more pity, less glitter and more glory, less insolence and more sense. "I have often endeavored," wrote Swift to Alexander Pope, "to establish a friendship among all sane men . . . They are seldom above three or four in a generation; and if they could be united, they would drive the world before them."

One such sane man he met—Voltaire. This rebellious young Frenchman, exiled to England for his too honest tongue—"It is my trade," he had said, "to say what I think"—sat at the feet of the "mad parson," absorbed his philosophy, wrote an imitation (*Micromégas*) of *Gulliver's Travels,* and returned to France with a new vision to abolish the hatreds and the injustices of the rulers of the world.

And the "mad parson" went on with his tireless search for a sane world. His body was racked with pain, and his heart was saddened repeatedly by the loss of his dearest friends. "The gift of a long life is bought at too high a price." To strengthen himself for the ordeal of a lonely old age, he wrote a prayer which was posthumously found among his unpublished papers. "Oh God, Thou dispensest Thy blessings and Thy punishments as it becometh infinite justice and mercy . . . Turn our thoughts rather upon that felicity which we hope they shall enjoy, than upon that unspeakable loss we shall endure."

Always thinking about the felicity of man—this cynic who faced mankind with a snarl.

VI

AND NOW his thinking and his suffering and his snarling had become erased into a merciful oblivion. His mind was a blank. One day, as he read *A Tale of a Tub,* it was pointed out to him that he was the author of this book. "Oh no," he said. "The man who wrote it was a genius." Again and again, when he saw his haggard face in the mirror, he remarked with an impersonal sadness, "Poor old man." And on his birthdays, when bells were rung and bonfires were lit in his honor, he asked, "Who is this man whom the people love so devoutly?"

October 19, 1745. A clear sky overhead, a clouded mind within. But for an instant the cloud lifted. "Oh God," he was heard to murmur, "have a watchful care of me on this my last journey."

And when he set out on the journey, an entire city came to bid him Godspeed. For they had learned to worship him as a man of great hatred and great love. A hater of injustice, a lover of men.

STERNE

Important Works by Sterne

Laurence Sterne

1713–1768

THE GRANDFATHER of Laurence Sterne was Archbishop of York who stood like a granite monument in one spot. His father was a soldier who moved restlessly like the wind from place to place.

"My birthday was ominous to my poor father, who was the day after my arrival, with many other brave officers, broke and sent adrift into the wide world with a wife and two children." He was "the Ulysses-like plaything of adverse gods at the War Office." And his destiny was also at the mercy of a prolific wife, who bore him a brood of feeble, anemic children. On orders to the regiment, she followed her husband "from Ireland to England, and from England to Ireland, from inland garrison to seaport town and back again, incessantly bearing and incessantly burying children"—until friends began to speak of Mrs. Sterne's losing one infant at such and such a place and leaving another behind on such and such a journey, as if they were so many unfortunate pieces of baggage addressed directly from heaven to the grave. Indeed, death seemed dressed for more than one kind of action under the King's regimentals. At Gibraltar the father of Laurence Sterne, "that much-enduring campaigner," was run through the body in a duel "about a goose." The affair took place in a small room; and Captain Philips put his rapier with such vigor through Captain Sterne's person, that he actually pinned him to the wall behind. Then, with infinite presence of mind, the wounded little officer politely requested Captain Philips that before withdrawing his instrument he might have the courtesy to brush off any plaster adherent to the point, "which it would be disagreeable to have introduced into my system."

Captain Sterne recovered from the wound. He retired for his convalescence to Jamaica—and there he died of a fever. "His malady first took away his senses, and then made a child of him; and finally in a month or two walking about continually, without complaining, he sat down in an arm-chair and breathed his last."

This mingling of the whimsical with the tragic—a destiny which pursued the little soldier throughout his life—continued in the life of his son, Laurence. Like his father, he was tossed about by the winds of chance and by the whimsies of his fellow men. Writing of his father, Laurence Sterne observed: "You might have cheated him ten times a day, if nine had not been sufficient for your purpose."

II

HIS FATHER had left his family "without a shilling in the world." Fortunately, however, a cousin came to the rescue. He invested his money in a classical education for the "lean and learned" youngster. "Who knows? Perhaps some day you will become an Archbishop like your grandfather."

Did his cousin know that Laurence's favorite book among the classics was Ovid's *Art of Love?* And that Laurence's absorbing pastime was flirting with the girls? After a due measure of Horace, Plato, Pliny, Cicero, Isocrates and the Lives of the Saints, he received his ordination and settled down as a clergyman in the Yorkshire parish of Sutton-on-the-Forest. He dabbled in politics with an uncle who was an influential churchman, received the benefice of additional parishes, and then looked around for a wife to add to his preferments. He courted Elizabeth Lumely for two years. No one ever wrote love letters quite like the letters of this semi-classical, wholly lovesick young preacher. "He sealed his kisses with quotations from Milton's *Paradise Lost,* and with allusions to the *Beggar's Opera,* and he underlined his sighs with footnotes from Pope's *Essay on Man.*" Elizabeth "owned she liked me, but thought herself not rich enough or me poor enough to be joined together . . . She fell into consumption, and one evening that I was sitting by her with an almost broken heart to see her so ill, she said: 'My dear Laury, I never can be yours, for I verily believe I have not long to live! But I have left you every shilling of my fortune.' Upon that she showed me her will. This generosity overpowered me. It pleased God that she recovered, and we were married . . ."

Their wedded life commenced well. The lady had musical tastes. "The vicar played on the bass viol and she accompanied him."

But it was a dull life. For Mrs. Sterne was a dull woman. All the heavier virtues dragged her down when she tried to accompany her husband on his intellectual hop, skip, and jump, so that the couple was unable to fulfill the first command of a happy marriage—to go through life as one. Sterne was a wit whose fancy lifted him on wings of laughter, while his wife plodded along, heavy-footed, sullen, unable to understand. He had decided that he was somehow—in spite of his clerical robes— a descendant of one of the most renowned families in fancy if not in blood—the family of the Yoricks of Denmark, the jesters at the King's court. Alas, poor Yorick! The jester of the King was dead. But long live his successor, the jester of the world!

For the world is sad and it must be amused. Away, then, with gravity! "Gravity is an errant scoundrel of the most dangerous kind—because he is a sly one . . . The very essence of gravity is design . . . a mysterious carriage of the body to cover the defects of the mind."

And so Laurence Sterne had adopted, in addition to the four

sacred Gospels, a group of four *secular* gospels—the gospels of painting, of fiddling and of laughter, and the divine service of books.

And for all that, he still found time for his favorite pastime— the "pursuit of happiness." A long list of ladies had kindled flames in the breast of the susceptible young parson. His "platonic dalliances" were the scandal—and the envy—of his parishioners.

Yet these dalliances did not stand in the way of his advancement. He still received preferments, and people still wondered at his versatility. He was appointed Justice of the Peace and he judged his fellow parishioners with a merry twinkle of self-ridicule in his eye. Never since the days of Friar Tuck was there such a spectacle in England as this Yorkshire parson, who buried the dead, baptized the born, and laughed, laughed, laughed uproariously till his sides ached.

Always laughter before duty. "Once, as Sterne was going over the fields on a Sunday to preach at Stillington, it happened that his pointer dog sprung a covey of partridges, when he went directly home for his gun and left his flock that was waiting for him in the church in the lurch." When he hired a servant, he called him, with delicious humor, "my sinful Amen."

Aware of his own imperfections, he sympathized with the imperfections of others. He found himself "attached in comradeship" to a group of cultured voluptuaries who called themselves the "Club of Demoniacs" and who foregathered at a country estate which they had nicknamed "Crazy Castle." Here they ate and drank and were merry, and discussed literature and love, and wrote sonnets to Venus and to her "godson" François Rabelais.

> *And in the evening when they met*
> *(To think on't always does me good,)*
> *There never met a jollier set,*
> *Either before, or since the Flood.*

In such pursuits, tucked in a corner of England, Sterne lived the first half of his life—obscure, contented, scolded and loved by his happy-go-lucky flock. For though he had many vices, he had one virtue in abundance—a heartful of kindness for every living soul.

His kindness had grown out of his suffering. Laurence Sterne was a sick man. His very looks belied his laughter. With his lean, lanky figure clad in black, his spider legs, his chest "utterly without stamina," and his face which consisted not so much of cheeks as of stretches of hollowed skin, he tried to convince the world— and himself—that he was what he was not. The man was slowly bleeding to death of infected lungs. His huge nostrils alone kept constantly quivering with the breath of his wit. Nature had built for him a framework of tragedy within which the spirit of laughter managed to keep the body alive.

III

FOR HOURS, after he had laid away his violin, he sat in his library and wrote. This library was the temple dedicated to his blessed trinity of humorists—"Lucian, my dear Rabelais, and dearer Cervantes"—men who had received sorrow and given joy. And close behind them were the lesser divinities in his affections— Montaigne, Pope, and Swift. Here in the library Sterne paid his devotions to the ancient, esoteric mysteries and became deeply immersed in the strange Kabala of the chuckle. And in this atmosphere he prepared a book that amazed and inspired and scandalized the world. A "new and original" book. Nothing like it had ever been written before. It had no shape, no logic, no dignity. He just observed the wisdom and the stupidity of the world, its tragedy and its comedy, its fears and its foibles and its hatreds and its loves, kneaded it all together into a story as rich in interest—and as empty of plot—as life itself, injected into it the tang of Rabelaisian humor, and called the astonishing concoction *The Life and Opinions of Tristram Shandy*.

He read the first pages of the book to some friends after dinner. And they promptly fell asleep. Deeply hurt, he walked over to the fireplace and was about to toss the manuscript into the flames when one of the company, still awake in one eye—an eye that saw far ahead—snatched the manuscript and saved it for the future.

Even after the book was published, Sterne was dubious about its reception. "It is so utterly a creature without a head or a tail"—the preface, for example, is written in the middle instead of at the beginning of the story. And its humor is so very much like the Devil in a posture of self-adoration. "You sport too much with your wit . . . It is like toying with a man's mistress . . . very delightful solacement to the inamorato, but little fun to the by-stander."

Yet he hoped that people might compare his story to that other story published in the same year—Voltaire's *Candide*—"the funniest book of all time." And he prayed to the muse of Cunegonde that the Shandy family might be added to the gallery of great fictional portraits.

And now he began to receive the reports of his London friends who had read advance copies of *Tristram Shandy*. "It is the opinion of the best judges, without exception, that your book cannot be put into the hands of any woman of character." "I hope you except widows," replies Sterne sarcastically, "for they are not at all so squeamish."

And then, when he comes up to London, he discovers that his Shandygaff has taken hold after all. *Tristram* has conquered. And Sterne is a celebrity overnight.

IV

IN THE Yorkshire dialect, "shandy" is a word which means "crack-brained, unsteady, gay." And this characteristic is true of the entire book down to the very typography. "The pages are sprinkled over profusely with dashes, stars, imitations of fiddles, tuning forks, pages numbered wrong (as though by a mistake of the binder), one page utterly blank of print . . . an odd series of zigzag lines, like a meteorological registry . . . dashes of every length from an inch long downwards . . ." And, as the Londoners began to read the book, they stared and wondered and scratched their heads—and then they read on and became absorbed. What curious ideas! What lovable characters! And what an Odyssey of outlandish adventures!

These adventures begin not with the birth of Tristram—indeed, he is not born until the third volume—but with the vagaries, the fortunes, the duties and the privileges of the embryonic manikin that is later to be created into a man. And then this potpourri of a novel hurries us on to an acquaintance with Walter Shandy, the eccentric father of this eccentric embryo. Walter Shandy is a man long on theory and short on practice. He always attempts to do the elaborate rather than the simple thing—with the result that he generally does nothing at all. When he has to scratch his right ear, he will invariably try to do it with his left hand around the back of his head. His hand will thus be twisted in pain and his ear will remain unscratched. Armed with a stunning array of mystical quotations and magical beliefs, he is a born orator whose great tragedy is that he has no audience. "He is like a perspiring juggler before a company of the blind."

Even his wife is blind to his talents, and quite indifferent to his talk. She never asks him any questions, and thus she never gives him the opportunity that he most desperately desires—to argue. "She went out of the world at last," observes Tristram, "without knowing whether it turned round or stood still . . . My father had officiously told her above a thousand times which way it was—but she always forgot."

And now we meet another character in the Shandy household —Walter's brother, Toby. Uncle Toby, a retired soldier who is spending his last days with the Shandys, is full of goodness and empty of thought. While his brother discourses on philosophical matters, Uncle Toby smokes his pipe and catches flies.

Catches them, only to set them free. "Go—says he one day at dinner, to an overgrown one which had buzzed about his nose, and tormented him cruelly all dinner time. . . . I'll not hurt thee, says my uncle Toby, rising from his chair, and going across the room, with the fly in his hand,—I'll not hurt a hair of thy head:—Go, says he, lifting up the sash, and opening the hand as he spoke, to let it escape;—go, poor devil, get thee gone, why should I hurt thee?—This world surely is wide enough to hold both thee and me."

Toby Shandy is a beautiful soul. And yet—note the irony of Laurence Sterne—this sensitive lover of God's creation is also a passionate admirer of man's destruction. He makes an eloquent—and pointless—defense of his admiration for war to his brother Shandy. "If, when I was a schoolboy, I could not hear a drum beat, but my heart beat with it—was it my fault? Did I plant the propensity there? When we read over the siege of Troy, which lasted ten years and eight months,—though with such a train of artillery as we had at Namur the town might have been carried in a week—had I not three strokes of a ferula given me, two on my right hand, and one on my left, for calling Helene a b——h for it? Did any of you shed more tears for Hector? And when King Priam came to the camp to beg his body, and returned weeping back to Troy without it,—you know, brother, I could not eat my dinner."

He hates to see the killed, but he loves to see the killing. Or, rather, he loves to see the ingenuity displayed in the *process* of the killing. For years he has made an intensive study of military tactics and he has reënacted, together with his servant, Corporal Trim, the campaigns of the Duke of Marlborough in Italy and in Flanders. Daily he analyzes these campaigns in the papers, and then he fights them all over again on the bowling green adjoining Shandy Hill. He employs his pipes for guns, and smokes them into a furious display of artillery. Shot for shot, command for command, he duplicates the exploits of the Duke. "When Marlborough made a lodgement, my uncle Toby made a lodgement too . . . There could not have been a greater sight in the world, than . . . to have . . . observed the spirit with which my uncle Toby, with Trim behind him, sallied forth—the one with the *Gazette* in his hand, the other with a spade upon his shoulder—to execute the latest maneuver. What intense pleasure swimming in his eye as he stood over the corporal, reading the paragraph ten times over to him as he was at work, lest peradventure he should make the breach an inch too wide,—or leave it an inch too narrow. But when the breach was made, and the Corporal helped my uncle up to the charge, and followed him with the colours in his hand, to fix them upon the ramparts— Heaven! Earth! Sea!—what a triumph for Uncle Toby!"

This is the family into which Tristram is born—a bit of drifting capriciousness in a capricious and drifting world. For five volumes he wanders in a physical and mental and moral labyrinth of unreason and humor, leading us out of nowhere through infinity and back into nowhere again, and providing us on the journey with the most unexpected absurdities and excitements and revelations and joys. The author leads us just as madly as the pen leads him. We pant as we follow this crazy carnival of masked characters as they whirl about without reason or rhyme, "each dragging his neighbor by the feet, head, coat, amidst the most promiscuous and unforeseen hubbub."

And when it is all over, we catch our breath and exclaim, "What a mad adventure! But what a hilarious madness!"

V

LAURENCE STERNE intended to continue the madness in a number of sequels to *Tristram Shandy*. Having left his hero in mid-air, he proposed later on to bring him down to the ground. In the meantime, he made a visit to London and found himself the lion of the literary world. Everybody paid homage to the "tall and hectic-looking preacher-poet of Yorkshire" in whom reverence and ribaldry were so intimately wedded. Garrick and Lord Chesterfield waited upon him. From morning till night his rooms were "full of the greatest company." Every jest with which he sent his companions into gales of laughter was passed to the coffee houses and through the newspapers to the world at large. Shandyism, the new "philosophy of nonsense," became the fashion "of all the men and of most of the women" in that "tolerantly licentious" age. Shandy salads were sold at the food stores. Horses at the Irish Sweepstakes were entered as Tristram Shandy. Cosmetics, clothes and even card games were named after the book.

And the fame of Shandyism spread across the channel. The French, unable to follow the weird language and the unorthodox punctuation of the book, kept asking one another, *"Qui le diable est ce Chevalier Shandy?"*

At last, having received his full measure of London adulation, and having arranged for Hogarth's "witty chisel" to illustrate the next edition of *Tristram,* Sterne made plans to sail for the welcome warmth of Southern France. For he could hear, through that thin blood of his, other voices calling him on and preparing for him a welcome less agreeable. "He's such a fine fellow," said the doctors who examined him. "Too bad he won't last the winter." And the news passed around as rapidly as any of his jests. "He bleeds the bed full and lies speechless for days after he has made a public appearance. *Voilà mon histoire!*"

He boards a ship at Dover. The passage is rough. He lies in his cabin. The wind seems to have him by the throat. "But, by Heaven, I will give death a merry chase yet. I will lead him a dance he little suspects. For I will gallop, without looking once behind me, to the banks of the Garonne; and if I hear him clattering at my heels, I'll scamper away to Mount Vesuvius—and from thence to Joppa—and from Joppa to the world's end. And there, if he follows me, I pray God he may break his neck!"

Death, however, is patient. He will not be cheated of his game. Laurence Sterne grows steadily worse. "Like a bale of cadaverous goods consigned to Pluto and Company, lying in the bottom of my chaise most of the route, upon a large pillow which I had the prevoyance to purchase before I set out," he enters Paris.

And then, a sudden miracle. He rises from his pillow and plunges into the social whirl for a final frolic with life. Within six weeks after his arrival in Paris, he has "danced with one half of her goddesses."

For a time, even death was nonplused. "Doubting of his commission, he turned away from the door, saying as he went, in apology for his intrusion, 'There must certainly be some mistake in this matter.' "

The French are amazed. "But he is marvelous, this Chevalier Shandy!" The Duke of Orleans asks him to sit for his famous collection of "eccentric men." One hostess appropriates him on Thursdays and invites "all those who are hungry and dry" to make a meal on his wit. Nothing is immune from this shandygaff wit of his. The queerest ideas are forever running through his head. In Paris he preaches a few sermons "from the heart rather than from the head,"—yet he seems at all times to be "tottering on the verge of laughter, and ready to throw his periwig in the face of the audience." . . . "I laugh till I cry," he writes, "and I cry till I laugh."

Here, as in London, feminine beauty overpowers him. "This clergyman," writes one observant Frenchman, "is in love with the whole female sex—and thereby he preserves his purity." He thrills to the touch of a lady's fingertips, loves to buckle her shoe, to sleep in the room next to hers at an inn. "It is all very innocent if you take it that way."

He is overmasteringly absurd in his energies, overmasteringly curious about the energies and the absurdities of others. He travels to the south of France on a mule beside his valet whom he has dressed in scarlet livery; he gives a macaroon to a donkey who had been munching an artichoke, in order to observe the change on the animal's face; he throws sous with a grand gesture to beggars who clutch at his jack boots; he rides miles out of his course just to carry on an interesting conversation with friars he has met on the way; he enters a glove shop and holds the wrist of the "grissette" who sells him the gloves—and when he has reached the twentieth count of her pulsebeat, a man enters. "It's only my husband," she observes—and so he goes on to the fortieth beat . . . He summons a sentinel at the theater to thrust out of his stall a burly German soldier who has refused to move his head so that a dwarf behind him might see the stage . . . "Are we not all dwarfs trying to get a view of the stage to see the meaning of the play? Are we not like . . . a tear of pride stole in betwixt every two tears of humiliation?"

And now he hears footsteps again. That "long-striding scoundrel of a scare-sinner" is gaining quickly. Sterne hopes that the encounter will take place at some lonely inn far from the concern of his wife and daughter and friends. And he hopes that when he enters the courtroom on the warrant that must come to all, his defense before the Great Prosecuting Attorney will not seem too impudent. Was there very little holiness in his life? Well, there was very little hypocrisy, too. To the fates he had always prayed: "Give me the blessings of wisdom and religion if you will. But above all, let me be man." He had never pretended to be anything else. "By G——," using one of Uncle Toby's most horrible oaths, *just let me be man.*"

"The *Accusing Spirit,* as he flew up to heaven's chancery with the charge, blush'd as he gave it in; and the *Recording Angel,* as he wrote it down, dropp'd a tear upon the word, and blotted it out forever."

SCOTT

Important Works by Scott

The Lay of the Last Minstrel
  (a poem)
Marmion (a poem)
The Lady of the Lake (a poem)
Waverley
Guy Mannering
The Heart of Midlothian
The Bride of Lammermoor
Ivanhoe
The Monastery

The Abbot
Kenilworth
The Pirate
The Fortunes of Nigel
Peveril of the Peak
Quentin Durward
St. Ronan's Well
Redgauntlet
Count Robert of Paris
Life of Napoleon
  (9 volumes)

Sir Walter Scott

1771–1832

In the fall of 1777, Mrs. Cockburn, a cousin of Walter Scott's mother, spent an evening with the Scott family. The next morning she wrote the following letter to her parish minister:

". . . I last night supped with the Scotts. They have the most extraordinary genius of a boy I ever saw. He was reading a poem to his mother when I went in. I made him read on; it was the description of a shipwreck. His passion rose with the storm. He lifted his eyes and hands. 'There's the mast gone,' says he; 'crash it goes!—they will all perish!' After his agitation, he turns to me. 'That is too melancholy,' says he, 'I had better read you something more amusing.' I preferred a little chat, and asked his opinion of Milton and other books he was reading which he gave me wonderfully. One of his observations was, 'How strange it is that Adam, just new come into the world, should know everything!' . . . When taken to bed last night, he told his aunt he liked that lady. 'What lady?' says she. 'Why, Mrs. Cockburn; I think she is a virtuoso like myself.' 'Dear Walter,' says Aunt Jenny, 'what is a virtuoso?' 'Don't ye know? Why, it's one who wishes and will know everything.' "

And then Mrs. Cockburn came to the climax of the letter to

her minister: "Pray, sir, what age do you suppose the boy to be? Name it now before I tell you. Fourteen? Twelve? No such thing. He is not quite six years old!"

II

THE little virtuoso of six had a prodigious mind, a vigorous body and a lame leg. At eighteen months he had suffered an attack of infantile paralysis. One of his legs had become crippled for life; but the rest of him, to use his own words, remained "healthy, high-spirited and sturdy." He learned to walk and to ride—and even to run—with the best of them.

He came, both on his father's and on his mother's side, of "gentle" blood. This gentility was to him a matter of pride but not of arrogance. Throughout his life he was a good fellow among good fellows. "Sir Walter speaks to a body," said a workingman many years later, "as if they was his blude relations."

From infancy he was as "restless as the whirlwind." He was always doing or saying something. His memory was like a sheet of blotting paper; he absorbed whatever he heard or read. He ran around the house reciting—or rather *shouting*—poetry. It was impossible for anybody else to be heard in his presence. The clergyman of the parish used to say of him: "One may as well speak in the mouth of a cannon as where that child is."

A "self-willed imp" with a voracious appetite for learning. When he entered school—at eight—he knew Shakespeare and Homer almost by heart. But he knew nothing of arithmetic. His teacher put him among the "duller pupils" at the bottom of the class.

At first the boys snubbed him because of his lame foot. "It's no use to argle-bargle with a cripple." But he challenged them to fight after fight, and sustained many a bloody nose, and finally won their respect.

And their admiration. For they learned that he could tell stories. "Jiminy, what stories!" About the Highlands and the

Lowlands, and the "bludy skirmishes" between the Highlanders and the Lowlanders in the No-man's Land of the Border.

But in between his reading and his fighting and his telling of tales, he found time for his arithmetic; and within two years he made his way to the first class. And two years later he was ready for college.

But a serious illness interrupted his schooling and almost ended his life. The bursting of a blood-vessel in the bowels. Weeks of agony, months of convalescence—and then he was ready to go on with his education. He entered college and prepared himself for his father's profession—the law. Walter Scott would have far rather been a soldier than a barrister, but a military life was out of the question for a boy with a crippled leg. And so he took his degree, and resigned himself to the copying of legal documents at his father's office.

But his mind kept roaming over the world, and his heart was filled with martial music. For a time indeed he enlisted in a volunteer cavalry corps and took part in the daily drills. His physical handicap, however, resulted in his discharge. He returned to his desk and to the adventures of his mind.

He began to write poetry, in emulation of "my fellow Scotsman, Robert Burns." His father tried his best to discourage him. "These unprofitable flights of your fancy will lead you nowhere." But Scott persisted. It was part of his duty as his father's apprentice to take trips into the Highlands in order to collect rents for his father's clients. On these trips young Walter met many a fascinating character and heard many a fascinating tale. And he himself was such a good teller of tales! And such a good listener! "Eh me," remarked one of the Highlanders, "sic an endless fund o' humor as he had wi' him! Never ten words but we were either laughing or roaring or singing."

Out of these "rent collecting raids" to the Highlands grew Walter Scott's poetry, and later on his Waverley novels.

III

HE FELL IN LOVE with a girl who refused to marry him, and he married a girl who refused to love him. But she admired him for the solidity of his character, the gaiety of his heart and the greatness of his mind. Theirs was a marriage of lasting affection —lasting yet not too ardent—just the sort of temperate climate necessary for the healthy growth of his genius.

He himself called his genius "a mere talent for scribbling." He dashed off a few Scottish poems and made a number of translations from the German. Though already twenty-eight at the time, he hadn't the slightest ambition for a literary career. By now he quite agreed with his father that "there's no living in the flights of the fancy." He wrote as an "avocation for the advocate's spare time." He was determined to make his career at the bar. He had been appointed Sheriff of Selkirkshire—a position which brought him a good income and consumed but a little of his time. It gave him plenty of freedom for his regular practice in the courts.

And plenty of time for his literary recreation. For several years he had been collecting old Scottish Border Ballads. He now edited the collection and prepared it for publication—not, however, for his own glory but for the benefit of a former schoolmate, the printer James Ballantyne. This man needed work to keep his printing business afloat and Scott offered the Border Ballads to a publisher on the sole condition that the printing should be done at Ballantyne's shop.

And thus it was in the service of a friend that Walter Scott entered upon his literary career.

The Minstrelsy of the Scottish Border—this was the title of the collection—was not a financial success. And Scott hadn't expected it to be. "My literary pursuits," he wrote, "are more a matter of amusement than an object of emolument."

Nor did he expect his first original poem, *The Lay of the Last*

Minstrel, to be a financial success. But it was, to his great surprise. His star definitely pointed not toward law but toward literature as his life's work. Yet even now—at thirty-four—he was unaware of his true calling. "As to my attachment to literature," he wrote, "I sacrifice for the pleasure of pursuing it very fair chances of opulence and professional honors." What he wanted above all was to become the least among the Scottish jurists. It was a keen disappointment to him when he became the greatest among the Scottish writers.

And the Scotsmen of his day took him at his own valuation. He "found a home," as he himself expressed it, "in every farmhouse" —not, however, as the great Poet of the North, but as the genial "Shirra (Sheriff) of Selkirkshire." And if you had asked his contemporaries to analyze their feelings, they would have told you that it was not even Walter Scott the Shirra that they adored, but Walter Scott the Man. He was so lovable and unaffected and modest, so full of anecdote, so free from pedantry, so utterly devoted to his friends. Even in his faults, as in his virtues, he was so delightfully human. "You will find me," he wrote to one of his readers, "a rattle-skulled half-lawyer, half-sportsman, through whose head a regiment of horse has been exercising since he was five years old; half-educated—half-crazy as his friends sometimes tell him; half everything, but entirely your much obliged, affectionate, and faithful servant."

"Entirely . . . your servant." This was the keynote of Walter Scott's character.

IV

WALTER SCOTT was generous, but he was prudent as well. Anxious to secure comfort for his family—he now had four children—he invested his savings in Ballantyne's printing business. And thus he became a partner in a venture which might have been successful but for two factors: Ballantyne's inability to size up a business situation, and Scott's inability to size up Ballantyne. For several years the business went creaking along, and Scott kept pouring more and more of his earnings into it. He was plunging steadily toward a tragic fall. But it was a long while before he became aware of it.

In the meantime he attended to his law practice which brought him a *slender* income, and he kept "dabbling" in poetry which netted him a *substantial* income. He wrote *Marmion*, the *Lady of the Lake*, and several minor poems. He took his literary honors with a shrug, and his literary blows with a smile. Once, when he heard about a disparagement of the *Lady of the Lake*, he burst into good-natured laughter. For the author of the disparagement was his own child, Sophia, a young lady of thirteen. James Ballantyne, having come across her in Scott's library shortly after the publication of the *Lady*, asked her how she liked the poem. "Her answer," he reported to Walter Scott, "was given with perfect simplicity: 'Oh, I have not read it. Papa says there is nothing so bad for young people as reading bad poetry.'"

Yet Scott's poetry, while far from great, was equally far from bad. The proof of the pie is in the eating; and the eater need not be an educated man to appreciate a tasty tidbit. One day Scott tried the effect of the First Canto of the *Lady of the Lake* —The Stag Hunt—on a farmer-friend, a man unlearned in booklore, but an intelligent and passionate sportsman. "He placed his hand across his brow," writes Scott, "and listened with great attention through the whole account of the stag hunt, till the dogs throw themselves into the lake to follow their master . . . He then started up with a sudden exclamation, struck his hand on the table, and declared, in a voice of censure calculated for the occasion, that the dogs must have been totally ruined by being permitted to take the water after such a severe chase."

To the illiterate farmer, as well as to the educated reader, the poem possessed the tang of life; and to this day, in spite of its singsong cadences and its occasional prolixity, the *Lady of the Lake* is tangful and alive.

The success of the *Lady of the Lake* was beyond expectation. It enriched not only the author, but every inn-keeper and coachman and ostler and gillie in the vicinity of Loch Katrine. For, from every part of Britain and even from the continent, "crowds had set off to view the scenery of the poem made famous by the Wizard of the North . . . and every house and inn in that neighborhood was crammed with a succession of visitors."

Loch Katrine had become a shrine and the poem had become a gospel and a battle-cry. In 1811, when a company of soldiers was fighting under Wellington in the Peninsula, their captain read aloud to them the description of the battle in the Sixth Canto. The soldiers lay flat on the ground and listened to the inspiring poetry while artillery fire of the enemy whizzed over their heads. Silent and rapt attention, save for "a joyous huzza whenever the French shot struck the bank close behind them."

The sales of the poem kept mounting from edition to edition. The royalties enabled Scott to realize a lifelong dream—the building of an estate in the country. And now, settled in this estate on the banks of the Tweed, the "laird of Abbotsford" opened the doors of his house and his heart to "all the people in the country, from the duke to the peasant." When his friends cautioned him against the extravagance of his good fellowship, he reassured them that all his visitors "paid their score one way or another." For everybody, however obscure, brought him the most precious of all gifts—a new friend. The currency of friendship was to him payment enough for the merchandise of hospitality.

He was growing gray now, as he wrote to one of his intimates, "but I cannot find that the snow has cooled either my brain or my heart." Indeed, far from *cooling* his brain and his heart, the advancing years were to *warm* them into new flights of imagination. Having written poetry up to his middle life, he had succeeded in becoming a second-rate minstrel. And now he turned his attention to prose and became a first-rate poet.

V

ONCE OR TWICE in his earlier years, Walter Scott had tried his hand at a prose novel, only to give it up as something beyond his power. In 1805 he had submitted seven chapters of *Waverley* to a friendly critic, William Erskine. "Throw them away," his friend had bluntly advised him. "These chapters are eloquent of the fact that you can't write fiction." Scott had not thrown the chapters away but had laid them aside. And now, in 1813, he came upon them accidentally while searching for fishing tackle in a desk that had been stored away in the attic. He re-read the opening of the story and decided, "just for the fun of the thing," to finish it.

And thus, without knowing it, Walter Scott had taken title to a gold mine.

Yet even after he had become aware of the *practical* value of his novels, he was not at all certain as to their *artistic* worth. He published them all anonymously; for, as he explained toward the end of his life, he thought it undignified for a sheriff to become a writer of fiction. He dashed off his novels surreptitiously, as if he were indulging in some secret, shameful vice; and when they were finished, he "whistled them down the wind"—to use his own expression—"and let them prey at fortune."

And the wind, receiving the precious cargo of his stories, wafted back to him an equally precious cargo of gold and glory. But it was an impersonal glory. Occasionally a discerning critic would guess at the authorship of one of his novels. When Maria Edgeworth had finished reading *Waverley,* she posted a letter to its "Unknown author—*aut Scotus aut Diabolus*" (either Scott or the Devil). But Scott neither affirmed nor denied his connection with the book. Once, when he sat at dinner with the Prince Regent of England, the Prince called for "a bumper . . . to the Author of Waverley," and looked significantly at Scott. The latter filled his own glass to the brim, and said, "Your Royal Highness looks as if you thought I had some claim to the honors of this toast. I have no such pretensions, but shall take good care that the real Simon Pure hears of the high compliment that has just been paid him."

His royalties now kept pouring into his coffers like a cataract, and Scott kept pouring them back into the bottomless sieve of Ballantyne's printing business. And all this time he was tragically unaware of the fact that the business was going from bad to worse. He bought more and more land, involved himself in a network of mortgages, entertained his hosts of visitors, gave dinners and dances to the countryfolk on the lawns of his estate, tramped (in spite of his lameness) over the hills and the valleys, rode to the chase, created his stories ("When, in the name of heaven, does he find time for it all?"), reveled in his honors (including a baronetcy), married off his children, wrote more novels, earned more money, plunged more deeply into Ballantyne's disastrous ventures—and then came the crash. Ballantyne was bankrupt, and Scott's entire fortune was wiped out.

The blow was as sudden as it was tragic. But it turned Scott from a good fellow into a great man. From now on he was the hero of a story more inspiring than any he had written. His debts, as a result of Ballantyne's bankruptcy, amounted to £117,000 (nearly $600,000). His friends advised him to declare himself bankrupt. As a lawyer, he had frequently given similar advice to his clients. But now he stubbornly refused to avail himself of this legal channel of escape. "No man," he declared, "shall lose a penny by me." When the members of his family tried to commiserate with him, he shooed them out of the room. "I hate red eyes and the blowing of noses." Stoically he set to work writing, writing, writing, in order to discharge "the entire debt." He turned himself into a living machine. One day two young men— Lockhart and Menzies—were dining at Menzies' home. Suddenly Lockhart saw his friend staring uneasily through the window.

"What's the trouble?" asked Lockhart. "Are you unwell?"

"No," replied Menzies. "I shall be well enough presently, if you will only let me sit where you are . . . There is a confounded hand in sight of me here . . . Ever since we sat down, I have been watching it—it fascinates my eye—it never stops—page after page is finished and thrown on the heap of manuscript and still it goes on unwearied—and so it will be till candles are brought in, and God knows how long after that . . . It is the same every night . . . Some stupid, dogged, engrossing clerk, probably . . ."

No, not a dogged clerk, but Walter Scott paying off his debt.

He fell sick from overwork. But he met his sickness like a Stoic. "It is the brave man's business to suffer and to work on." When he was unable to sit up, he dictated his manuscript from his bed. There were times when he clenched his teeth in pain. But as soon as the spasm was over, he went on with his dictation. His wife died. He laid her away—"the solitude is terrible"—and went on with his work. He wrote novels and poems and biographies; he paid off a quarter of his debt, half of it, three quarters. Under the strain of his exertion, his mind broke down like his body. He fell into the error that he had paid off his entire debt—a blessed delusion. In his more lucid moments he wrote the description of a sick man—a character in one of his novels. It was really a description of himself: "The easy chair filled with cushions, the extended limbs swathed in flannel, the wide wrapping-gown and nightcap, showed illness; but the dimmed eye, once so replete with living fire, the blabber lip, whose dilation and compression used to give such character to his animated countenance—the stammering tongue, that once poured forth such floods of masculine eloquence, and had often swayed the opinion of sages whom he addressed,—all these sad symptoms evinced that my friend was in the melancholy condition of those in whom the principle of animal life has unfortunately survived that of mental intelligence . . ."

Yet, in the intervals of his suffering, Scott's mind rose to the completion of another novel—*Robert of Paris*. And then he was ready to rest. "The plough is nearing the end of the furrow."

His friends sent him off on a Mediterranean cruise, in a frigate generously offered by the Admiralty. Among those who came to bid him Godspeed were lairds and ladies and one "common man" whom he admired above all—William Wordsworth. On shipboard he started two new novels—for in the twilight of his forgetfulness there were lightning flashes of urgency. "There's something I *must* do before I die." One day he received news of Goethe's death. He begged the captain to end the cruise. "At least Goethe died at home. Let us to Abbotsford."

He arrived on July 11, 1832. Though scarcely able to walk, he begged to be put into a chair at his desk. "Now give me my pen and leave me for a little to myself." But when his daughter put the pen into his hand, his fingers could not close on it.

They put him to bed. He lingered for two months, and then he closed his eyes in utter tranquillity. "No sculptor ever modelled a more majestic figure in repose."

And no wonder he looked so peaceful. He had paid his full debt to his Creditor in Heaven.

BALZAC

Important Works by Balzac

Louis Lambert

The Wild Ass's Skin

Jesus in Flanders

Eugénie Grandet

Droll Stories

The Unknown Masterpiece

Père Goriot

The Peasants

The Country Doctor

Seraphita

The Atheist's Mass

A Daughter of Eve

Cousin Bette

Cousin Pons

Vautrin (a drama)

Pamela Giraud (a drama)

Honoré de Balzac

1799–1850

$\mathbf{A}$s a child he played on a little red violin for hours at a stretch. He made excruciating sounds on it—and he could not understand why people did not feel the beauty of his music. At school, instead of doing his lessons, he wrote a treatise on the human will. And he did not know why the teacher destroyed it in a fury. His questioning eyes looked so intense that folks thought him dull with dreaming. But occasionally his mother was startled at the profound words that came from his lips. "Honoré," she exclaimed to the seven-year-old, "it is impossible that you can understand what you have just said!" Honoré was his name because he had been born on St. Honoré's Day. What a challenge for a boy to have been godfathered by a saint, and a saint of honor, too!

His father was a supply clerk for the army. He had much of "Montaigne, Rabelais and Uncle Toby" in him. He was an imaginative optimist who bequeathed to his son an estate of dreams, and nothing else. His high school teachers gave him up as a failure and abandoned him to his dream acres. "This fat little fellow goes around in a state of intellectual coma," they reported. And Honoré walked out of high school, down the streets, and haunted the libraries for fantasies and facts. Like a ghost he glided into the Sorbonne and listened unobserved to the lectures of the mighty. Neither Victor Cousin nor Guizot realized how far and to what regions their words on history and politics and philosophy were traveling.

His mother, a woman of extraordinary shrewdness, called him back into this world and told him that he must study law. Father Balzac, who was now seventy-four, had been placed on the retired list. The family was in straitened circumstances. The call to duty stopped Honoré's steps one day as he was taking his regular walk in the Père-Lachaise cemetery—a favorite spot where he fed his deepest inspirations, weighed his mightiest thoughts, launched his most ambitious plans.

He came home and announced to his family, "No law. I want to be a writer."

Au diable! His mother, who was a genius in her own way, thought of a plan to wake her son from his latest dream. She told him that he could not work at home, since the quarters were too small. She hired an attic and furnished it with the barest necessities. She bestowed upon him this gift of discomfort in the hope that it might cure him of his "crazy ambition."

Honoré blessed her. And when he sat down amidst the filth and the vermin, he felt that he was sitting on the throne of his spiritual ancestors—the starving kings of the pen. Ah, but it was heavenly to indulge himself in this greatest of his dreams!

A friend who came to see him has left us this record of his visit: "I entered a narrow garret furnished with a bottomless chair, a rickety table and a miserable pallet bed, with two dirty curtains half drawn around it. On the table were an inkstand, a big copybook scribbled all over, a jug of lemonade, a glass, and a morsel of bread. The heat in this wretched hole was stifling, and one breathed a mephitic air." Balzac was in bed with a cotton cap on his head. "Welcome, my friend, to the abode which I have not left except once for the last two months. During all this time I have not got up from my bed where I work at the great masterpiece."

On the table lay a recently completed drama—the "master-piece" for which the author was luxuriating in so much filth. Balzac picked it up one day and came to read it to his family. No favorable response. He brought it to an authority on the drama at the Académie Française. "Will you kindly examine this work, Monsieur, and tell me what I should do in the future." Monsieur read the manuscript and replied, "In the future do anything but write." Honoré merely shrugged his shoulders. "Tragedies, I guess, are not in my line."

But he went on composing in his garret. Unable to *sadden* the world, he decided to *amuse* the world. Having failed to write inspired tragedies, he would write perspired pot-boilers. Sensational fiction for the pulp magazines. His head was teeming with plots—and his heart and his purse were empty. "I am hungry, Laure," he wrote to his sister. "Will ever my two immense desires be satisfied—to be famous and to be loved?"

He worked at a white fever, turning out stories after a set formula. He wrote sixty pages a day. In three years, under various pseudonyms, he completed thirty-one volumes of adventure—and still he was neither loved nor famous. The royalties for his work almost always took the form of notes payable in the future. And all his obligations, too, he promised to pay in the future. Somehow he never quite managed to get a grip upon the present. And as the bills kept constantly running ahead of his income, he felt that he must turn out his dream-stories faster and ever faster.

But finally it was manifest to the dreamer that he must find another job. For pleasant dreams come only to well-fed stomachs wrapped in warm clothing. He needed an income independent of his writing—a weekly salary. But how? Well, he had a head full of schemes and he could launch plans—in his conversation—that simply fascinated people. One of these plans was to become a publisher. He spoke of his proposed venture with such vehement gestures and such eager enthusiasm that a wealthy businessman bought him a publishing house. The house collapsed like a bubble. But the sponsor, who had lost seventy thousand francs in the business, was still bewitched under the magic of Balzac's eloquence. He introduced Balzac to his brother, another wealthy man, who transformed the publisher into a printer.

The printing business, like the publishing business, went down under the guiding hand of Balzac. But his tongue retained its magical persuasion. He enticed his friends to buy him a type foundry. He guided it promptly into disaster, and his relatives came forward with sufficient funds to save him from bankruptcy and his family from disgrace.

He started a newspaper and dreamed it away. And then he went back to his writing with a merry chuckle. No, indeed, he bore no malice against anybody. True, it was his evil destiny and the dishonesty of his associates—he felt convinced—that had tripped him up. Certainly he himself had never been in the wrong about anything. But why bother about such matters? He was far too happy with his dreams. A hundred thousand francs in debt before he was thirty? *Eh bien!* He hung his rooms in blue calico—the color dazzled him. And to his sister he wrote—it was an effort to find money to post the letter—"Ah, Laure, if you did but know how passionately I desire (but hush! keep the secret) two blue screens embroidered in black (silence, ever!)" Tormented, worn out? He could not get the screens out of his mind. "Always the screens," he murmured in his sleep. It was a fixed idea. What if he had no bread in his stomach? He had something far more important—beauty in his soul. At dinner time he would take a piece of chalk and draw upon his table a circle to represent a plate. And then he would write down within this plate the name of his favorite dish. And thus he fasted and chewed and swallowed the most exotic dishes that his mind could conjure up. And the saliva would come to his mouth, and tears of happiness would spring to his eyes.

Yet there were moments when despair clutched at his heart. At these moments it was only the love and the understanding of a woman considerably older than himself that kept him from committing suicide. He had come to her in one of his blackest moods. "Don't console me. It is useless—I am a dead man." But the moment she spoke a word of cheer—"By God, you are right! My genius will make me live."

Meanwhile, on the tracks of Providence, his train was running on time. With all the silly confusion of his life, he was arriving at his destination. The absurd quantity of his fiction was shaping the quality of his intellect. Painfully, with the unpaid bills pricking him like sword-points, he acquired a profound knowledge of the world and a great sympathy for suffering. Out of the whirring energy of his ambition, out of the steam and the smoke and the sweat of his struggles, there arose the artist's vision—"a vision as brief as life and death, deep as an abyss, great as the sound of the sea . . . Work calls, all the ovens are heated, the ecstasy of conception conceals the subsequent distress. Such is the vision of the artist who is the humble instrument of a will apparently the freest, in reality a slave."

II

TALES and novels came now from the press under his real name. Stories of the rising bourgeoisie—the shopkeepers, the bankers and the purse lifters—the civilization whose god was money and whose soul was steam. Balzac chortled with glee at the stir he made. "I have good news to tell you, little sister; the reviewers are paying me better for my articles. Hé! hé!—Werdet tells me that my *Country Doctor* was sold out in eight days. Ha! ha!—I have wherewith to make faces at the November and December bills that disturb you. Ho! ho!—There are many millions in *Eugénie Grandet!*" And he dreamed of himself sitting in the Institute, in the Chamber of Peers, in the Ministry of the Government. And why should not the authors and the dreamers steer the helm of the Government? "Are not those who have made the tour of the world of ideas the most fitted to govern men? I should like to see the fellow who would be astonished if I should receive a portfolio!"

And then he looked at his bank book, and the rosy light faded out of his dreams. It seemed that the more he wrote, the greater his debts. This was a marvelous defiance of the laws of logic. He surveyed the rooms that he had furnished upon the first indication that the winds were in his favor. Splendid books, antique chairs, carved tables, the finest works of art, Saxony porcelains, Chinese tapestries. And, harassed, he went breathlessly back to his work. Toil in luxury for the Countess B——. He wrote about the greatest scoundrels and the most audacious roués. He let loose the tainted odors of society with a fury as if he had let loose the seven winds from the bag of Aeolus. And he sat and worked in a white robe like a Dominican monk. He wore red morocco slippers bordered with gold, and he girdled his ample body with a gold Venetian chain from which he had suspended a golden folding-stick, a gold knife, and a pair of golden scissors. And he drank copious draughts of steaming coffee to keep awake. Writing was a ceremony as solemn as a mass—commencing at two o'clock in the morning when the high priest roused himself from bed and took up his pen. By the light of four candles he peered into the unholy garbage from the Paris banquets—the leftovers of love and scandal. At six in the morning he took his bath and drank several cups of coffee. Then he corrected the proofs for the printer. From nine in the morning until noon the boys hurried back from the printer to the writer, trying to decipher the hastily-inserted pages, the crosses and the asterisks, and the arrows pointing toward the newly improvised words until the proof sheets looked like the secret book of a medieval astrologer.

Toil for luxury. An eye for beauty crystal clear, so clear that it cannot reflect the lights and the shadows of the women who concern his own happiness. A master of the history of the heart in his books, he is a fool for the merest woman in life. They are an opaque luxury whose colors deceive him and do not allow his mind to peer through. He falls madly in love with a Marquise. "One evening I was everything to her, and the next morning I was nothing . . . In the course of the night a woman—the woman whom I loved—had died." Then a "foreign lady" who lived a lonely life in a chateau in Poland, having nothing better to do, wrote him love letters wrapped in mysticism. He met her secretly in Switzerland, exchanged kisses with her under the very nose of her husband, and gave eighteen years of his hope, his strength and his life to the unreciprocating countess beyond the Vistula.

"Work, always work. Heated nights succeed heated nights, days of meditation follow days of meditation; from execution to conception to execution." And it was just as easy to buy a mansion and to live a grandee's life as to write a story. "I shall not live like a bourgeois while thinking like a demi-god." Aha, here is a tiny pyramid of money, the basic food of life. And a few weeks later, the pyramid has melted away. One hundred and seventy thousand francs in debt by the time he is forty. Rapid figuring. The interest alone on that amount would come to six thousand francs a year. He looks at the gold cane he carries, drives in his tilbury behind a high-stepping horse with a tiny pet tiger perched beside him. He writes a novel in three days, completes another in six weeks with only eighty hours of sleep—an average of two hours a day—and then he falls into a fit of exhaustion in the elegant garden of his mistress.

When his novels failed to produce the necessary funds, he turned to the stage. He wrote a play in sixteen days—and it was refused. He then submitted the idea for another play, and the idea was accepted. Hurriedly he sent for Gautier. "Here you are at last, Theo," he cried impatiently when Gautier arrived. "You idler, dawdler, sloth! You ought to have been here an hour ago! Tomorrow I am going to read to Harel a grand drama in five acts."

"And you want to read it to me and hear my advice?" Gautier seated himself and prepared for a long reading.

"The drama is not written!" said Balzac simply.

"Good heavens! Well, then, you must postpone the reading before the producer for six weeks."

"No, we must hurry to write the drama and to get the money.

I've a large debt to pay. Now listen, Theo. Here's how I have figured it out. You will write the first act; Ourliac will write the second; Laurent, the third; de Belloy, the fourth; I, the fifth. I will then read the entire play to Harel tomorrow at twelve, as arranged."

"Well, then," said Gautier, "relate the subject to me, explain the plot, sketch out the characters in a few words, and I will get to work."

"Ah," cried Balzac with a magnificent gesture, "if I have to relate the subject to you we shall never finish!"

However, the play was written. One of his friends gives us a vivid description of Balzac during rehearsal. "He was almost unrecognizable from worry and overwork. His perplexities had become public property, and people used to wait at the door of the theater to see him rush into the street . . . wearing enormous shoes with the leather tongues outside instead of inside his trousers. Everything he wore was many sizes too big for him, and it was covered with mud from the boulevards."

Shortly before the performance he wrote: "I have gone through many miseries. But if I have a success, my miseries will be completely over. Imagine what my anxiety will be during the evening when *Vautrin* is being acted. In five hours' time it will be decided whether I pay or do not pay my debts."

The play was not a success. The "villain" of the piece decided to act his part in comedy. When he took off his hat, he showed a wig dressed in the form of a pyramid—a coiffure which was the exclusive prerogative of King Louis Philippe. The Duke of Orleans léft his box and stamped out of the theater. It was difficult to finish the performance for the roars and the hisses and the cat-calls and even the threats of the audience. The official censor immediately banned the play from the stage.

But during that first performance Balzac was unperturbed. He was fast asleep on a bench in the back of the theater, in the midst of another dream.

III

ANOTHER FRUITLESS DREAM, and a low ebb in his fortune. He escapes from his debtors in woman's clothes and masquerades in finery. He dodges in and out of garrets and country estates, depending on the direction of the wind. He steals into the houses of his friends, discusses morals and literature and love from five o'clock in the evening until five o'clock in the morning with George Sand, that other "great man" of the century—and then a new book. And new debts.

He calls his publishers the vultures that eat the flesh of Prometheus. "Some day," he writes to them, "and that day is not far off, you will have made your fortune out of me; our carriages will pass in the Bois; your enemies and mine will burst with envy. Your friend, H. de B." And then a microscopic hand in postscript, "Apropos, dear friend, I have nothing left, so I have raised 1500 francs from Rothschild and drawn a draft for that amount on you, due ten days after sight."

But he was still hopeful that some business scheme would put him on his feet and that he would be able to dream in luxury. He had read that the ancient Romans had exploited silver mines in Sardinia. He was certain that there must be silver in those mines still to be exploited. He spoke to a merchant about this theory, drew up a partnership with him, and read in the papers one morning that his partner, in collaboration with a government agency, was exploiting the mines in Sardinia without him.

But he held on to his hopeful dreams. Late one night he awakened his two friends, Gautier and Sandau, and told them that there had come a voice to him in a trance and that this voice had given him the location in which Toussaint L'Ouverture had buried a treasure. Unfortunately the plan remained academic. None of the vagabond authors had the money to get to Haiti.

But Balzac planned on. He went into business with his brother-in-law and devised a system of inclined planes for railways. He dreamed of building canals from Nantes to Orleans, of transporting oaks from Poland to France, of raising pineapples on an acre of city soil—if only he had a few thousand francs to begin with. He collected the sayings of Napoleon and sold them for four thousand francs to a hatmaker who believed that they might help him to get an appointment into the Legion of Honor. And then he decided that he would acquire a monopoly of all the statuary, tapestries and paintings of Europe and act as auctioneer to the world. He would purchase the Apollo Belvedere, for instance, and let all the nations bid for it—oh, if only he could have a little country home!

And then one day he comes into possession of a home of his own. But afraid that his creditors will multiply at the rumor of his affluence, he tells all the people who visit him, "Nothing of all this belongs to me, you understand; friends of mine live here. I am their servant." And the visitors look around at the house in amazement. "Who are the strange folk who live here and keep Honoré de Balzac as their servant?" For the rooms are practically bare of furniture. And the stucco walls, at regular intervals, carry the most grandiose descriptions scrawled in a familiar hand— "Here is a veneering of Parian marble." . . . "Here is a mantelpiece in Carrara marble." On the ceiling—"Here is a painting by Eugene Delacroix." And on the floor—"Here is the most wonderful mosaic fresco ever done by the hand of man."

And Balzac carries a gold cane with the following motto translated from the Turkish: "I am the conqueror of all difficulties."

Supernatural messages come to him. Magnetism haunts his mind. He believes that he is a *polar* person. He declares that when he has mastered a secret, he will be able to command every man to obey him and every woman to love him.

And so he dreams a thousand droll stories and probes into the human passions and weaves his fantastic way from earth to heaven over a rainbow of arabesques. Though by accident of birth he is descended from day laborers, he looks upon himself as a member of the one true nobility—a royal brother to Haroun-

al-Raschid, the Prince of the spinners of plots and the entertainers
of men.

And what a wealth of beauty in the spinning of his tales! He
is unafraid of the charge of too much color. Even vice, he declares, is only the desire to know everything. He will tie his destiny
to Faust and Paracelsus. He suffers no *real* illusions about the
world. At the moment of his highest ecstasy he will die like
a gorgeous insect splendidly adorned for a love festival—and
crushed under the foot of a passer-by. "Why then all this puny
striving after tinsel?" you will ask. By heaven, it is not the tinsel
that we care for. Balzac told his soul in secret—few of his millions of friends had heard him whisper it—"I have no dread of
poverty. If disgrace and contempt were not a beggar's lot, I
would beg, to be enabled to solve in peace the problems that fill
my mind. At times I grasp the universe of thought, I knead it, I
mould it, I pierce it, I comprehend it . . . But the man who
sees two centuries ahead of him dies on the scaffold . . . That
is why I have my gardens and my business schemes, to lull, to
cheat the evil spirit that would erect the scaffold for a man in
rags . . . By God, I shall shout the truth even in my silence. Let
the angels build hospitals for suffering souls. But until they do,
I shall build them a palace of dreams . . ."

IV

AS A YOUNG DREAMER of thirty-odd years, he conceived the stu-
pendous plan of writing a cycle of novels and fusing them into
an entire Human Comedy of manners. He rushed over to his
sister's house—as always when a great dream possessed him—and
he entered like a drum major, imitating the booming of martial
music and the rolling of the drum. And then he cried out, "*Ma
petite,* congratulate me!"

And he went about his business humming tunes, tapping
friends on the shoulder, playing the happy buffoon, as the plan
of his epic venture slowly germinated into actual completion.

Exalted, depressed, pompous or penniless, a most unstable fellow in practical matters, he never swerved throughout twenty years from his task. Other novelists wrote one or two or ten books—momentary outpourings of their art when the mood seized them. But what novelist had ever conceived of writing ninety-six books, each to serve as a single stroke of the brush in a consecutive picture of life? The Human Comedy of the Earth—a worthy companion-piece to Dante's Divine Comedy of Heaven.

But Balzac did something more than to write a mere companion-piece to Dante's poem. He was an artist living in an environment of modern science and not in an atmosphere of medieval faith. He planned to do for the kingdom of men what Buffon had done for the kingdom of animals—to write an exhaustive document on the comparative moral anatomy of the human species. And why not? Animals had been catalogued and specified according to types. "Soldiers, workmen, scholars, statesmen, merchants, seamen, poets, beggars, priests are types as distinct from one another as wolves, lions, ravens, vultures, and sharks." For the motives that guide the world of man, reasoned Honoré de Balzac, are the passions of animals—particularly the passion of self interest. "Politeness merely adorns man, and hypocrisy disguises him . . . The animal persists in man with this difference —that the mind of man being vaster, his wants and his perils are greater."

And thus he constructed in the museum of natural human history a panorama of hopes and desires and ambitions and struggles and rivalries and loves and hatreds and flatteries and fears—an exhaustive picture of all the inhumanity of the human race under the reign of Napoleon I and of Louis Philippe. Balzac was a great admirer of the Little Corsican. He often liked to compare himself to him. "This man is the soldier with the sword, and I am the soldier with the pen . . . Yet *I* shall succeed where Napoleon failed. For I shall conquer the world."

And the *Human Comedy* did conquer the world. It brought to the fore a new world with a new standard—the standard of the bourgeoisie. New men, new occupations, new hopes and a new faith. The faith in the common man. The religion of Democracy. The miner in his gas mask, the laborer in his heavy culottes, the little shopkeeper behind his counter—these were the heroes of the new literature, the new order, the new life. Aeschylus and Shakespeare and Corneille had written dramas about noblemen and kings. And now Balzac issued his challenge to the readers of these dramas: "My bourgeoisie novels are more tragical than your tragic plays."

Like Shakespeare, Balzac paints every variety of human character—the shadows as well as the lights. And, like Shakespeare, he remains uncontaminated by the mental diseases and the moral degradations that he has elected to describe. He paints the decline and fall of the nobility and the emergence of the bourgeoisie—the banker, the fortune hunter, the parvenu. His novels are an epic of sordid lust—an overpowering thirst for material success. He is the poet-laureate of the capitalistic urge. Money is the only yardstick to human worth. It is the lifeblood that flows in the veins of his characters. It supplies the oxygen to their lungs, the food to their brains, the gospel to their hearts. The clink of gold is their music, their poetry, their philosophy, their religion, their life. It is the stuff their dreams are made of. Under its magic spell they create beauty and perpetrate crimes. The Stock Exchange is the arena for heroic battles and infamous treacheries. Money breeds, coin attracts coin, a five-franc note is jealous of a ten-franc note and struggles to increase. Money is the cosmic force that rules the earth. It is the Prospero and the Caliban, the God and the Devil who shake the world between them.

And Balzac stalks into the parlors and the counting rooms, and tears away the veils of hypocrisy from his characters and lays bare their souls. But he scorns to judge them. For how could he judge? Man classifies all things by abstractions—good, evil, virtue, vice —words that have a different meaning for different people. The justice of man is blind. "God alone in His justice sees." And what of this foolish earth of ours? "Does it exist in a *universe* of folly?"

To this question, Balzac gives a negative answer. The universe does move toward a logical end, and that end cannot be a society constituted like ours. A frightful void lies between us and heaven. Man is not a finished creation; if he were, God would not be. And yet from all this, "from the spectacle of our society—a society within which philanthropy is a magnificent error, and progress a meaningless cry,—I gained a confirmation of the truth—that life lies within us and not without us; that to rise above our fellows for the purpose of commanding them is only to magnify the career of a schoolmaster; and that men who are strong enough to lift themselves to the level at which they can enjoy the sight of heaven, ought not to turn their gaze upon their feet."

With this philosophy in mind, Balzac divided the people of the world not into heroes and villains, good men and bad, but into *doers, thinkers* and *seers.* At the lowest level are the men of action —the fighters, the merchants, the money-changers, the captains of hustle and push. Next come the men of thought—the scientists, the scholars, the philosophers, the teachers, the guides. Finally come the men of vision—the poets, the artists, the musicians, the prophets, the saviors of the world. It is the destiny of man, believed Balzac, to rise from action through abstraction to sight. And then, when the final stage is reached, the material flesh of man will return to its divine origin—the spiritual world of God . . .

Balzac never completed his grandiose plan. He was an artist rather than an artisan; and it is the artisan alone who can ever complete his task. Every novel in the *Human Comedy* was written in an agony of toil. His style was obscure. The fires of his inspiration were often darkened with the smoke of a heavy phraseology. But to the end of his life he struggled with the burden of his creation, and he left a monument all the more magnificent for its unfinished strength.

V

AND THEN, as he approached fifty, Destiny wrote the final chapter to the Human Comedy of his own life. The Countess Hanska, with whom he had exchanged clandestine kisses for eighteen years, lost her husband. At last she could be his. "I will not be a farthing in debt, my dear," he wrote to her in a delirium of delight. "I will have five hundred thousand francs in commissions, not counting the returns from the *Human Comedy,* which will amount to that much more. Thus, beautiful lady, you will be marrying a million or more, if I do not die."

He took a home and bought chinaware, carpets, damasks, medallions, clocks, pictures and chandeliers—all ready to be unpacked on the eve of their marriage. It was to be their honeymoon home, a lordly pleasure-house awaiting its queen.

But Madame Hanska had long wearied of Honoré de Balzac. By now she was completely indifferent to the genius that had been her plaything in idle moments. For five years longer she resisted him. And then, worn out by his siege, she married him. "I am at the summit of my happiness," wrote Balzac to his sister. "I am at the climax of my dream."

And then he awoke. The woman of his dream was middle-aged. Her arms and legs were swollen with gout. Often she was unable to walk.

Yet she felt in no wise inferior to her Prince Charming. She and her doctors had their secret. Balzac was a dying man. In the month of May, the month of life and love, Victor Hugo visited his fellow author and noted succinctly, "Married, rich,—and almost dead."

The sheer exhaustion of his energy—an energy unparalleled in the history of literature—had at last broken the sturdy body. His eyesight had been the first to go. And then his heart broke down. And gangrene settled in his leg.

The final month, ensconced in a magnificent house, lying on

a sofa covered with red and gold brocade, his face purple with pain, his legs rotting away. Yet his head was still a volcano of projects. "He fell in love with visions and then deserted them for still more beautiful visions."

On the last day, Victor Hugo came to pay his respects. He entered the house of the fabulous little man and tried to read the secret of life in the dying face. But all he saw was death and decay. "There was a colossal bust of the author in the salon. The bust of the marble was like the ghost of the man who was to die ... As I approached the bed I saw his profile. It was like that of Napoleon. An old sick-nurse and a servant of the house stood on either side of the bed. I lifted the counterpane, and took the hand of Balzac. The nurse said to me, 'He will die about dawn.' "

He died at night. It must have been night over France, for the people took scarce notice of his passing. But even in the daytime of his life they had given him no glory. When he had applied for membership in the French Academy of letters, the pompous gentlemen slammed the door in the "face of the clown."

"Glory," Balzac had observed, "is the sunlight of the dead."

DUMAS

Important Works by Dumas

Alexandre Dumas, *Père*

1802–1870

ALEXANDRE was four years old when his father died. As his mother walked out of the death chamber, she saw the little fellow climbing up the steps and dragging a heavy rifle after him.

"Where are you going, child?"

"I am going to heaven."

"Good gracious, what for?"

"To fight a duel with God for killing my father."

Like his Three Musketeers, Alexandre was from his earliest childhood an impetuous fighter against insuperable odds.

II

HE CAME of a stock of adventurers and fighters. His grandfather, the aristocratic Davy de la Pailleterie, followed the call of the blood and set sail from Normandy for the island of San Domingo. Here he lived like an Emperor Jones, surrounded by a host of black slaves. One of these slaves, Louise Dumas, bore him a mulatto son to whom he gave the name Thomas-Alexandre.

This son of Davy de la Pailleterie inherited the effervescence of his father. "I want to enlist in the army."

"Very well," said his father. "But you must enlist under your mother's name. I'd be disgraced if a mulatto soldier bore the noble name of Davy de la Pailleterie."

And so Thomas-Alexandre joined the French army (1793) under the name of Dumas, and within seven years he rose from the rank of private to that of general. A peculiar, courageous, tender, thoughtful, lovable fighting man—this mulatto aristocrat with the black skin and the chestnut hair. He stormed the Pyrenees, he took two thousand prisoners, he defended a bridge single-handed against a regiment of Austrians, he fought always in the front rank of his division—and once, after a battle, he fainted dead away. "Are you wounded, General?" asked his aide-de-camp when Dumas opened his eyes.

"No, but I have killed so many . . . so many . . ."

He fought under Napoleon as a fiery republican, and a fiery republican he remained when Napoleon assumed the dictatorship. He was dismissed from the army in disgrace.

In the meantime he had married and had become the father of a strapping man-child—nine pounds in weight and eighteen inches in length. And—"thank God!" exclaimed the mother—the child was born white. Pink skin, light hair, blue eyes. The only evidence of his mulatto descent was a thickness about the lips.

They named the child Alexandre.

And the child, from earliest infancy, grew strong in body and in mind and in the spirit of rebellion. "That wicked man (Napoleon) has disgraced my father. I shall fight all my life against wicked men."

III

HIS MOTHER tried to make a scholar out of him; but he hated learning. Then she tried to turn him into a violinist; but he hated music. Finally she tried to interest him in the priesthood; but he ran away from his home and for several days lived in the woods.

His mother gave up in despair. "The only thing he can do is write a good hand. But any idiot can do that."

But Alexandre was far from an idiot. He had a quick eye, an open mind, and a heart that embraced the world. Though averse to book learning, he was rapidly learning to read the kaleidoscope of current events. And the greatest events were afoot in those stirring days. In June, 1815, Alexandre saw a carriage dashing through the main street of Villers-Cotterets. Behind the curtain he glimpsed the outline of a man—firm, straight, determined. "It's Napoleon, speeding on to Waterloo." A few days later, he saw the same carriage dashing through the street in the opposite direction. Behind the curtain, the outline of the same figure— dejected, slumped in his cushions, crushed. "Napoleon, running away from Waterloo."

After the defeat of Napoleon, Alexandre's mother tried to recoup her fortune and her place. She offered her son the choice between adopting the old aristocratic name de la Pailleterie, or retaining the obscure and humble name Dumas.

"I shall remain Alexandre Dumas," said the young rebel.

But what was Alexandre Dumas, the grandson of a black slave, to do for a living? His neat handwriting provided the answer to the problem. He became a "copy clerk" at the office of Maître Mennesson, a liberal notary and friend of the Dumas family.

At this office the long-legged youngster of sixteen did more reading than writing—much to the vexation of his employer. He went through Voltaire and many of the other writers who had fanned up the flames of the revolution.

But just now he was interested in a flame of a different sort. He had suddenly discovered the seductiveness of his tall graceful figure and his dazzling white smile. And he proceeded to seduce Adèle Dalvin, a young girl of the town.

When his campaign with the young lady proved all-too-easily successful, he began to cultivate his new talent assiduously. He became the Don Juan of Villers-Cotterets.

And then, a new ambition. If he was destined to cut a brilliant figure in the world, why waste his talents on a little provincial town? Why not go to Paris?

But how? His mother was too poor, and his own earnings were too meager for the luxury of a trip to Paris.

Yet for Alexandre's will there was always a way. In his idle hours he had become an expert billiard player. One evening at the tavern he challenged everybody to a game of skill at the billiard table—and left home with his pockets full of the necessary funds for the trip.

When he arrived in Paris, he made his way to the Théâtre Français and into the dressing-room of the great tragic actor, Talma. There was no stopping this streak of lightning in human form.

The old actor was delighted with the spirit of the young adventurer. "What, my friend, is your business?"

"I'm a notary's clerk, sir. But I'd like to be a writer."

"Why not? Corneille too, you know, began as a notary's clerk."

"Thank you, sir. And please, sir, would you mind touching my forehead for good luck?"

"Not at all," laughed the actor. And placing his hand upon Alexandre's forehead, he said: "I hereby baptize thee poet, in the name of Shakespeare, Corneille, and Schiller."

The actor had spoken these words more in banter than in seriousness. But to Dumas it was no bantering matter. Poet in the name of Shakespeare, Corneille, and Schiller? *Parbleu,* but he would make the prophecy come true! "I'll prove it to Talma and to all the rest of the world. And right away!"

He went home and sat down to a dramatization of Scott's novel, *Ivanhoe.*

IV

HE COULD FIND no producer for *Ivanhoe.* Nor for his next play, nor his next. But he kept on hoping, and philandering, and begetting illegitimate children, and writing plays and stories, and trying again and again and yet again to force his talents upon the attention of a stubborn world. Whenever a producer or an editor refused to see him, he merely smiled at the secretary and said, "Thank you, Mademoiselle, I'm not easily discouraged. I shall come again."

And finally his smiling persistence gave him his chance. One of his plays, *Queen Christina of Sweden*, was accepted for production at the Théâtre Français. The cast was selected, the rehearsals were under way, and the young playwright was definitely headed in the direction of success—when suddenly he threw away his chance. He did this out of an impulse of generosity. Another playwright—an old man who all his life had tried unsuccessfully to reach the footlights—had just written, like Dumas, a drama on the Swedish queen. "Let the poor fellow have his fling," said Dumas, "before he makes his earthly exit." And he gallantly withdrew his own play in favor of the other.

And then he proceeded to write a new play, *Henry III*, and secured a producer and waited feverishly for the opening performance.

The night of February 11, 1928. Dumas begins to dress himself for the theater. He has laid out all his clothes in advance. "Hurry, I mustn't be late!" He puts on his shoes, his trousers, his shirt—and suddenly discovers that he has forgotten to buy a collar. He snatches a pair of scissors, and cuts a collar out of cardboard.

And then the cardboard cavalier rushes to the theater and looks through the hole in the curtain. The house is packed to the doors!

The performance was a triumph. The tumult of applause at the final curtain turned into a delirium of frenzy when the author appeared, "his head uplifted so high that his disordered mop of hair threatened to take fire from the stars." The mulatto with the paper collar had become the new king of the Parisian stage.

And Dumas entered into his kingdom as if born to the purple. He bestowed his smiles and accepted his honors and drank the sweet air of success like "a youth who is feeling the coming of dawn." New plays, new triumphs, new mistresses.

And then—a new adventure. The writer became a fighter. Charles X had issued an edict suspending the freedom of the press. The Parisian intelligentsia revolted against the edict, and Dumas joined the revolt.

In this rebellion Dumas did much more shouting than shooting. His own part in the fighting was like that of "the fly on the coach-wheel." But he managed to get his face smeared with perspiration and powder, and to carry off the major proportion of the applause. "M. Dumas," exclaimed Lafayette as he embraced him, "you have just achieved your finest drama."

Dumas thanked Lafayette for the compliment, and offered his services as an organizer of the French peasantry. Lafayette accepted the offer. Dumas arrayed himself in a blaring uniform—he had an African weakness for tinsel—lacquered boots, trousers of king's blue, scarlet coat with silver epaulettes, and shako with waving red plumes and a tri-colored cockade. He then set out with an adjutant—a counterfeiter whom he had saved from the galleys—and harangued the peasants and amused them and failed dismally in his effort to organize them.

The revolution was a fiasco. The rebels had merely succeeded in replacing a *bad* king with a *worse* king. Dumas reluctantly turned away from his political failure to his literary success. He wrote a play—*Antony*—with a new twist to the eternal triangle, and all Paris flocked to revel in its "indecent and dramatic intensity." In the enthusiasm of the first night, the ladies tore away the skirts of his coat. "Mon dieu, what a daring young dramatist! And what a delightful young man!"

And the daring, delightful mulatto with the gaudy waistcoat and the flashing teeth continued to ride the whirlwind of his destiny. The birth of a child, the desertion of a mistress, an attack of cholera, another successful play, another abortive revolution, a flight to Switzerland to escape arrest as "a dangerous republican"—and then, a sudden ambition to enter the priesthood. "Why not? I, the creator of the new drama, will become the founder of a new order."

But he gave up the idea almost as soon as he had conceived it. He was too volcanic by far for the quietude of the cloister. The pleasures of the earth were too savory to be replaced by the promises of heaven. "I had rather remain a pagan and pay the price."

And a pagan he remained to the end of his days. He amused the menfolk and seduced their wives and produced his plays and covered himself with "glory and glass beads" and faced his successes and his setbacks with a good-natured nonchalance. He met his praises with a shrug and his insults with a smile.

Yet occasionally, when an insult was too venomous, he seasoned his smile with a salty retort. One day a surly young nobleman boasted of his ancestry in the presence of Dumas. And then he turned to Dumas and asked pointedly, "Tell me now about *your* ancestors."

"My father," replied Dumas, "was a creole, my grandfather was a Negro, and my great-grandfather was a monkey. My family, it seems, began where yours leaves off."

On another occasion he met Balzac, his embittered rival, at a literary salon. Balzac, in an effort to clip the wings of the successful young playwright, remarked, "When my talent is used up, I shall write plays."

"Better begin at once, then," snapped Dumas.

V

On FEBRUARY 6, 1832, a "talented young girl" from the Montparnasse, Ida Ferrier, made her debut in Alexandre's latest play, *Térésa*. After the ovation at the final curtain, the actress flung herself into his arms. "M. Dumas, you have made my reputation. How can I ever repay you?"

"Easily enough," he said, flashing his irresistible smile upon her . . .

For several years she kept repaying him for his kindness—but not in legal tender. And then, to everybody's surprise, they were married. "Dumas resigned to a domestic life—the lightning contented to be chained!"

But the chains hung loosely upon his impetuous strength. Again and again he left his fireside for adventures abroad. And he allowed his wife generously to seek for her own adventures at home. "Live and let live," was his motto.

Always searching for new excitements, new amours, new applause. The triumphs of the theater had begun to pall upon him. The fires of rebellion had died down throughout the world. His quicksilver energy must find a fresh channel. But where? And how?

Ah, he had it! Historical fiction. He would stir the dead past back into tumultuous life. Walter Scott, the King of Romance, was dead. Long live the new King, Alexandre Dumas!

Feverishly he set to work on his first historical romance—*The Three Musketeers*. To help him with his historical research, he engaged the services of Auguste Maquet—a scholar with a flair for plotweaving. As for himself, he cared little for the *dead facts* but he cared a great deal for the *living truths* of history. "It is permissible to violate history," he said, "on condition that you have a child by her."

Tirelessly he worked at his novel—from seven in the morning until seven at night—his sleeveless shirt unfastened at the throat, his noonday lunch remaining often untouched at his side. If a visitor happened to drop in during his working hours, he waved a greeting with his left hand and went on writing with the other.

He worked always at high tension. But it was the tension of a man at play. He lived with his characters, he talked to them, he jested with them. One day an English visitor heard an outburst of laughter issuing from Dumas' workroom. "I shall wait until your master is alone," said the visitor to the servant.

"But my master *is* alone," replied the servant. "He is merely enjoying a *bon mot* that he has heard from one of his characters."

He lived with his characters by day and with his cronies by night. And when people asked him how he managed to feel so fresh after his daily grind, he replied that his daily output was no grind at all. "I don't produce my stories. The stories produce themselves within me."

"But how?"

"I don't know. Ask a plum tree how it produces plums."

He had that rare mysterious gift for creation. And that even rarer mysterious gift for friendship. At all times he kept open house and open heart. The Dumas "lunch hour" lasted from half past eleven to half past four. Always there were new guests arriving, and always the servants had to run out to the butcher for more cutlets. On the days when Dumas was able to relax from his work, he mingled freely among his guests—many of whom were uninvited but none the less welcome. "Will you be kind enough," asked a friend, "to introduce me to that gentleman over there?" "Sorry I can't do it," replied Dumas. "I haven't been introduced myself."

His generosity was like a bottomless sieve into which he kept pouring away all his earnings. He was forever in debt. The bailiff had become the most familiar of his visitors. Once a friend asked him for his contribution to help bury a poor devil of a fellow who had just died. Dumas took fifteen francs out of his pocket. "And who," he asked, "is this poor dead man?"

"A bailiff."

"So you're burying a bailiff!" cried Dumas. "Here's another fifteen francs—bury two of them."

VI

WHILE Dumas' pockets were running empty, his fame kept rising from height to height. From the turning of history into fiction, he now advanced to the turning of fiction into history. His *Monte Cristo*—a book on which he again collaborated with Maquet—is a texture of pure romance. Yet so vivid are the characters that to this day the guides at Marseilles point out to the visitor the houses of Mercedes and of Morel, and the cells of

Edmond Dantès and of the Abbé Faria at the Château d'If. Out of clouds and vapors, Dumas created solid habitations and living men.

Yet it was not the purpose of Dumas to create. He wanted merely to entertain. An author's business, he said, is to *write* joyfully in order that his readers may *live* joyfully. "What's any art worth that doesn't make people gay?" He pretended to be neither a poet nor a scholar. His sole aim was to be an expert teller of tales. "You write about events that you have never studied," observed a captious critic. Whereupon Dumas retorted: "If I had studied events, when should I have found time to write?"

He allowed Maquet and his other assistants—his enemies accused him of running a regular "fiction factory"—to supply him with the sterile facts. And then he took these facts and blew into them the fire of imagination and the breath of life.

And so he sat in his workroom until the evening of his career, "like the Arabian story-teller who prolongs the vigil of his tribe under the starry sky of the desert." And toward the end of the vigil the cup of his success grew somewhat acrid with the bitterness of envy. Yet in the very bitterness there was a mixture of pride. For the object of his envy was his own son. Alexandre Dumas *fils* had written a story—*The Lady of the Camellias*, known on the stage as *Camille*—whose popularity outrivaled the popularity of any of the stories of Alexandre Dumas *père*. The father and the son tried to outdo one another, and taunted one another, and loved one another to the point of adoration. "I have raised a child," said Dumas *père* jocosely, "who has turned out to be a serpent." "And I," rejoined Dumas *fils* playfully, "have raised a father who has turned out to be a child."

An irrepressible, laughter-loving and adventure-loving child to the end. Though advanced in years and physically overplump with the sweetmeats of success, he remained mentally as turbulent as of old. Wherever there was a revolution, he threw himself into the center of the whirlpool. In 1848 he was ready to lead the National Guard to Paris. But the National Guard refused to follow. In 1859 he joined Garibaldi and not only contributed his fortune of 50,000 francs but offered to contribute his very life to the cause of Italian freedom. Four years later he accepted a commission to lead the Greek rebellion against the Turks—only to discover that the man who had organized the rebellion, the Prince of Skandenberg, was an impostor.

His mercurial energy was forever straining to be translated into action. He could never rest. Once, at the age of sixty-three, he returned to Paris from a "revolutionary" visit to Italy. His son met him at the station. It was ten o'clock at night. "You must be pretty tired after your exertions, father. Let me take you home."

"No," cried Dumas *père*. "I want to see Gautier before I go to bed." And off he dragged his son to his old crony's house at Neuilly.

The house was locked when they arrived. Dumas raised a hullabaloo and awakened Gautier out of his sleep.

"Who's there?"

"Dumas the father and Dumas the son."

"But we're all in bed."

"What, in bed at this early hour? Come on, you lazybones, get up, everybody!"

It was four o'clock in the morning when the father and the son returned from Gautier's house. "And now, Alexandre," said Dumas *père*, "I want you to get me a lamp."

"What for?"

"I've got work to do."

The son left his father at his desk and went to sleep. When he awoke, it was long past dawn. On the desk lay three completed articles for three magazines. Dumas *père* was shaving and singing before a mirror.

"How do you feel, father?"

"Fresh as a daisy, son." And then, with a twinkle in his eye, "We youngsters, you see, don't tire as easily as you old men."

VII

AT LAST the youngster of sixty-eight put aside his pen and lay down to rest. Not that he was tired of his old adventures, but that he was anxious to try something new. He had just passed through his final romance—with an American actress, Adah Menken. A short, swift, passionate storm that ended in tragedy when the actress was killed in a fall from her horse. Dumas went to his son's house. "My boy, I have come to you to die."

He fell silent after that. And whenever his friends shook their heads sadly and remarked that Dumas had fallen into a decline, his son retorted: "A mind such as my father's can never fall into a decline. If he refuses to speak to us in the language of today, it is because he is learning to understand the language of eternity."

HUGO

Important Works by Hugo

Marion de Lorme (a drama)
Hernani (a drama)
The Hunchback of Notre Dame
The King Amuses Himself
  (a drama)
Napoleon the Little (a political
  treatise)
Les Misérables
The Toilers of the Sea

The Man Who Laughs
Ninety-three
Legend of the Centuries
The History of a Crime
The Supreme Pity
Several volumes of
  dramatic and
  lyric poetry

Victor Marie Hugo

1802–1885

In 1865, Victor Marie Hugo was an exile on the Island of Guernsey. "Napoleon the Little" had banished him from Paris because of his too-ardent love for humanity. On April 29 of that year he received a letter—so widespread was his fame—addressed to *Victor Hugo, Ocean*. On the same day he sent a letter, in care of the American Minister to Belgium, addressed to *My Fellow Citizens, the World*. In this letter he expressed his sorrow at the assassination of Lincoln. "The thunderclap at Washington has shaken the earth . . . How frightful a cataclysm!" And then Hugo went on to comfort the American people in words as prophetic today as they were in 1865: "The American people is a colossus of bronze: traitors may scratch its surface, but they cannot overthrow it . . . America has become the guide among the nations . . . the nation pointing out to its sister nations the granite way to liberty and to universal brotherhood." The exile then concluded his letter by signing himself "a devoted citizen of the Republic of Mankind."

There are those who regard Victor Hugo and Abraham Lincoln as the Head and the Heart of the Nineteenth Century.

II

STRANGELY ENOUGH, the child that was to become one of the most ardent of European republicans was brought up with a reverence for monarchy. The father of Victor Hugo was a general in Napoleon's army. When Victor was eleven years old, he saw Napoleon riding through the streets of Paris. "What struck me in my sacred awe when the Emperor appeared . . . was not the sight of the noisy crowd that followed him . . . singing in chorus . . . it was the sight of this sovereign man, moving mute and brave, with the air of a god of bronze." Until well into his mature life, Victor Hugo regarded the emperors of France as partaking of the solidity of bronze and the solemnity of God.

His love for the empire came not so much from his father as from his mother. Madame Hugo's feet were always shod with green, for green was the color of the French kings.

And green, too, was the color of Madame Hugo's eyes. She was always jealous of her husband. And her husband was always jealous of her. And not without cause. Their married life was a constant succession of reconciliations and separations—of strange women in the house of General Hugo, of strange men in the house of Madame Hugo.

As for Victor, he adored both his father and his mother—in spite of the fact that the irregular life of his parents meant a childhood of restless wandering for himself. From Paris to Bordeaux, from Bordeaux to Segovia, from Segovia to Madrid, from Madrid back to Paris. As a result of this constant wandering little Victor picked up a rather desultory education—a helter-skelter knowledge that made up in variety for what it lacked in solidity. "This child," said a friend of his mother's, "knows a little about everything." "Yes," replied his mother lugubriously, "and he knows precious little about anything."

And so he flitted about from school to school, and sipped hastily of this flower and of that, until at thirteen he came upon a great discovery—the poetry of Virgil. He made a translation of Virgil's *First Eclogue*, and was rewarded with a thrashing from his teacher, Decotte. For Decotte himself had just finished a translation of the selfsame *Eclogue*. How *dared* this little upstart set himself up as a rival?

Victor wiped away his tears, and went on with his poetry. He composed an ode in a school contest—Decotte was not one of the judges—and carried off the first prize. He wrote an epic, a drama and a novel. His teachers dubbed him the "sublime child."

And the sublime child proved himself precocious not only in literature but in love. At seventeen he became engaged to Adele Foucher, a girl of sixteen. "Do you remember, Adele, it was on the twenty-sixth of April, 1819, one evening as I sat at your feet, that you asked me to tell you my greatest secret . . . And then I confessed trembling that I loved you; and after your reply, my Adele, I had the courage of a lion . . ."

Two years later they were married. What a handsome couple— this girl with the brave black eyes and the wistful smile, and this boy with the mouth of a poet and the brow of a soldier! And what a joyous wedding—an occasion of "honey and milk, and flowers and fruit and foliage, and laughter and love!"

Yet there was one discordant note. In the midst of the wedding feast a man rushed in with an axe and made straight for the bridegroom. They barely managed to pin him down. "A madman!" It was Victor's older brother, Eugene. He had gone insane with jealousy. He, too, had wanted to marry Adele.

The stormy scene at the wedding was the beginning of a stormy life for Victor. And the shifting winds brought joys and sorrows in equal measure. A successful volume of poems, a successful drama, applause from the public, praise from the critics, the ribbon of the Legion of Honor, the birth and death of a child, the death of his mother, and the betrayal of a devoted friendship. The dearest of all his friends, the critic Sainte-Beuve, had gone back on him. He had tried, though without success, to seduce Hugo's wife.

It was with this bitter thought in his heart that Hugo attended the opening night of *Hernani*. A momentous occasion. This unconventional drama of Victor Hugo's was to be the opening battle between the Romanticists and the Classicists, "the fire of the new and the ashes of the old." Hugo had boldly challenged the enemy to the fight. "In this play," he had declared, "I smash into bits all theories, prosodies and systems. I tear down the old plaster which covers the façade of beauty. From now on, there are neither rules nor models . . ."

The play was produced in a tumult of catcalls and cheers. At the final curtain the cheers prevailed. The entire audience gazed rapturously upon the newly-crowned King of Romance. But Hugo was oblivious to the tempest of adoration. His eyes were centered upon the box in which Sainte-Beuve was sitting. The eyes of Sainte-Beuve were fixed upon Adele.

III

AT HUGO'S URGENT REQUEST, Sainte-Beuve promised that he would never see Adele again. But Sainte-Beuve didn't keep his promise. He persisted in meeting her and writing to her—in secret, as he thought, but the secret did not escape Hugo.

And Hugo tried to forget his sorrow in his work. He wrote a novel, *Notre-Dame de Paris*. He began it on the fourth of September, 1830, worked on it in a frenzy of passion through the fall and the early winter, and finished it on the fifteenth of January.

The story of a holy temple—an edifice of stone with a living soul. "Side by side with the old Cathedral (of Notre-Dame)," writes the French historian, Michelet, "Victor Hugo has built a Cathedral of Poetry as firmly seated on its foundations as the other, and with towers equally high."

More applause, more heartaches, more work. And then, the birth of a new love—for the "Fire-Bird" Juliette Drouet. This beautiful actress, whose body had been the plaything of many men, now made a gift of her heart to one man. For fifty years she remained passionately devoted to Victor Hugo.

And Victor Hugo remained passionately devoted to Juliette Drouet. Not that he had ceased to love Adele. His affection for her remained steadfast. But it was the affection of a son for a mother rather than that of a husband for a wife. And Adele seemed to be satisfied with that quiet sort of affection. Her feelings toward Hugo—and, for that matter, toward Sainte-Beuve—had always been platonic rather than possessive. Love to her was a distant sun. She enjoyed its slanting warmth and was content to stay out of its vertical blaze.

But the emotions of Hugo and of Juliette—she, too, had the spark of poetry within her—were like an overmastering flame. They never knew love's "sad satiety." Half a century after their "first night" he still responded to the intoxication of her kisses. "I kiss your body and your soul. You are beauty; you are light. I adore you!"

Juliette, the object of Hugo's adoration, was a nameless child of the people—a foundling. And to Hugo she symbolized all the nameless people of the world. Through the "consecration of her love" he gradually became transformed from a Bourbon to a bourgeois, from a royalist to a socialist. From now on, he declared, his life would be inspired with a "somber fidelity to fallen things." Whatever power he possessed, he declared, would be employed "in the defence of powerless men."

This remained his guiding principle to the end of his days. In 1830, and again in 1848, he joined "the cause of the people"— risking on both occasions not only his reputation but his life. In the Revolution of 1848, he stood fighting on the barricades. "I am dead with fatigue," he wrote to Juliette, "having spent three days and nights awake, in the fray, with no bed to sleep in, almost no food or drink, and only an occasional moment in which to sit down on a pavement by way of rest . . ."

While he was away at the barricades, his house was ransacked by the very people whom he was trying to save. From room to room they went, hacking, tearing, breaking, until they finally came to Victor Hugo's study. On a high desk near the window— Hugo always wrote standing up—the insurgents saw a number of scattered sheets. The leader of the insurgents, a former schoolmaster by the name of Gobert, glanced at the sheets. They were the beginning of a story. He then looked at the title page. "H'm, not a bad name for a novel."

"What is the name?" asked one of his companions.

"*Les Misérables.*"

IV

HUGO began the writing of *Les Misérables* in Paris. He finished it at Guernsey, whither he had been banished for his opposition to the tyranny of Napoleon III. The tempest of his destiny kept still pursuing him. Life and death kept dealing him alternate caresses and blows. Election to the Academy—and the drowning of his daughter, Leopoldine, in an estuary of the Seine. Recognition as the greatest poet of France—and the untimely death of another daughter. Pilgrimages to the Island Shrine of the Seer— and the unfortunate love affair followed by the insanity of still another daughter. Such were the events that surrounded the composition of *Les Misérables*. As he wrote this epic of human sorrow, God touched him on the shoulder and turned his gaze from earth to heaven. "The earth called me *Poet,* and heaven echoed *Prophet.*" Through his sufferings he had become the prophet of hope. "I have faced the terror of death, and I have found beyond it the flower of life."

The flower of life, the hope of the hopeless, the gospel of the humble, the lovingkindness of God for all His suffering creatures —this is the theme of *Les Misérables*. The transformation of suffering into pity, of pity into love. A wild and turbulent and tender book that swept the world with a cleansing fire. On the day of its publication the Parisians had besieged the Pagnerre bookshop at six in the morning. Within a few hours, they had carried off fifty thousand copies of the book. Victor Hugo, the lone prisoner upon the rock of Guernsey, was hailed as the *First Citizen of the World*.

And the First Citizen took his honors with a "modest pride" and grew younger as the years went on. "Under my white hair lives the love of springtime . . . Light knows no old age." He had become a Titan of physical and of mental endurance. Up at dawn, a plunge into the sea, and at his desk—standing up—before the sun rose. Afternoons, a bit of relaxation with his crayons —for he loved to draw as well as to write—and then a long walk over the seashore facing the sun and the spray. Never a stick to help him over the rocks, or an umbrella to shield him against the rain. He feared neither the heat nor the cold. "I am immortal. Nothing can hurt me." His appetite was enormous. Several platefuls of meat at a single sitting. There were days when two chickens were not enough to satisfy his hunger. Hearty eating, hearty thinking, and a hearty acceptance of the sorrows as well as of the joys of life. "Sorrow is but a prelude to joy." The symphony of life, if only we can attune our ears to it, resolves into a triumphant chord. In this absolute trust he faced the death of two of his sons, and of his wife Adele. And in this trust he faced the German invasion of France in 1870—he had now returned from his exile at Guernsey. "Everybody to the front, citizens! Let all the towns rise up. Let all the fields take fire! . . . Cities, cities, cities! make forests of pikes, multiply your bayonets, harness your cannon; and you, village, take up your torch! Let every man, rich, poor, laborer, peasant, clerk, bring forth or pick up from the ground whatever resembles a weapon or a missile! Roll rocks, pile up paving stones, change furrows into trenches . . . tear forth the stones from our sacred earth, stone the invaders with the bones of our mother, France . . ." And then, with a prophetic light in his eyes, "Fear not the defeat of today. Center your hearts and your hands upon a single goal—victory in the end!"

And it was in this selfsame trust—a trust in the wholesomeness of human sorrow and in the purposefulness of human toil—that he wrote one of the most beautiful of his novels—*The Toilers of the Sea*.

Here, in its mutilated brevity, is the story:

Lethierry, the uncle and guardian of the charming Deruchette, befriends the adventurer Rantaine. The latter repays the favor by stealing 50,000 francs from Lethierry. This money, saved over a period of forty years, has been intended for Deruchette's dowry.

Now Deruchette is the object of a great and silent worship. Gilliatt, a young man of doubtless courage but of doubtful birth, adores her from a distance. He feels too humble, however, to tell her of his love.

One day Gilliatt rescues a young curate from the high tide. The curate offers him a sovereign, which Gilliatt refuses. He accepts a Bible instead.

An interesting situation. A beautiful girl whose dowry has been stolen; a young man of lowly station who is desperately in love with the girl; and another young man, of higher station and learning. The old inevitable triangle. But let us go on and see how the author develops the theme and how he interweaves the fates of the other characters with the fates of these three young people.

Deruchette's uncle Lethierry owns a steamboat, the *Durande,* which is commanded by Captain Clubin. Lethierry has lost all his other ships, and all his hopes are centered in the *Durande* and its captain. He is an honest man, this captain, and well worthy of his master's trust.

On one of his trips, Captain Clubin runs across Rantaine, the scoundrel who has stolen Lethierry's money and who is about to escape from the country with a fortune of 75,000 francs. Clubin compels Rantaine, at the point of a pistol, to deliver the money to him. He then sets sail to bring the money back to Lethierry.

And now the author produces a complication in order to prolong the thread of the story. The steamship *Durande* is wrecked. Clubin sends the passengers off in the long-boat, and calmly awaits death on the sinking ship.

Lethierry's hope for Deruchette is practically at an end. The *Durande* is a total loss—except for the engines which Lethierry himself has designed. If only he could recover the engines, he might build another ship around them. And life might go on.

Is there anyone who can find a way to save the engines? If there is any man who can do it, he shall have the hand of Deruchette.

There is one man in the crowd who undertakes this almost impossible task. It is Gilliatt.

He sets out for the wreck. It is situated underneath a precipice in the channel. In order to reach it, he must climb down by means of a knotted rope. It is a superhuman task, fraught with the greatest danger. Day after day he toils and starves himself; for part of the food which he has brought along with him has been swept away by the sea. He lives on shellfish and crabs—whenever he can get them.

Once, as he wades into the shallow waters of a cave, he is attacked by a devil-fish and barely escapes with his life.

And thus Gilliatt toils on—a symbol for all the toiling human creatures who struggle and suffer and hope that their struggles may steer them into the haven of their dreams.

And now the author begins to prepare us for the climax. He takes Gilliatt into the further recesses of the cave where he discovers the skeleton of a man. By means of a belt with a name upon it, Gilliatt is able to identify the skeleton. It is that of the ship captain, Clubin. Tied firmly to the belt is an iron box. The box contains 75,000 francs.

Gilliatt takes the money and returns to his toil. Deruchette shall have her dowry; and Lethierry, his engines.

Finally Gilliatt succeeds in rescuing the engines. He is ready for his own reward—the hand of Deruchette.

In the evening he approaches the house in which she lives. A nightingale is singing. In his heart, too, there is a song.

Deruchette is in the garden. She is not alone. The young curate whose life Gilliatt has saved is with her. Deruchette and the curate embrace. Gilliatt turns away and leaves them to their love.

Deruchette and her lover are married. They set sail for England. Gilliatt stands on a rock at the water's edge and watches the ship. The tide is rising. It comes up to his knees, his shoulders, over his head. And thus ends the life of one of the toilers of the sea.

But he has had his reward. For he has won not the *hand* but—what is far more important—the *happiness* of Deruchette.

V

HUGO'S EIGHTIETH BIRTHDAY. "Flowers! We must have flowers!" one of his friends has declared. And the whole gay way between Nice and Paris has been lined with wagon-loads, train-loads of flowers. And his house is literally buried in roses. And fifty thousand children, beautiful living flowers, are singing and dancing in honor of *grandpère Hugo*. And over the avenues of Paris, half a million workers march singing Hugo's favorite anthem, the *Marseillaise*.

The height of his triumph, the depth of his sorrow. For shortly after the celebration of his eightieth birthday, his "dearest friend" Juliette passed away. "And if you were dead I should love you still," he had written to her shortly before the end. "And if I were dead I should love you yet . . . You dead, I should die . . ."

And with Juliette's death, Hugo ceased to live on earth and began to look forward to the greater life beyond. Of the reality of this greater life he hadn't the slightest doubt. "If an ant, at the moment when I was about to crush out its life, were to join its two miserable paws in prayer to me, I should be kind to it. Why then should not God be kind to me? . . . I supplicate Him to grant eternal life to you . . . to me . . . to all . . ."

Though he had lost his lover, his wife, and all his children save one—Adele was still alive but hopelessly insane—he was not alone. For he lived amidst his grandchildren—an oak surrounded by a circle of hardy saplings. He called them to his side when he was about to receive the summons. "My sweet angels, I am leaving you. I feel that God is calling me. I am going to see again my other little ones who are in heaven. You will not see me again, but I shall always be with you, near you, much nearer than I am now. And I shall bless you as I bless you now."

He died on May 22, St. Julia's day, the name-day of Juliette.

His friends had expected a "royal burial." Yet they were not surprised when they learned of his final request:

"I desire to give fifty thousand francs to the poor . . . I desire to be borne to the cemetery in the hearse of the poor . . ."

And at the end of his request he penned a simple statement of his faith: "I refuse the prayers of all churches . . . I believe in God."

FLAUBERT

Important Works by Flaubert

Madame Bovary
Salambbô
*The Sentimental
  Education*

*The Temptation of
  Saint Anthony*
*Bouvard and
  Pécuchet*

Gustave Flaubert

1821–1880

IN 1840 a strange, shy, grumpy, handsome, slovenly, proud, sensitive and caustic young fellow of eighteen came to Paris to study law. "He looked like a Greek God dressed in a red flannel shirt and blue overalls." He spoke little; and when he did open his mouth, "his tongue was dipped in a cask of vinegar." He showed an utter contempt for the conventions; and he looked upon everybody, including himself, as an utter fool. "The very first nincompoop I see every day is myself, in the morning, when I go to the mirror to take a shave." And the very last one, he added, "is whatever person I happen to speak to before I go to bed."

Who is this peculiar fellow? the students wanted to know.

"Flaubert. Gustave Flaubert. His father is the surgeon-in-chief at the Rouen Hospital."

"It must be wonderful," said one of the students to Flaubert, "to be the son of so great a celebrity."

"What's wonderful about it?"

"Why, think of all the lives he saves."

"Yes," snorted Flaubert. "My father saves the stupid for future stupidities."

II

HE WAS peculiar from the very first. Always interested in the morbid side of life. As a child he climbed the wall of his father's hospital in order to look at the corpses in the theater. He found a special fascination in lunatics and idiots, and he fancied that lunatics and idiots found a special fascination in him. A born observer, he began to take notes of people almost as soon as he had learned to write. The son of a dissecter of human bodies, he grew up to be a dissecter of human souls. When he was a mere tot, he composed plays and acted them with his sister on a home-made stage—the family dining table. Not content with his plays, he also wrote a novel and two "scientific" essays—on Corneille and on Constipation. All this before he had reached his teens.

But he had to hide himself away from his father when he wrote. For Doctor Flaubert was decidedly averse to a literary career for his son. When Gustave tried to read him one of his "masterpieces," the doctor fell asleep. He was anxious to turn Gustave into a good surgeon, like himself. And like Gustave's brother, Achille. "We are a respectable family, we Flauberts, and we want no vagabonds or poets among us."

And so Gustave was sent to a respectable school, and for eight years he dreamed and observed and wrote, and ridiculed his fellow students and befriended them—for, like most cynics, he was at bottom a gentle soul—and at eighteen he told his father flatly that he would not be a doctor.

His father was ready to compromise. "If you won't be a doctor, then you'll have to be a lawyer." And off he packed him to Paris to study law.

But Gustave was stubborn. "I am a Barbarian. I have a Barbarian's obstinacy." And a Barbarian's love for adventure. "I am descended from Sicilian pirates." He, too, would be a pirate, a rover of the spirit, a seeker after the gold of the perfect phrase. "I mean to be a writer and nothing else."

His father gave him up as a hopeless case. And Gustave, relieved, abandoned his law books and turned to *Don Quixote*—"the Bible of human folly." This book became the primary source of Flaubert's philosophy, the cardinal principle of his faith. "The trouble with men is not that they are scoundrels, but that they are fools." Under the influence of this philosophy, he wrote a number of plays and novels dealing with the more somber aspects of life—the story of a man who has lost his soul just as Peter Schlemihl has lost his shadow, the tragedy of a cataleptic who is buried alive and who dies blaspheming his destiny, the adventures of a creature whose mother is human and whose father is an ape—fantastic and immature tales that he wrote only for his own amusement and for the amusement of his friends.

And these friends of Flaubert's were even more pessimistic than himself. "We were a group of droll youngsters who lived in a strange world . . . We beat out a familiar path between madness and death . . . Some of these youngsters killed themselves; others died in their beds; one who strangled himself with his necktie; several who took to drink in order to drive away their thoughts . . ."

Flaubert, however, was able to maintain a healthy balance between madness and suicide. And this was due to three of his more conventional friends—Ernest Chevalier, Alfred le Poittevin, and Maxime du Camp. While Gustave had a morbid interest in literature and in death, these three young men had a wholesome interest in literature and in life. Chevalier was a combination of the poet-politician—a man with his head in the clouds but with his feet on the ground. Le Poittevin, the son of a successful businessman, was himself destined to be successful in business. (Le Poittevin's sister, it is interesting to note, was the mother of de Maupassant.) Du Camp, the editor of the *Revue de Paris,* had appointed himself as Flaubert's guide not only in the gardens of fancy but in the ways of the world. He drew Flaubert out of his solitary shell; he induced him to meet people; and he took him (1849) on a trip to the Orient.

This trip to the Orient was one of the enchanting episodes in Flaubert's life. "Never shall I forget the experience—the colors and sounds of Egypt, the Nile, Syria, Palestine, Malta, Constantinople." He found a special fascination in the Pyramids. "When we reached the bottom of the hill on which the Pyramids stand, I set my horse at full speed. Du Camp did likewise . . . At the sight of that grandeur, my brain whirled . . . It was sunset. The three Pyramids, all rosy, seemed drowned in light . . ."

Three Pyramids. Three friends. And one mistress. He met Louise Colet, the girl who was to become his mistress, at the studio of the artist Pradier. She was a poetess of little talent and great charm. Many of the literary lights of Paris, though they were left cold at the beauty of her poetry, were quite ardent over the poetry of her beauty. Once, when Victor Hugo bewailed the mutilation of the Venus de Milo, she remarked that the arms of this famous statue had been recovered.

"They have?" asked the surprised Hugo. "Where are they?"

"Under my sleeves," replied Louise Colet.

When the shy Flaubert met this forward young courtesan, he surrendered to her his heart, his mind, and his entire critical faculty. "She is not only the most *beautiful* but the most *talented* young woman in Paris!" he exclaimed with a lover's blindness.

Yet he never married her. For one thing, his mother disapproved of such a marriage. His father had died, and Flaubert now lived (at Croisset, near Rouen) with his mother. Madame Flaubert, a neurotic little lady, was too possessively attached to her son. "I will share him with no other woman—not even an angel from heaven."

But Flaubert himself was averse to marriage. He was willing to give his beloved everything save the complete possession of his body. This body of his was but the shadow of himself. He lived in a world not of things but of ideas. "I have never," he said, "really embraced a woman. Not even Louise. What I have held in my arms is the semblance of love, but not love itself."

This "semblance of love" was sufficiently strong, however, to influence the entire course of his life. For it was under the inspiration of Louise that he perfected his literary style and launched upon the series of novels that were to place him in the front rank of the creators of the world's literature.

Yet the inspiration of love and the devotion of friendship were but passing shadows in the world of his ideas. Flaubert was essentially a man of solitude. He lived alone with his thoughts. He broke with Louise, and he broke with his three friends, and he retreated within the hermit shell of his genius. That caustic tongue of his, and his equally caustic pen. When du Camp, out of sheer kindness, gave him practical advice on the publication of one of his books, he took it as an affront. "I do not blame you for publishing your own stuff. And I thank you for your kind intention in advising me as to the publication of mine. But this mania of yours concerning my welfare is rather comical to me . . . We are no longer on the same road, you and I. We do not sail in the same boat. May God lead each of us where each of us wants to go—you to a safe harbor, I to the open sea."

And so he left his friends and his intimates and his loves and set sail for the open sea of an uncompromising literary career.

III

As a writer, Flaubert was a rare combination of the romanticist and the realist. "There are two distinct men within me," he wrote. "One of them is in love with noise, with lyrism, with great eagle-flights, with all the sonorities of phraseology and all the high summits of ideas. The other searches and probes the reality as deeply as he can, loves to bring out small facts as well as great ones, and would like to make you feel almost materially the things which he reproduces. This one enjoys laughter and takes pleasure in the animalism of mankind."

All his life, Flaubert hovered between the two worlds of fancy and fact. At times he went soaring into flights of imagination, at other times he went groveling into the muck of material existence.

And whichever was the world that he happened to be living in at the moment, he always wished that he were living in the other. He never spoke of the book that he was writing; he constantly spoke of the book he was going to write next. The sequence of his books was therefore an invariable alternation between the realistic and the romantic: *Madame Bovary, Salambbô, The Sentimental Education, The Temptation of Saint Anthony, Bouvard and Pécuchet.* This alternation was not merely accidental; it was the result of a perpetual inner conflict between the artist and the scientist, the poet and the cynic, the comforter and the despiser of mankind.

But whatever he wrote, he was always the consummate artist. "In the beginning is the word." To Flaubert, a word was not merely the conveyer of a thought. It was a living entity—with a voice, a perfume, a personality, a soul. He polished and repolished his pages—frequently devoting an entire day to a single phrase—until the society of the words upon those pages had been reduced to a perfect singing unit. If at all possible, he never used the same word twice on the same page. "It is wrong to offend the *ear,* just as it is wrong to offend the *heart,* of my readers."

Yet he had little respect for the *mind* of his readers. "The human mind is tragically stupid." This abysmal human stupidity both repulsed and attracted him. He studied it as a conscientious doctor studies a loathsome disease—in order that, having determined its cause, he might be able to discover its cure. It has been said that Ernest Renan always tried to find a little wisdom even in a fool, but that Gustave Flaubert always tried to discover a little folly even in a wise man. But here again, it was the doctor in Flaubert—his male ancestors had been doctors for centuries—that liked to probe into the human personality, insisting upon a periodical and thorough examination in order to discover and to eliminate the disease upon its first appearance.

It was in this effort to discover and to eliminate disease—the disease of bourgeois paltriness—that he conceived and wrote the greatest of his novels, *Madame Bovary.* This book, like Goethe's

Faust, is the biography of an erring soul. But whereas Goethe's hero, in spite of his bungling, is guided by an instinct for the one *true* way, Flaubert's heroine, in spite of her planning, is misled by an instinct for the one *false* way. The way from ennui, through transgression, to death. The story of Emma Bovary is a realistic picture of a romantic soul. Emma is the daughter of a kindly, sensual and lighthearted farmer overburdened with vanity and devoid of religion. From earliest childhood she has been brought up to live beyond the horizon. "The fruits of the next field always taste sweeter—in imagination—than the fruits of your own field." Brought up in a convent, she has become saturated with the subtle erotic flavor of the pious legends that she has been allowed to read on Sundays as a relaxation. Returning from the convent to the farm, she finds herself once more in the midst of her ugly surroundings and her romantic dreams. She longs to leave the sounds and the sights and the smells of the stables and the fields. Away from the Here to the Elsewhere. She longs to find someone who will make this pilgrimage possible for her. A young man appears. Charles Bovary. He is neither good nor bad, neither clever nor stupid. Just an average nobody, an ordinary bore. But to Emma he is the Prince Charming who will rescue her from her own boredom. She marries him.

But the moment after her marriage, she returns to her restless dreams. For Bovary represents the commonplace Here, and Emma is always yearning for that glorious Elsewhere.

And now another man comes—as she believes—to her rescue. Leon. Young, elegant, romantic. A brief moment of ecstasy, a peep into the heaven beyond the horizon, and then he leaves her.

Reality once more—heavier, duller, more oppressive than ever. The days drag along on leaden feet. Even her dreams are now weighted down with the monotony of her boredom.

And then the next lover comes, and she throws herself into his arms with utter abandon. "She was entering into a wonderful something where all would be passion, ecstasy, delirium. An immensity of blue space surrounded her; the summits of romance glistened in her thoughts and ordinary existence appeared far, far below, in the shadows between the heights."

A new dream, with her new lover (Rodolphe). Together they travel in fancy to faraway places—to Spain with its tambourines, to Italy with its blue skies, to the Orient with its minarets and its bazaars.

But this dream, too, is soon ended. A quarrel with Rodolphe, and Emma sinks back into a reality which now borders on despair. Her actual world is unbearable, her romantic world is shattered, and there is nothing left but forgetfulness. She seeks this forgetfulness in a frenzy of sensual excitement. She meets Leon again and throws herself into his arms—this time, however, not as a lover but as a courtesan. Her dream now is not to escape from *reality,* but to escape from *herself.*

And thus she falls from degradation to degradation—from Leon to an operatic tenor, from the operatic tenor to a notary's clerk. She has even stopped dreaming. Her life has become a confused, desperate and panicky escape.

And then, the final choice between the gutter and the grave. Emma chooses the grave. For the gutter would be but another relapse into reality. But death is that fearful, hopeful journey beyond the horizon. The last great excursion into the Land of Romance.

Emma Bovary is romantic to the end.

IV

WHEN Flaubert published *Madame Bovary,* the critics condemned him as a moral leper. The French government had him arrested on the charge of "foisting pornographic literature upon the public." After a stormy trial he was acquitted—not, however, without a verbal lashing on the part of the presiding judge. It took the French public to convince both the critics and the government that *Madame Bovary* was an honest transcript of life, and that in its fidelity to the truth it was no more immoral than the honest description of an avalanche.

And Flaubert, indifferent alike to the storms of vituperation and the tempests of applause, sat like a monk within the shelter of his home and alternately scorned and amused the world into a better frame of mind. "I am a satirist, to be sure. But satire is the salt that enables mankind to digest the flatness of life."

The most solitary man in Europe, his friends dubbed him. He spent the greater part of the year at Croisset, going up to Paris only occasionally for a chat with George Sand or a dinner with Victor Hugo and a few other congenial souls. A huge bulk of a figure, with the mustache of a pirate and the eyes of a child. Though he loved his occasional contacts with his fellows, he loved even more to be left alone. He lived in a long, low house on the Seine, with five windows in his study on the second floor. "Whichever way I look, I see the universal sky."

A solid old house, and a solid old man with solid settled habits. He rose regularly at ten o'clock, read his letters and papers, ate a light breakfast at eleven, took a walk along the river, returned at twelve-thirty and sat down to work until seven. Then he ate his dinner, took a brief stroll in the garden, and returned to his desk for "another bout of work" which lasted until the wee hours of the night.

He lived almost entirely in his books. "A crusty old misanthrope," said his neighbors. Yet they didn't know that this "hater of his kind" had sacrificed most of his fortune for some distant relatives who needed it more than himself.

And thus he lived alone, dispensing his charity without expectation of thanks, and writing his novels without desire for fame. "In the final analysis, a man lives in his ideas. That is where he finds his only amusement and receives his only reward."

And it was in the midst of his ideas—he was engaged in writing his novel *Bouvard and Pécuchet*—that Death took him by the hand and led him into newer scenes for greater works.

HAWTHORNE

Important Works by Hawthorne

Twice Told Tales
The Blithedale Romance
Mosses from an Old Manse
The Scarlet Letter
The House of the Seven Gables

The Marble Faun
The Dolliver Romance
Tanglewood Tales
The Snow Image
The Great Stone Face

Nathaniel Hawthorne

1804–1864

HAWTHORNE'S LIFE was a poetical symbol of creation, just as Hawthorne's creations were a poetical symbol of life. Born of a seafaring race, he sat secluded on the seashore and quietly recorded the eternal struggle between the sand and the surf. To a more active personality this passive aloofness might seem to be a waste of time, a mere childish game in the face of the serious problems that confronted the grownups of the world. Yet "even a child's game," as Hawthorne observed, "becomes magnificent on so grand a scale." While the others were trying desperately to trace their names in the sand, Hawthorne watched the inrushing of the waters as they washed away the traces. "Draw the letters (on the sand) gigantic, so that two strides may barely measure them, and three strides for the long strokes! Cut deep that the record may be permanent! Statesmen and warriors and poets have spent their strength in no better cause than this. Is it accomplished? Return then in an hour or two, and seek for this mighty record of a name. The sea will have swept over it, even as time rolls its effacing waves over the names of statesmen and warriors and poets. Hark, the surf wave laughs at you!"

Hawthorne made it his business to watch these tracings and

effacings of human endeavor, and to hand down to history the characteristics of the letters cut into the sand just before the waters swept them away. He was especially interested in the character of the dying Puritanism of his day. He caught its spirit and preserved it from oblivion just before it gave way to the more spectacular optimism of the post-Civil-War days.

II

WHEN Hawthorne decided to devote himself to literature, he knew that he was doomed to a career of poverty and suffering and neglect. For literature in America was not a salable commodity. Indeed, under the Puritans the courting of the muses had been regarded as a sin, just like the playing of cards or the drinking of whisky or the kissing of another man's wife. The earliest American dramas, in order to pass the censorship of the Puritans, had been euphemistically called "Moral Lectures." In Hawthorne's day the censorship had been somewhat relaxed, but authorship was still a hazardous occupation. Yet Hawthorne was willing to take the risk. For he came of an adventurous stock. The Hathornes—it was Nathaniel Hawthorne who added the *w* to the name—had been ship captains for some generations past. They had the sea-blood in their veins. To launch upon unknown perils was second nature to that family.

Moreover, Hawthorne's early training had unfitted him for a business or a professional career. He was brought up to be what the modern psychologists would call an introvert. He lived within the circle of his own thoughts. Born at the turn of the century (1804), he lost his sailor-father as a child. His mother shut herself up, together with Nathaniel and her two little girls, in a lonely Salem house. Here they were cut off from the rest of the world as if they had been confined within a ship in the middle of the Atlantic. And even within the family group each member was taught to live a separate life. It was a strange little monastery to which the peculiar Puritan nun condemned her children. Each of them ate and played and read and brooded in a different room, so that Nathaniel found himself obliged to create a world of imaginary characters for his own companionship.

Furthermore, he sustained at an early age a severe injury to his leg, and this injury crippled him for several years and kept him from playing with other children. Sensitive by nature, and influenced by the morbidity of his mother, he stayed indoors all day and went out only at twilight or after dark for a ramble through the fields or along the seashore. As a result of this practice, he became acquainted with nature in her most somber moods. Throughout his life he saw the world dressed only in a gray or a sable cloak. We find this mood reflected throughout his literary style. His language has the melancholy sweetness of a world singing itself to sleep.

III

AT SEVENTEEN he entered Bowdoin College and there he met two students who later were to make a mark in life—Henry Longfellow and Franklin Pierce. In his academic studies he suffered the customary fate of the genius who is too deep for his instructors. He received very low marks. When he graduated, he returned to Salem and settled down "to dream of life"—to use his own expression—"instead of living it." He wrote stories and read them to himself and then threw them into the fire. Unable to become an actor in the drama of life, and unwilling to remain a mere spectator, he decided to serve as an observant commentator. He read in the morning, wrote in the afternoon, and took long walks at night. He looked at the dark landscape and peopled it with the shapes and the passions of bygone ages as well as of his own generation. He became an explorer of the unseen, a searcher into the mystery of the human soul. He took the dry bones of history, clothed them with flesh—a pale and unearthly but beautiful flesh—and then he plunged these frail characters into sin and analyzed their reactions with the severity of a Puritan and the compassion of a poet. We find this strange combination of his genius, this constant struggle between his piety and his pity, even in the earliest of his published works—the collection of stories known as *Twice Told Tales*. One of the most characteristic of these tales is *The May-Pole of Merry Mount*. It is the story of a young man and a young woman who came into the stronghold of New England Puritanism with a touch of wild Paganism in their hearts. To the Puritans, life is a stern reality; but to these Pagan youngsters, it is nothing but a joyous dance. They are sinners and they must be punished for their sins. And so, as they celebrate their wedding around the May-Pole, Governor Endicott descends upon them with his soldiers, strips the May-Pole of its flowers and condemns the terrified couple to a life of physical hardship and moral gloom. But here the poet in Hawthorne raises his voice against the Puritan in him. As the couple turned away from the scene of their happiness, the severe old governor "lifted the wreath of roses from the ruin of the May-Pole, and threw it, with his own gauntleted hand, over their heads." Blows for the ugliness of their sin; roses for the beauty of their suffering. It was a new note in American literature.

But the American public was not as yet attuned to this new kind of literature. The book was a financial failure.

IV

HAWTHORNE'S CLASSMATES were getting ahead in the world. Longfellow was a professor at Harvard, and Pierce was a member of the United States Senate. But Hawthorne was still drifting along. For a time he managed to get a job as a weigher of coal in the Boston Custom House. But a new President (Harrison) was elected, and Hawthorne was swept out of his job in the undercurrent of the political "spoils system."

He then invested his savings—about one thousand dollars—in the coöperative colony of Brook Farm. Here, he thought, he would be able to live without the necessity of fighting for a living.

It was an experimental period in American history. All kinds of -isms were springing up—Socialism, Feminism, Transcendentalism, Anarchism, Communism, Fourierism and what not. The idealists were ready to usher in the millennium. Brook Farm, under the leadership of Margaret Fuller, was to become one of the garden spots of the New Heaven on Earth. And, to prove their practical qualifications for their job, the members of Brook Farm appointed Hawthorne—of all people!—as the financial adviser of their colony.

And so we see Hawthorne in a new role—that of farmer-financier. He has laid aside his pen and taken up a pitchfork. Instead of spreading ink over the paper, he is now spreading manure over the fields—a most incongruous figure, an angel in a dung heap. He stood this sort of life for about a year and then returned to Salem. He had lost all his money in the Brook Farm experiment. But he had found there the material for the *Blithedale Romance,* his one colorful novel. Unlike the somber characters of his other books, the people in this story are bathed in the warmth of the noonday sun.

He was now thirty-eight years old—a figure of extraordinary beauty and pathetic futility. He had the body of a Hercules and the head of an Apollo. But his eyes were the eyes of a frightened child, or rather of a haunted stranger from an alien world. He shrank from the society of others. He felt more at home among the characters of his stories than he did among the inhabitants of Salem. He took a lonely seat upon the heights and began to transform life into fiction—a fiction, however, that was more living than life.

Absorbed in his art, he wanted to live entirely undisturbed by the intrusions of the world. He resented, "with an inward antipathy and a headlong flight," the approach of anyone who dared to break into his meditative solitude. "From such a man, as if another self had scared me, I scramble hastily over the rocks, and take refuge in a nook which many a secret hour has given me a right to call my own."

Yet he wasn't entirely alone In the summer of 1842 he married the one woman—Sophia Peabody—who was destined to bring him the happiness of a fulfilled life. They moved to Concord, the town of revolutionary memories and of rebellious spirits such as Bronson Alcott, Ellery Channing, Ralph Waldo Emerson and Henry Thoreau. Here he felt a little more at home, a little less removed from a life that held so much in common with his own. Yet even here he emerged only upon the rarest of occasions from his diffident aloofness. He rented a shabby house in an out-of-the-way corner of the town. Wrapping himself in his tattered dressing gown—"I may not be a landlord," he said, "but I have the biggest *rents* in the country"—he sat down to go on with his creation of Pagan characters against a Puritan background.

For four years he barely managed to get along on the proceeds from his stories, and then he was visited by a stroke of good fortune. The Democrats had once more regained the Presidency, and Hawthorne was appointed Surveyor of Customs at Salem. His salary was twelve hundred dollars a year—a fabulous sum in the Salem of 1846.

But his luck held only till 1849. The election of Zachary Taylor as President meant the dismissal of Hawthorne from the customhouse. His plight was pitiable. Though only forty-five, he felt like an old man. He had a wife and two children to support, no savings to fall back upon, and no prospects for a new job. But three things came to his rescue: the courage of his wife; the generosity of his friends; and the faith of his publisher in his ability to produce a literary masterpiece.

His wife greeted his dismissal from the office as a piece of good news. "At last," she smiled bravely, "you will have the leisure to write that great novel." She built a fire in his study, tidied up his desk, helped him on with his dressing gown and made him sit down to write. Then she went upstairs and came back with a hundred and fifty shining gold dollars, a sum that she had secretly saved up for just such an emergency.

A few days later Hawthorne learned that he was as unexpectedly rich in the affection of his friends as he was in the devotion of his wife. He received a substantial check, together with a touching letter signed by George Hillard, one of the Cambridge group of intellectuals of whom Longfellow was the head. "It occurred to me and some other of your friends," wrote Hillard, "that you might at this time be in need of a little pecuniary aid. I have therefore collected, from some of those who admire your genius and respect your character, the enclosed sum of money . . . I know the sensitive edge of your temperament; but do not speak or think of obligation. It is only paying, in a very imperfect measure, the debt we owe you for what you have done for American literature . . . Let no shadow of despondency, my dear friend, steal over you. Your friends do not and will not forget you . . ."

In his reply to Hillard, Hawthorne wrote: "Your letter drew—what my troubles never have—the water to my eyes . . . There was much that was sweet—and something too that was very bitter—mingled with that same moisture . . . The money, dear Hillard, will smooth my path for a long time to come. The only way in which a man can retain his self-respect, while availing himself of the generosity of his friends, is by making it an incitement to his utmost exertions, so that he may not need their help again."

And so, incited "to his utmost exertions," he went on with the writing of his book. But he did not believe in himself. One day his publisher, James T. Fields, came to visit him in Salem. He found Hawthorne in his study, hovering over a stove.

"Have you prepared anything for the press?" asked the publisher.

"Why, no," replied Hawthorne, "what publisher would ever risk a book from me, the most unpopular writer in America?"

"I would."

"But I really have nothing worth while," Hawthorne insisted.

Fields opened the door and was about to leave, when Hawthorne took a batch of manuscript from one of the drawers.

"Perhaps," he said hesitantly, "you might care to look over this bundle of rubbish."

The publisher took the bundle home, and that night he wrote Hawthorne an enthusiastic letter. The manuscript which he had just read was the rough outline of *The Scarlet Letter*.

V

THE action of *The Scarlet Letter* does not begin at the beginning. Hawthorne uses the flash-back method in this novel. The scene opens upon Hester Prynne's discharge from prison. Hester, a woman with a great yearning for love and a great capacity for suffering, emerges from the gloomy fortress with a three-months-old baby in her arms. On the breast of her gown, in scarlet cloth, appears the letter A.

Outwardly serene, but with agony in her heart, she walks to the pillory.

On the outskirts of the gaping crowd stands a small man. He has an intelligent brow and cruel eyes. This man is Dr. Roger Chillingworth, Hester Prynne's husband. He has been abroad for a number of years and is now a stranger in this town.

The popular minister of the town, Arthur Dimmesdale, a young man whose courage is not equal to his devotion, is seen pushing his way through the throng. He comes to Hester's side and urges her to name her fellow-sinner. But Hester stubbornly refuses to yield to his urging.

And now, without any further delay, the author begins to weave the strands of the web that entangles the life of the four leading characters—Hester, Dr. Chillingworth, Arthur Dimmesdale, and little Pearl. On the night following Hester Prynne's discharge from the prison, her child falls ill and Dr. Chillingworth is called in.

"I have greatly wronged thee," murmurs Hester.

"It was my fault as well as thine," replies her husband. "I am a man of thought, you a woman of beauty. What right had we to marry?"

Roger Chillingworth understands, but he does not forgive. His mind and his heart are not in harmony. He is determined to learn the name of her fellow-sinner and to punish him.

Hester takes up needlework for a living. The worthy people of the town are at first insistent upon taking her "sin-child" away from Hester. But Mr. Dimmesdale finally prevails upon them to let the child remain with her.

"You take, my friend, a strange interest in this poor woman," smiles Roger Chillingworth.

Mr. Dimmesdale's health is failing. Dr. Chillingworth appoints himself as his physician. He moves into the same lodging with the minister. For he is determined to ferret out the secrets of Dimmesdale's heart.

Note how the author brings these two men together physically in order to interweave the threads of their mental and moral reactions. Chillingworth becomes the incarnated conscience of the guilty minister.

Dimmesdale regards Chillingworth with increasing horror. Time and again he tries to confess his sin from the pulpit, but his courage always fails him.

Once, in the dead of night, he mounts the pillory where Hester has stood exposed in her shame. He believes that everybody is asleep. Yet there are three people who see him: Hester and Pearl, who are returning from the home of a dying woman—and Dr. Roger Chillingworth.

In mock pity the doctor takes him home. "You should not study so hard, good Master Dimmesdale!"

The strands of the plot have now been interwoven into a definite and tragic pattern. The story moves rapidly forward to its inevitable climax. Hester plans an escape from the baleful influence of Roger Chillingworth. She takes passage for England. Dimmesdale and Pearl are to go with her.

But they find that Chillingworth is not so easily to be shaken off. Hester learns that he, too, has booked passage on the same ship for England. This information comes—note the skill of the author—on a very important holiday: the day on which Mr. Dimmesdale has been chosen to preach the election sermon in honor of the newly appointed governor. Thus the height of Mr. Dimmesdale's fame and the culmination of his tragedy come together on the selfsame day. For it is no longer possible for Dimmesdale to conceal his sin with Hester. Better the present confession, with its attendant disgrace, than the future torture of Chillingworth's endless probing into the deepest recesses of his soul.

And so Dimmesdale preaches the election sermon to an adoring congregation; and then, in a dramatic gesture, he mounts the pillory together with Hester and little Pearl.

"People of New England," he cries, "at last, at last I stand where seven years since I should have stood . . ."

And now comes the moment of tragic revelation:

"Lo," he continues in a ringing voice, "the scarlet letter which Hester wears . . . I, too, have my scarlet letter!"

He tears away the ministerial robe from his breast. Seared upon his flesh stands out the scarlet letter A.

Then, as the populace stares at him in amazement and pity, his head sinks down upon Hester's bosom. He has paid for his sin with his life.

VI

"THE SCARLET LETTER," like most of the other novels and short stories of Hawthorne, represents the moral history of New England—the struggle between the Puritan love of religion and the Pagan religion of love. But the book is not only a picture of New England; it is a picture of Hawthorne himself, a man with a Puritan body and a Pagan soul. There is a little of Hawthorne in all the characters of the book—in the severity of the judges, who punished Hester Prynne for her transgression with Arthur

Dimmesdale; in the relentlessness of Chillingworth, who set himself up as the avenging conscience of the young priest; in the irresolution of Dimmesdale, who concealed a heart of flame under the ashes of a conventional code; and in the defiance of Hester Prynne, who wore the symbol of her pain like a consecration on the garment of her love.

In this book Hawthorne represents two kinds of sin: the sin of love against convention, and the sin of convention against love. And of the two, the latter is to Hawthorne the more inexcusable. Hawthorne the poet tries to break away from Hawthorne the moralist. Puritanism has run its course in America. Something new must take its place. Just what that something new may be, Hawthorne does not pretend to know. Perhaps it is represented by the character of little Pearl, that vague and wild and ethereal offspring of the Puritan and the Pagan, beautiful and evanescent like the flash of a sunbeam in a dream, but promising something more complete, more attuned to the heart of the world, than either of the parents. Hawthorne lived too early in American history to write the story of little Pearl grown to maturity. That task remained for some future novelist.

Hawthorne represents a transitional period in the mental history of America. He belongs to those intellectual pathfinders who try to break away from the errors of the past. He begins to doubt the old Calvinistic picture of the human race—a mob of sinful creatures who are caught in a trap between a cruel Taskmaster in Heaven and a cruel Executioner in Hell. Hawthorne is the child of Puritans. His ancestors have hanged Quakers and burned witches. But he is also the father of rebels. In the final analysis, his sympathies are not with the judges and the jailers, but with the victims. The most sympathetic, and indeed the most *noble,* character in *The Scarlet Letter* is Hester Prynne.

Yet Hawthorne is groping his way. He is not as yet sure of his ground. Like his characters, he lives in a world of twilight and mystery. Objects are indistinct. Distances are blurred. The horizon is in a haze. There is no telling where the earth ends and

Heaven begins. But one thing he knows—that the mistakes of the past will be transmuted into the hopes of the future. "At some brighter period, in Heaven's own time, a new truth will be revealed, in order to establish [the human race] on a surer ground of mutual happiness."

A surer ground of mutual happiness—the eternal quest of the inspired poet and the moral pioneer.

VII

THE REST of Hawthorne's life can be told in a few words. When Pierce was elected to the Presidency, he appointed his novelist classmate to the American consulship at Liverpool. While living abroad, Hawthorne was just as aloof from society as he had been at home. He familiarized himself with the *history* rather than with the *people* of England. At the expiration of his consulship he took a trip to Italy; and there, too, he lived in the past rather than in the present. Then he returned to America and to the place where he felt most at home—the borderline between the present and the past as mirrored in the lives of a provincial folk.

So immersed was he in the problems of his provincial dramas, that he was hardly aware of the national tragedy that was being enacted before his eyes. When the Civil War broke out, he dismissed it with a shrug. "I approve of the war," he said, "but I don't know what we are fighting for."

But he, too, was fighting in a war—a war of the human soul to extricate itself from the meshes of its environment. He pictured this war in *The House of the Seven Gables,* in which the sins of the fathers weave a net against the happiness of their children. He returned to this battle in *The Marble Faun,* in which a wild and half-human creature out of the past comes to life amidst the serious human problems of the present—Hawthorne's favorite theme of sin and suffering. And at the very end of his life he was engaged in another, unfinished, battle of the soul against the inevitable decrees of Destiny—*The Dolliver Romance.* In this book he tried to find the elixir of life, the conquest of death, the universal human pass to immortality. It was the irony of fate that just when this novelist-philosopher was seeking eternal life, he died (May, 1864).

And with him died a mental epoch in American history.

THACKERAY

Important Works by Thackeray

The Great Hoggarty Diamond *Henry Esmond*
The Yellowplush Papers   *The Newcomes*
Barry Lyndon   *The Virginian*
The Book of Snobs   *Lovel the Widower*
Vanity Fair   Numerous essays
Pendennis   and poems

William Makepeace Thackeray

1811–1863

Born in Calcutta, he lost his father at five and was shipped off to England to live with his aunt at Chiswick. He was an odd-looking child, like a pumpkin on a beanpole. His aunt put her husband's hat upon the little fellow's head—a rather oversized hat—and found to her horror that it fitted exactly. She took him to her family doctor for an examination. "Don't be alarmed," the doctor reassured her. "The child has a large head, but there's a good deal in it."

Yet the large and capacious head of young William took a long time to develop. At the Charterhouse School, where he was enrolled as a day-scholar, he was somewhat less than mediocre. "Though he stayed there several years," wrote his classmate, George Venables, "he never rose high in the school, nor did he distinguish himself on the playground." Yet the "pretty, gentle, moony little fellow" displayed even at this period a dash of the dry humor that was to distinguish him in his later years. "I like my school," he wrote to his mother in Calcutta. "There are so many good boys to play with." And then he added a subtle postscript: "There are 370 in the school. I wish there were 369."

He wrote regularly to his mother and to his stepfather, Major

Carmichael Smyth. He always confessed to them how lazy he was today and promised them how industrious he was going to be tomorrow. But that industrious tomorrow never came. When he graduated from the Charterhouse School, he needed additional tutoring to prepare him for Cambridge. He got this tutoring from his stepfather—Major Smyth and his wife had now moved to England—and he matriculated at Cambridge in February, 1829. Here, too, he lived a sensitive, solitary and undistinguished life. "If only somebody could stir him out of his laziness!" exclaimed one of his teachers. "Why, this fellow could do anything if he chose—but he never chooses." That was precisely the trouble with Thackeray. He could never settle down to one thing. One day he would translate Horace; the next day he would make funny sketches; the day after that, he would write satirical verses. Everything he did was good, but not good enough. He didn't concentrate on anything sufficiently to become an expert at that one thing.

Certainly he didn't concentrate on his studies. After two years of drifting at the university, he was invited to leave—without his degree.

And so he left the university and drifted along through the world. He traveled to the continent, and visited the museums and the theaters and the libraries, and made sketches, and wrote poems, and observed the vanity and the pity and the beauty of life. A long, lanky, taciturn young aristocrat—he had inherited about $100,000—with a voracious ambition for glory and an infinite distaste for work. A paradox in appearance as well as in temperament. He had the body of a giant, the face of a cherub and the nose of a clown. He had broken his nose in a fight at the Charterhouse School, and he remained disfigured for life. "Were it not for my broken nose," he once remarked jestingly, "I might have got a job as a circus giant. When I applied for the job, the showman examined me critically, and then shook his head. 'You're nigh tall enough, young man, but I'm afraid you're too hugly.' "

Idle days, playful nights—and a bitter experience. The growing pains of a gifted mind. In the course of his drifting he found himself one evening in a gaming house. A thrilling but expensive business. Within a few months he was stripped of his entire fortune.

And then he settled down to the serious business of life.

II

HE TRIED ART for a while, but realized that his talent was inadequate. And then he decided upon literature. In his travels he had seen "many cities and men"—and everywhere the same busybody aimlessness. "And behold, all is vanity and a striving after wind." He would be a modern Koheleth, an observer of the passing show and, if possible, a humble commentator upon the meaning of some of its obscure passages.

To this end, he began to write poems and essays and stories—and most of them were rejected. And there was good reason for their rejection. Thackeray wrote at cross purposes. He was by conviction a despiser and by inclination a lover of humanity. The editors failed to understand him because they couldn't place him. He was that most paradoxical of literary combinations—a sentimental cynic. He saw the stupidity of life, but he saw it through a mist of sorrow.

For Thackeray himself had entered upon a great sorrow at the very threshold of his career. He had married a beautiful Irish girl, Isabella Shawe, and she had given him two daughters and "the happiest foretaste of heaven that ever came to any man." And then she fell sick of a fever. Her body recovered, but her mind died. And Thackeray's happiness died along with her mind. He entrusted her to the care of a friendly family, and threw himself into the maelstrom of a club-life for which he had but little taste. "My social activity is but a lifelong effort at forgetting."

And his literary activity was a lifelong effort at deriding. He mocked at his fellows because he pitied them. Jesters, as G. K.

Chesterton reminds us, are the most serious people in the world. There is no malice in Thackeray's satire. The hand is the hand of Esau, but the voice is the voice of Jacob.

And this is why he found it so hard to build up a literary reputation. The public couldn't make head or tail out of a writer who used a whip only to caress. Even his own children, as they grew older, upbraided him for the subtlety of his humor. "Why don't you write *simple* humor, like Dickens, so that everybody will understand you?"

Thackeray was keenly disappointed at his inability to sell his literary wares. Unable to get into the magazines, he started a magazine of his own, *The National Standard*. The venture only enabled him to make a "gaby" of himself. But "if thou hast never been a fool," as he observed in *Lovel the Widower*, "be sure thou wilt never be a wise man."

The magazine failed, and Thackeray continued to learn wisdom through his folly. Little by little his compositions were finding lodgment in the obscure corners of the magazines. "A writer of slight essays, of scraps of pretty verses, nothing more," observed one of the editors. Whereupon Thackeray retorted, "I'll show you that I am a better man than you think."

It took him a long time to show. While Dickens, his junior by one year, was the toast of London, Thackeray was "that obscure young satirist whom nobody ever reads." He wrote a superb story, *The Great Hoggarty Diamond*—"what is there better in Fielding or in Goldsmith?" asked John Sterling—and several magazines turned it down. He applied for a job as editor of the *Foreign Quarterly Review*—"please to think of your humble servant, who could really, I believe, do the duty very well"—and his application was thrown into the waste basket. He offered to write a series of articles for *Blackwood's Magazine*—"I belong to a couple of clubs in this village and can get together plenty of rambling stuff" —but his offer fell upon deaf ears. It was a discouraging business, this futile effort to make a living by the pen. But he stuck to it—

"what else can I do?"—and finally, after twelve years of uninterrupted failure, he won a slight measure of success.

The first of his moderately successful compositions was *The Irish Sketch Book*. The book reached a sale of 1000 copies. Thackeray could hardly believe his eyes when he read the report. "At last," he exclaimed with a wry grin, "I am almost as popular as Dickens, whose books sell about 100,000 each."

And then, with the munificence of the man who had "arrived," he advised a literary friend in Ireland, the novelist Charles Lever, to come and try his fortune in England. He even offered to help him financially—an offer which, as Lever humorously observed, is like teaching your friend to swim when you yourself are struggling to keep your head above water.

The intoxication of his first success soon wore off, and Thackeray returned to his obscurity and his sadness. A friend of his, referring to *The Irish Sketch Book*, remarked that it must be great fun to write a book of such sparkling humor. For answer, Thackeray told him a little story. One day a sick man came to a doctor's office to be examined. "You're too melancholy," said the doctor. "What you need is something to cheer you up. Why don't you go to the pantomime and watch the antics of the famous clown, Pulcinello?"

"I," said the sick man, "am Pulcinello."

Thackeray laughed, he said, because he felt so much like crying. "What funny things I've written," he observed in one of his letters, "when fit to hang myself!"

III

HE CONTINUED TO WRITE his funny stories and poems and articles, and the public repaid him with a handful of pence and a scattering of applause. Indeed, the public hardly knew his name. In his exaggerated desire for anonymity, he had assumed a number of pen names—*Titmarsh, Yellowplush, Ikey Solomons, Major Gahagan, Folkstone Canterbury, Goliah Muff, Leonitus Huggle-*

stone, Fitzboodle, Mrs. Tickletoby, Paul Pindar, Fitz-Jeames de la Pluche and *Frederick Haltamont de Montmorency*. This assumption of many disguises was but another paradox in his paradoxical character. Though hungry for personal fame, he did everything in his power to keep himself impersonal.

Yet Thackeray found ample justification for his pseudonyms. "My secondary ambition," he said, "is to be famous; but my primary ambition is to make a living for my children." And he was able to make his living only through the continual bombardment of the magazines at so much—or rather at so little—per word. "It may so happen to a literary man," he explained in one of his letters, "that the stipend which he receives from one publication is not sufficient to boil his family pot, and that he must write in some other quarter. If Brown writes articles in the daily papers, and articles in the weekly and monthly periodicals too, and signs the same name to them all, he weakens his force by extending his line." And so, in order that he might not intrude his name too often, he concealed it altogether. "Who is this new writer?" asked a magazine reader on one of those rare occasions when Thackeray signed his own name to an article. "His work is so amateurish compared to the work of Titmarsh."

Thackeray was now "nearly come to forty year" and remained still anonymous and obscure. He felt bitter about his obscurity. "My friend," he wrote in one of his articles, "black boots, clean knives, do anything, but don't turn literary man." For literature, he observed on another occasion, is neither a business nor a profession; it is a misfortune.

Yet he stuck to his misfortune. For he was determined to show the world that he was "a better man than you think." This determination resulted (1847) in that interesting literary experiment—*Vanity Fair*, "a novel without a hero."

Thackeray wasn't at all certain about the value of *Vanity Fair*. "I wonder whether this will take, the publishers accept it, and the world read it." And at first it didn't take. Thackeray submitted the opening chapters to *Colburn's Magazine,* and the editor returned the manuscript. "This man," he said, "can't write fiction." The editor of another magazine returned the story with the comment, "The words are as light as feathers of lead." Still another editor, Macvey Napier of the *Edinburgh Review,* observed that "one requires to be very much on one's guard in accepting the work of mere strangers . . . In a journal like the *Edinburgh* it is always of importance to keep up in respect of names."

Several other magazine and book publishers refused *Vanity Fair* before the editor of *Punch* finally accepted it.

The public was slow to recognize the merits of the book. But the critics and the writers saw at once that here was a new landmark in English literature. "I brought away the last four numbers of *Vanity Fair,*" wrote Mrs. Carlyle to her husband, "and I have read them during the night . . . Completely beats Dickens out of the world." And Abraham Hayward, in a review that appeared after only a few installments of the novel had been published, prophesied that *"Vanity Fair* is assured of immortality as ninety-nine hundredths of modern novels are sure of annihilation." Several other reviewers hailed the book as a masterpiece. But it remained for the novelist, Charlotte Brontë, to provide the full measure of appreciation for this work of her fellow-craftsman. Her own recently published novel, *Jane Eyre,* had created a sensation. Yet in the midst of her triumph she found the time and the generosity to acclaim a rival work which, in her opinion, deserved an even greater triumph. "There is a man in our own days," she wrote in the preface to the second edition of *Jane Eyre,* "who to my thinking comes before the great ones of society, much as the son of Imlah came before the throned kings of Judah and Israel; and who speaks truth as deep, with a power as prophet-like and as vital—a mien as dauntless and as daring . . .

"Why have I alluded to this man? I have alluded to him, Reader, because I think I see in him an intellect profounder and more unique than his contemporaries have yet recognized; because I regard him as the first regenerator of the day . . . because I think no commentator on his writing has yet found the comparison that suits him, the terms which rightly characterize his talent. They say he is like Fielding: they talk of his wit, humour, comic powers. He resembles Fielding as an eagle resembles a vulture: Fielding could stoop on carrion, but Thackeray never does. His wit is bright, his humour attractive, but both bear the same relation to his serious genius that the mere lambent sheet-lightning playing under the edge of the summer cloud does to the electric death-spark hid in its womb. Finally, I have alluded to Mr. Thackeray because to him—if he will accept the tribute of a total stranger—I have dedicated this second edition of *Jane Eyre*."

It took a supreme novelist to understand a supreme novel like *Vanity Fair*. This story, not only without a hero but also, in a technical sense, without a plot, is a very slice of our hero-less and plot-less human existence. The entire book may be summarized in a single stanza which Thackeray wrote several years after the publication of *Vanity Fair*:

> *O Vanity of Vanities,*
> *How wayward the decrees of Fate are;*
> *How very weak the very wise,*
> *How very small the very great are!*

IV

THACKERAY had now acquired a full measure of glory and a comfortable living. But he was still unhappy. For he too, like the characters in his novel, was a puppet of *Vanity Fair*—riding perpetually on the merry-go-round of human ambition and aiming forever at something just beyond his reach. When he got a house, he wanted a coach and four; when he got a coach and four, he wanted a position in society; when he got a position in society, he wanted a seat in Parliament. And, although he hadn't the slightest aptitude for politics, he ventured to offer himself as a candidate for a seat in the House of Commons.

Fortunately for himself—and perhaps also for England—his

sense of humor prevented him from trying too hard for his election. When Lord Monck, presiding at one of his rallies, said "May the better man win," Thackeray retorted with a smile, "I hope not!" He knew that the rival candidate, Edward Cardwell, would make a much better statesman. Cardwell was elected, and proved to be a very good statesman indeed.

And Thackeray went on with his writing, the one thing at which he himself was the better man.

But his ambition kept driving him on. He undertook a series of lectures, "for the children's sake." He accepted all sorts of invitations to hear himself flattered—"this feast of flattery is all the more welcome after so long a period of starvation." He paid two visits to America, and came back full of honors and indigestion. "Now the dear children are provided for, the great anxiety is taken from my life, and I can breathe freely for a time."

But he didn't breathe freely. He was still restless, still anxious to attain the unattainable. He must exchange his cabriolet for a brougham, his footman for a retinue of servants, his little house for an estate. He must keep up in his mad race with the gentry of Vanity Fair. "Tom Carlyle," he wrote to his mother, "lives in perfect dignity in a little £40 house at Chelsea, with a snuffy Scotch maid to open the door, and the best company in England knocking at it." But this sort of secluded glory was not to his own taste. He wanted to be a man about town. "Look at the popularity of Dickens!" He, too, must be a lion roaring in the parlors and the taverns of the world. What a comfort it was to have Lord Flamdoodle grasping him familiarly by the hand, and Lady Flamdoodle smiling upon him with that gracious *aimable liberté*, and the waiters nodding to one another in hushed admiration as they served him at dinners given in his honor. He loved to tell the story of the two Irish waiters whom he overheard while dining in St. Louis. "Do you know who this man is?"—"No, tell me."— "This man is the famous Thacker."—"What's *he* done?"— "Damned if I know, but he's a great man."

And with each succeeding novel he kept adding to his greatness, and the tongues of the people kept wagging in his honor, though damned if they knew why. For, to paraphrase a contemporary critic, everybody admired him and nobody read him. Even his greatest novel, *Henry Esmond*—"I stand by this book," wrote Thackeray to his American publisher, James T. Fields, "and I am willing to leave it where I go as my card"—even this novel was labeled as "the most beautiful and least popular story in English literature." The public devoured the reviews and discussed the characters and lionized the author and bought the book—and left it on the library table with the pages uncut.

Let us cut the pages and briefly glance at the story of *Henry Esmond:*

In the last days of the Stuarts there lived in the house of Lady Castlewood a little fellow who did much thinking and little talking. His name was Henry Esmond—the illegitimate son, as everybody thought, of the Viscount Thomas Castlewood. As the little boy grew older, his education was entrusted to the Jesuit Father Holt, the spiritual adviser of the Castlewoods.

In due time, the master of Castlewood died in the service of the deposed King James, and Francis Castlewood took over as the new master of the house.

Henry Esmond accepted his changed fortune in his quiet, thoughtful way. New masters, new burdens. And one new supreme joy. The young and pretty Lady Castlewood—she looked like the daughter rather than the wife of Francis—took kindly to Henry. And Henry regarded Lady Castlewood with a feeling akin to worship. And he came to love her two children, Beatrix and Frank, with the love of a devoted brother.

At first there was peace in the Castlewood household, and then a double sorrow descended upon it. An attack of the smallpox disfigured Lady Castlewood's beautiful face; and her husband began to seek consolation for her disfigurement in the arms of other women.

Yet the Viscount's coldness toward his wife did not prevent his jealousy when another man, Lord Mohun, tried to pay court to her. He challenged Lord Mohun to a duel; and although Henry, now a full-grown man, endeavored to fight in his master's place, the Viscount insisted upon taking his own revenge—and was killed in the act. Just before his death, the Viscount confessed that Henry Esmond was the legitimate son of Thomas Castlewood, and therefore the rightful heir to the Castlewood estate. But Henry's devotion toward Lady Castlewood and her children was greater than his love for personal glory. He burned the confession—and remained "a servant in the house."

Not only that, but a *detested* servant. For, as he lay wounded and imprisoned for the part he had played in the duel, Lady Castlewood denounced him as the cause of her husband's death.

Life under these conditions was unbearable for Henry. He enlisted in the army, fought and bled under Marlborough, rose gradually to the rank of colonel, became an aide to General Webb and finally, while campaigning in the Low Countries, ran across his old tutor, Father Holt. The priest told him the true story of his origin. Henry's father, Viscount Thomas Castlewood, had married his mother, a weaver's daughter, and then had deserted her. She had died in a convent, and his father had taken him as a "charity child" into his household.

But still he kept his origin to himself. He must not hurt those he loved, though they no longer loved him.

One day, while he was praying at the Cathedral of Winchester, he found to his joy that his prayer was answered. For Lady Castlewood stood there before him. As soon as their eyes met, their hearts renewed their old contact.

And now a new emotion came into the heart of Henry Esmond. A passionate love for Lady Castlewood's daughter, Beatrix, now a sixteen-year-old maid of honor at the royal court and as beautiful a coquette as ever shattered English hearts. For ten years Henry kept centering his hopes upon her, but in vain. She would have none of this penniless and nameless soldier while so many brilliant courtiers were singeing their wings at the candleflame of her charms.

And now Henry's old love for the Castlewoods discovered a new outlet—a devotion toward Beatrix's brother, Frank, a youngster as reckless and as charming and as lovable as his sister. Henry campaigned with him and protected him through several battles, and attended to his education, and took a paternal and somewhat apprehensive interest in his marriage to a Dutch noblewoman considerably older than himself.

In the meantime, Beatrix went on with her now rather weary pastime of breaking hearts. And finally she came to the breaking of her own heart. She was rapidly advancing beyond the springtime of her beauty, and she remained still unmarried. The men had a way of "dying" for her and proposing to her and becoming engaged to her—and then leaving her for a more eligible catch. As for Henry Esmond, she still kept refusing him in the hope of getting a better man.

At last she got her man—the Duke of Hamilton, a widower who was double her rank and twice her age. Henry Esmond, submitting to his defeat, offered her as a wedding present a beautiful diamond necklace which he had received from Lady Thomas Castlewood, his father's (second) wife.

But the Duke of Hamilton refused the offer. His bride, he insisted, must not accept the gift of a man without a name.

Whereupon Beatrix's mother replied angrily: "Henry Esmond is not a man without a name. He is Viscount Castlewood's lawful son and true heir to the estate. We are merely the recipients of his bounty."

And then milady explained that she had heard the story of Henry's origin from the old Viscountess. "And he has never breathed a word of it to anybody."

The eve of the wedding between Beatrix and the Duke of Hamilton. A duel between the Duke and the old Castlewood nemesis, Lord Mohun. Hamilton is killed in the duel, and Beatrix is left once more alone.

But still she refused Henry. For now she had another man

dangling after her—this time the greatest catch of them all, the young Stuart Prince, pretender to the British throne.

The Prince, however, was interested in Beatrix not as his wife but as his mistress. Henry Esmond and Beatrix's brother, Frank Castlewood, had both espoused the cause of the Stuart Prince. When they learned of Stuart's designs upon Beatrix, however, they broke their swords, denounced the Prince, and left him to his own evil fate.

And then, as the pretender and Beatrix escaped to France, the air of London was electrified with the fateful cry: "Queen Anne is dead! Long live George Hanover, the new King!"

As for Henry Esmond and Lady Castlewood, they turned to each other for solace, and their solace ripened into married love. The renewed love of their olden days. "For the oldest loves are the newest—and the best."

V

THACKERAY'S EXPERIENCE in an old friendship was akin to Henry Esmond's experience in an old love. Charles Dickens had always been one of Thackeray's earliest and best friends. But a quarrel had arisen—among literary compeers it takes but a spark to be fanned into a flame of dissension—and for several years the two men didn't speak to each other. And then one evening—Thackeray was now in his fifty-third year—the two met on the stairs of the Athenaeum, and Thackeray impulsively held out his hand to Dickens. The latter returned the greeting, and the old quarrel was patched up.

It was as if Thackeray knew that he must make haste to say hail and farewell to his old friend. For it was only a few nights later—December 23, 1863—that he went to sleep for the last time. The Master had called the roll; and Thackeray, like the beloved Colonel Newcome in one of his novels, responded gently, "*Adsum*—I am here."

DICKENS

Important Works by Dickens

Pickwick Papers
Oliver Twist
Nicholas Nickleby
Barnaby Rudge
The Old Curiosity Shop
Martin Chuzzlewit
A Christmas Carol

Dombey and Son
David Copperfield
Bleak House
Hard Times
Little Dorritt
A Tale of Two Cities
Great Expectations
Our Mutual Friend

Charles Dickens

1812–1870

THE WORLD OF CHARLES DICKENS was a world of lovable, foolish, blundering, blustering, mischievous, playful and hopeful children. And he himself was one of them.

Yet his own childhood was far from being either playful or
hopeful. Small and sickly and undernourished, he suffered from
periodic fits of convulsions. "This child," said his father, "will
never live to experience the bitterness of maturity."

His father was a boon companion to bitterness, and he shared
it all-too-generously with his family. A clerk in the naval station
at Portsea, he earned his money too slowly and spent it too
rapidly. As a result, he was compelled to swim perpetually against
a rising tide of debts. When Charles was two years old, his father
was transferred to London. This meant a slight increase in salary
and a tremendous increase in the opportunity to spend it. And,
to add to his troubles, John Dickens was not only profligate but
prolific. Within a few years he brought eight children into the
world.

And left it to a kindly Providence to raise them. As for himself, he went to live in the security of the debtor's prison at
Marshalsea.

Under an environment such as this, there was but little prospect for Charles to receive a formal education. The three R's at his mother's knee, a smattering of Latin at a school kept by the Reverend Mr. Giles, an occasional visit to the theater under the patronage of his cousin, James Lamert—and at the age of eleven Charles Dickens was ready to graduate from learning to earning.

At first he earned a few pennies by singing comic songs to the water-front characters at Limehouse. "This boy," exclaimed one of the delighted cockneys, "his a reggeler progidy, so 'elp me!" But Charles was wasting his talents in the suburbs of Vagabondia. There was not enough money to be earned in singing to these stepchildren of the world. And so his father, with the help of James Lamert, got him a more "solid" job—as a paster of labels in a blacking factory at Hungerford Stairs.

It was a dreary business standing in the front window of the factory, pasting labels from sunrise to sunset, while the crowds of passersby stopped to make remarks about the "queer little fellow with the clever fingers." Week ends, however, he felt like a rich man with his "fabulous" salary of six shillings (about a dollar and a half). Spending tuppence—an extravagant price!—on a bit of stale pastry for himself, he took the rest of the money to his parents. Sundays he walked with his father—John Dickens had now been released from the debtor's prison—out of cockneyland into fairyland. One of his favorite objectives in this "fairyland of the rich" was the gorgeous mansion on Gads Hill. "Some day, if you persevere and work hard," said his father, "you may live in this very house."

"What an impossible dream!" thought Charles.

II

As DICKENS GREW OLDER, he worked hard and persevered and became ambitious. If he couldn't live in a *real* fairyland, perhaps he might be able to create a *fictitious* one. He decided to become a writer.

He began his writing career as the founder and editor of a newspaper at the Wellington House Academy—a school which he attended for a short period between jobs. And he was his own newsdealer. He sold his paper for marbles and pieces of slate pencil, and regarded himself quite a successful businessman.

But his parents needed something more than marbles and slate pencils to live on, and so they took him out of school (at fifteen) and put him to work in a lawyer's office.

Dickens, however, didn't want to be a lawyer. He was determined to be an author. He taught himself shorthand, and

> *Began to record the cosmic show*
> *Of panting humanity on the go.*

By day he was now (at twenty) a parliamentary reporter; and by night, a writer of fictitious sketches of London life. He signed these sketches with the pen name of *Boz.*

Some of these sketches were published—without pay—in a paper called the *Monthly Magazine.* When he saw the first of his *Boz* stories in print, he walked down to Westminster Hall "and turned into it for half an hour"—we are quoting his own words— "because my eyes were so dimmed with joy and pride that they could not bear the street . . ."

It was a zestful and eventful and indefatigable life that young *Boz* was leading in those days. The most earnest of hustlers in his worktime, the most vivacious of companions in his playtime. "What a face is his to meet in a drawing-room!" exclaimed Leigh Hunt. "It has the life and the soul of fifty human beings."

Yet his face hadn't the life and the soul—or rather his purse hadn't the shillings and the pounds—to win the one human being he loved above all others. Maria Beadnell, the daughter of a bank manager. "Dickens is a nice young fellow; but as a writer of stories, he'll never be able to support me in style."

And so Dickens lost Maria. She married a wealthier suitor— who within a few years became a pauper. And Dickens went on with the writing of his stories—and became one of the richest men of England.

III

DICKENS was in his early twenties when the first shower of gold descended upon him. His *Sketches by Boz* had come to the attention of the publishers, Chapman and Hall, who commissioned him to write a monthly serial around the sporting pictures of the popular artist, Robert Seymour. This serial was ordered as a routine piece of hack-work. Under the inspired pen of Dickens, it turned out to be the immortal *Pickwick Papers*.

The first few numbers of the *Pickwick Papers* were not very popular. Yet they gave Dickens sufficient courage to marry the "second choice" among his young female acquaintances—Catherine Hogarth. And then there came a sudden blow, the suicide of Robert Seymour, and an equally sudden stroke of good luck, the selection of Hablot Knight Brown (who adopted the pen name of *Phiz*) as the new illustrator.

From that moment the success of the *Pickwick Papers* was assured. *Boz* and *Phiz* made a perfect team. They stimulated each other to heights of "sublime nonsense"—passages that wept with laughter and laughed with tears.

And Dickens too, as he wrote the *Pickwick Papers*, was compelled to weep in the midst of his laughter. For he lost Mary Hogarth, his wife's sister, who had been living with them since their marriage. For two months he was unable to go on with his serial. "Since the appearance of the last number of this work," explained his publishers, "the author has to mourn the sudden death of a very dear young relative to whom he was most affectionately attached, and whose society had been for a long time the chief solace of his labours."

He never completely recovered from his grief. Every death scene that he wrote thereafter was but the reopening of an old wound. When he resumed his *Pickwick Papers*, he was a sad and sage old man of twenty-four.

And the toast of London. The entire city had blossomed out into Boz cabs, Pickwick ties and Sam Weller corduroys. "There isn't a place in England," wrote a contemporary, "to which Boz has not penetrated . . . Dr. Benjamin Brodie takes it to read in his carriage between patient and patient; and Lord Denman studies Pickwick on the Bench while the jury are deliberating." A man on the point of death said to his priest, "Thank God I can now die in peace. I have just read the last number of *Pickwick*."

As a result of his popularity, the publishers overwhelmed Dickens with commissions for articles, stories and novels. And he accepted them all. "Life is so short, and my fancy is so full of characters that beg to be brought into life." He almost killed himself with overwork. In one year he wrote simultaneously three novels, edited a magazine and, in his spare moments, dashed off an operetta and a farce.

And in the evening he cut a lively caper in society—not the society of the gentry, but of the intellectuals, "the salt of the earth." One of the most interesting of all the Dickens characters was his own smiling figure—"a flower come to life in the drawing-room," resplendent in his bright green waistcoat, lavender trousers, scarlet necktie and a pair of eyes that beamed a loving "God-bless-you" upon one and all.

He burned his candle at both ends, and rejoiced in the glow. He squandered his money and his health, and piled up his books, and increased his fame and multiplied his family—but with a woman he did not love. Though not unattractive physically, Catherine was awkward—"she manages to scrape her shin against every chair"—and niggling and suspicious and prone to sudden and unjustifiable outbursts of temper. This, it must be admitted in all fairness, is the picture we get of Catherine through the eyes of Dickens. Without a doubt there was something to be said for *her* side of the story, too. Unfortunately, she hadn't the talent, like her husband, to say it. At any rate, it required a woman of extraordinary tact to be the wife of a celebrity who was the adoration of all the women of England. And Kate Dickens had no extraordinary tact.

Whatever the cause of their marital incompatibility, Charles Dickens had to season the sweetness of success with the wormwood of discontent. For the present, however, he swallowed the mixed drink of his destiny and went on with his work.

IV

AT THIRTY he paid his first visit to America—a visit which began in mutual anticipation and ended in mutual disappointment. After a triumphant tour of lectures and dinners and demonstrations in Boston, in New York, in Philadelphia, in Baltimore, in Washington and in a dozen other American cities, he came to look upon the New World, and the New World came to look upon him, as somewhat of a sentimental humbug. Familiarity had bred contempt, and each was prone to exaggerate the faults of the other. "There is altogether too much spitting in America," he said. And then he went on to describe how once, on a railway journey, "the flashes of saliva flew so perpetually and incessantly out of the windows all the way, that it looked as if they were ripping open feather-beds inside, and letting the wind dispose of the feathers." And Dickens, complained America in turn, "is biting the hand that is pouring money into his pockets. He is nothing but an ungrateful parasite."

While each side exaggerated the shortcomings of the other, there was nevertheless sufficient ground for complaint on both sides. Dickens suffered from the "piracy" of the American publishers, since the American copyright law permitted the publication of his books in this country without any compensation to him. He referred to this injustice in several of his lectures. And his audiences resented this airing of a private quarrel at a public gathering. His departure from America therefore brought a mutual sigh of relief to everybody concerned. As one of his English admirers facetiously remarked: "I wish both Mr. Dickins and the 'Merrikins joy of their bargin."

Dickens returned to England and to a long series of battles for the underdog. Joyous battles through the medium of fiction. With the pen of a caricaturist and the heart of a poet, he scolded and amused and threatened and wheedled the English government into one reform after another. His books, as Thackeray with something of an envious justification observed, were written for an audience of grownups with the mentality of children. And Dickens thanked him for the observation. "Precisely. I am writing for the human race."

A race more stupid than vicious. But since men were only bearded children, you could laugh them out of their stupidity by dangling before them a Punch and Judy show of their own images in distorted attitudes. A trip through the novels of Dickens is like a visit to a pavilion of convex and concave mirrors. See all these people and their funny antics—Micawber, Pickwick, Weller, Serjeant Buzfuz, Charles Cheeryble, Smike, Smeers, Quilp, Scrooge, Dick Swiveller, Bob Cratchit, Tom Pinch. Who are they but ourselves parading behind those grotesque looking-glasses? Our very names are twisted into funny shapes. Yet what a remarkable likeness! And how indelibly fixed they become in our memory! Note how in a few phrases Dickens is able to perpetuate the picture of a man. "Jonas Chuzzlewit kept tucking all his valuables into a strong-box until they finally tucked his own valueless body into the strong-box of his coffin."

England, it has been said, has produced two of the world's greatest artists—Reynolds, the painter of the human body, and Dickens, the cartoonist of the human soul.

V

BUT Dickens was more than a painter. He was a superb story-teller. His facility in plot weaving was the envy of the more philosophical yet less imaginative Thackeray. "What is the use of my trying to run before that man, or by his side?" once exclaimed the author of *Vanity Fair*. "I can't touch him; I can't get near him."

Yet in all the diversified stories of Dickens there is something of his own life. "This man," remarked a contemporary, "seems to have been everywhere, to have known everybody, and to have shared in every man's experience." Every novel is the author's allegory of his physical and spiritual pilgrimage through the world. This is especially true of the novels of Charles Dickens— and of *David Copperfield* in particular. "If you want to know my life," said Dickens, "read *David Copperfield*."

But this book, it must be emphasized, is a *fictitious* story of his life. "The *true* particulars about my life," he once remarked to the French translator of *David Copperfield*, "I keep to myself."

David Copperfield is the distorted yet recognizable image of Charles Dickens as seen through the mirror of his comic genius. The very initials of David Copperfield (D.C.) are the initials of Charles Dickens (C.D.) transposed. Like Charles, David is a child of poverty; but unlike Charles, he is compelled to live with a cruel stepfather, Edward Murdstone. At eleven, both David and Charles go to work in a blacking warehouse; and here again there is an intermingling of fiction with fact. While David is employed at the warehouse, he lodges with Mr. and Mrs. Wilkins Micawber and their brood of little children. This Micawber lodging-house is in reality the home of the Dickens family. Wilkins Micawber is Charles Dickens' father—an adorable, shiftless, boisterous and improvident believer in the goodness of Providence, a man who always expects something to turn up yet never moves a finger to start the turning. Pressed by his creditors, Mr. Micawber is thrown into a debtor's prison, falls constantly into the clutches of unscrupulous exploiters, and finally, with the help of David's aunt, is enabled to make a new start in Australia. Which is probably where Charles Dickens would have liked to see his own father, safe and sound and beloved, but as far out of his sight as possible. For the ne'er-do-well John Dickens was a constant drain upon his son's purse and a constant embarrassment to his son's peace of mind.

The rest of the story, too, is a skillful interweaving of the real and the fanciful. David, like Charles, serves as a lawyer's clerk, learns stenography, becomes a successful author, and marries a sweet and insipid little creature. And here the similarity breaks off again. David loses his wife—the modern psychoanalysts would call this a wish fulfillment on the part of Charles Dickens—and marries a woman more congenial to his own character.

As for the rest of the story—the marriage of the maid Peggotty to the coachman Barkis who is always willin', the hypocrisy and the exposure of Uriah Heep, the betrayal of Little Emily and the death of her lover, Ham, in his effort to rescue her betrayer, Steerforth, from the shipwreck—all these episodes and characters belong to the imaginative part of Charles Dickens' life. Imaginative, yet to the author none the less real. For in the mind of the creative artist it is difficult to define the border between the fictitious and the factual. "I live," said Dickens, "with every one of my characters."

VI

THE OLDER HE GREW, the more passionately he loved to associate with other people. His life had become a merry-go-round of jovial excitement. He was forever writing new books, making new friends, learning new dance steps. His daughter tells us how once, having been introduced to an intricate step, he jumped out of bed in the middle of a cold night and began to practice it to his own whistling—and to the annoyance of his awakened family.

An irresponsible, restless, capricious, extravagant child. How easily his money kept rolling in! And how rapidly it kept rolling out! He was aware of the whirligig intoxication of his life, and he rejoiced in it. "Heigho," he cried jubilantly, "I am three parts mad and the fourth part delirious!"

His mind, already active far and away beyond the activity of most other minds, had now entered upon a new avenue of excitement. And his tiring body followed recklessly after. He became a theatrical producer, manager and actor. Up and down the countryside he traveled, with a company as madcap as himself, reviving old plays, writing new ones, flirting with the "periwinkles," and leaving everywhere behind him a trail of good will and laughter.

He liked especially to produce plays for children. For he best understood *them*, and they best understood *him*. In all the busy whirl of his activities, he was never too busy to entertain them. His house was always full of children—there were now ten of his own, to say nothing of the "innumerable" little playmates who came to visit them. And time and again, his daughter records, "Uncle Boz" would leave his work in the middle of a sentence to have a romp with the "diminutive rascals."

In his attitude toward children, Dickens revealed himself not only at his funniest, but at his tenderest. A friend of his relates how he was walking with Dickens through the slums on a cold winter night. "At the door of one of the penny lodging-houses (it was growing towards morning, and the raw air almost cut me to the bone), I saw him snatch a little child out of its poor drunken mother's arms, and bear it in, filthy as it was, that it might be warmed and cared for." Another of his friends gives us an equally charming picture of Dickens as the two of them were walking through the Hungerford Market. In front of them a coal-heaver was carrying a child whose rosy, smudgy face was peeping over its father's shoulder. Dickens winked at the child, and the child winked back at Dickens. And then, this common bond of understanding having been established between them, Dickens bought a bag of cherries at a fruit stand, and fed them to the child one by one without the father's noticing anything of the little comedy.

All life, as Dickens and the children knew, could be turned into a comedy if you only looked at it in the right way. Destiny, too, was feeding its cherries to Dickens, and giving him great joy and a pleasant taste in the mouth.

And final indigestion. Dickens had bought Gads Hill, the "palace" his father had once told him he might some day possess if he persevered and worked hard. And the possession of this house and its upkeep meant more perseverance and more hard work. And more friends, and more entertainment, and more irritation on the part of his wife—and a final definite break with her.

And then, a breakdown in his health. But no interruption to his work. Expenses were mounting, and a hungry public was clamoring for more and more of his stories and of his personal appearances. He undertook a series of public readings from his own novels—in England, in America. And everywhere he was overwhelmed with torrents of gold and applause. From Exeter he wrote to a London friend, "I never beheld anything like the personal affection which they poured out upon me." In New York a woman stopped him in the street and said, "Mr. Dickens, pray let me touch the hand that has filled my home with so many friends." It seemed as if "everybody who has read my stories is now anxious to hear me re-read them." And no wonder. For "this man," as a Boston lady remarked, "is a veritable magician . . . a whole stock company in himself . . . He seems to be physically transformed as he passes from one character to another; he has as many distinct voices as his books have characters." There were times when the entire audience would be carried away on a stream of hysterical adulation. There was no stopping the outbursts of laughter and tears and the clapping of hands and the stamping of feet and the frenzied shouts of *encore, encore,* and yet another *encore!*

And Dickens humored his admirers with his encores, and gathered his earnings, and drained himself of his strength. After a five months' tour of America he came back with a hundred thousand dollars in his purse—and with the stamp of death upon his face.

Though his heart was still the heart of a child, his body was now the body of a very old man. "The least excitement," wrote a friend in her diary, "will make the blood rush into his hands until they become at times almost black." His digestion had become so impaired that he was unable to touch solid food. His daily menu consisted of a few biscuits soaked in cream, a cup of beef tea, a glass of sherry, and an eggnog with a dash of rum to give it "a human taste." He suffered from continual insomnia, and he felt a peculiar numbness in his left foot, "as if part of me were already dead."

Yet he went on with his readings—through the spring of 1869 and then, after a brief midsummer rest, throughout the fall and the winter of 1869 and into the spring of 1870.

And then he no longer had the strength for the exertion. "From these garish lights," he said at his final appearance, "I vanish now for evermore with a heartfelt, grateful, respectful, affectionate farewell."

It was only a few weeks later that he made his first appearance before his new public. An immortal audience of laughter-loving children—"for of such is the kingdom of heaven."

DOSTOYEVSKY

Important Works by Dostoyevsky

Poor Folk
The Double
The Landlady
The Family Friend
The House of Death
Letters from the Underworld
Crime and Punishment

The Gambler
The Idiot
The Demons
The Brothers Karamazov
The Eternal Husband
The Dream of a
*   Queer Fellow*

Feodor Mikhailovich Dostoyevsky

1821–1881

ORIGINALLY the Dostoyevskys were a Catholic family from Lithuania, with Norse blood in their veins. Sprung from the loins of a Greek Orthodox priest, they were proud, intolerant and devout. And very poor. They were hungry for the word of God—and hungry for wheat. They moved into the Ukraine, changed their religion to something more in keeping with the strain of Norman blood within them, and sought food and the eternal answer to the eternal question of the soul. They were a tribe of nomad intellectuals who would go anywhere on an impulse—into heaven or into damnation, but never into obscurity.

Feodor was born in 1821 of this strange breed of Norman Catholicism, brooding splendor. His father was staff doctor in a Moscow hospital for the poor. And that was right. It was impressed upon the boy that intellectuals exist not by virtue of their intellect, but because they are staff doctors to the poor . . . In the winter, Moscow is pierced with a wind that leaves not only a melody in the ear but a stab in the heart. Doctor Dostoyevsky's hospital is crowded with every sign of Nature's hard dealing with man. In the summer, when the wind is warm, children with one leg and old folk wasting away with filth and disease are seen hobbling over the hospital garden next to Feodor's house—mad question marks against the smiling landscape.

The garden of the sick. This was one of Feodor's first recollections. His consciousness became early aware of life's amazing paradox—the suffering of man amidst the beauty of nature. The quaking clash of the oppositeness of life shook him to the depths.

A high wall shut Feodor's house from the garden. But as soon as he was able to walk, he found that nothing separated him from that beauty, and that suffering. There was a gate in the wall. He opened it . . . And then one night his father in a terrible frenzy slammed the gate in his face and told him never to open it again. But Feodor knew that the gate was waiting to be opened by someone who would defy a thrashing, even *welcome* a thrashing. He decided that so long as his father held the key as a jailer, he would thrash himself three times a day for the joy it would bring him as a sufferer along with those who suffered on the other side of the wall. Sufferers in the midst of beauty. One had to be in pain in order to walk in a garden . . .

Doctor Dostoyevsky was very strict with Feodor and his brother Mikhail. Always, when there was a gate through a wall, he shut it. And when there was no wall, he built one. The boys were not allowed to associate with anyone outside of the family. As a result of this strictness, Feodor grew up to be a recluse. When he entered the engineering school at Petersburg—he was sixteen at the time—the teachers and the pupils alike regarded him as a snob. His only companions were his dreams. "I dream of the great and the beautiful. I live in a world of dreams. I am writing a romantic drama."

He lived in the abstract because his father had never allowed him to live in the concrete. What did he know about a romantic drama? His father had commanded his young puritan offspring never to mention women—except in dramatic verse. At sixteen the young Russian devils of the engineering school knew all about women. They taunted and abused the white-skinned little monk-poet in their midst.

But after a while, friendship came stealing in upon him through a forbidden channel. For he had met some literary folk like himself—fellow dreamers who read Pushkin and wrote poetry. And who occasionally sought the companionship of women. Feodor had become passionately attached to these young men. But this attachment was beyond the comprehension of his father. "Build a wall around yourself. Keep away from the contamination of your fellows." Feodor had written to his father, begging him for a little money to buy a new suit of clothes, to dine out in comfort with his friends and—yes—to *sin* a little. To these requests Feodor received nothing but angry retorts. His father had moved from the hospital to a country estate. The expenses of this estate, he complained, were eating up all his resources. His sons, he declared, would be beggars when he died if they did not cease asking him for money—"always for more money . . ."

Feodor noticed that the handwriting was unsteady. Too much vodka—an old weakness of his father's. And one day he received a letter from his father's house—not in that pitifully unsteady handwriting, but in the hand of another. And he read that his father had taken a trip to overlook some property and had never returned . . . Found smothered to death under the cushions of his carriage . . . The coachman had disappeared with the horses. And it was whispered that this was a crime of vengeance committed by the serfs who could no longer stand the cruelty of the landowner Dostoyevsky. And many of the villagers, it was rumored, had taken part in the plot . . .

Feodor never mentioned his father's name again. But the murder of the elder Dostoyevsky, and its probable cause, produced a violent turmoil in his soul. With a curse as of Cain upon him. He looked into the night.

II

AND the night was filled with visions. They intrigued him and terrified him and pointed to a great moral. And he put these visions down on paper—psychological stories of adventure, dramas that were enacted not _outside_ but _within_ his characters. And an abstraction.took form in the shape of a monster that held him by the eye. The Russian people. He would interpret it, work for it, _slave_ for it. He would carry fire and water for its genius . . . and massage it into expression from the huge feet up to the head. At Petersburg among the intellectuals he had seen only the head. Now for the feet. These suffering millions that made up the feet, he had observed, expressed themselves most freely in the drinking house over a glass of vodka. Shy and fastidious as he was, he went into the dram shops of Petersburg to listen to the "stepchildren of Mother Earth." He was not the sort of man that strangers talk to. His face was homely and morose, and his eyes were out of focus. And so he invited men not for conversation at the table, but for a game of billiards where the face is lowered and the ears are keen.

A poor player and good listener, he lost money and gained wisdom. And one day a manuscript of his fell into the hands of a discerning Russian critic. The critic sent for Dostoyevsky. "Young man, do you know what you have just written? No, you do not. You cannot understand yet."

Dostoyevsky had called his manuscript _Poor Folk_. It was the story of men who had been only half-created—pitiable bits of clay misshaped by the fingers of clumsy angels. Crippled bodies and souls. Human paradoxes. Idiots with beautiful eyes. Giants with twisted limbs. Dostoyevsky looked at the lives of these poor folk, and he found therein neither reason nor rhyme.

And then he turned to the intellectuals again. _They,_ at least, would help him find an order in creation, a meaning in life. These intellectuals would change the face of society, would overthrow the Czar in Russia and set up a republic of free men. Not God but Man himself must be his own Saviour. The mind of Man must be put to work in order to kindle the heart of Man from suffering into ecstasy.

Feodor comes to the parlor consultations of these radical intellectuals who would change the heart of the world. He adds his own voice to their outcries against the injustice of the government officials. At one of the meetings he is arrested. A perfunctory trial, and then he is marched off to the Peter Paul Fortress, to await his doom together with the other political offenders.

His body is imprisoned. But how can they imprison his mind? How can they lock up infinity within the four walls of a cell?

And now they put him into a coach and take him to the Semenov Drill Grounds. It is the Christmas season. The air is brisk. Other coaches arrive with other political prisoners. Troops stand at attention, ready to carry out the sentence of the military court—death. A priest, with a crucifix in his hands, leads the prisoners to a platform draped in black. Batch by batch they are brought to face the firing squad. Feodor is in the third batch. He figures that he has about five minutes to live. Strange how alert his mind can be at such a moment . . .

And then, as the soldiers raise their rifles, a horseman gallops up to the platform with a message from the Czar. A reprieve for the prisoners. Their death sentence has been commuted to an exile in Siberia. A grim jest for the Little Father. One of the men, as he hears of his reprieve, goes raving mad. Another cries bitterly, "Better if I had been shot!" For they know that the death-in-life of Siberia is a punishment worse than death.

III

ON CHRISTMAS EVE they marched Dostoyevsky from the Peter Paul Fortress to the train for Siberia. At the first stop, a woman pressed a Bible into his hands. It was the only practical guidebook for a traveler going into that wasteland. Between the pages of the Bible he found a note for twenty-five roubles—enough to buy him tobacco, linen, soap and white bread.

But not enough to buy him peace of mind. It was not easy for a fashionable and comfort-loving young man to pass his time in a convict's suit with his arms and legs in chains. His hands, which had never worked with anything heavier than a pen, were busy now at hard labor. Shy and timid to a fault, he was thrown amongst the most notorious thieves and murderers of Russia. The irredeemable were his constant companions. They intruded in his thoughts and threatened to commit a crime far more dreadful than any they had perpetrated before. This crime was the knife-less murder of a mind.

But Dostoyevsky's mind refused to be slain. In the excess of his bewilderment the great problem of human destiny once more agitated him. And he found that the prison camp in Siberia was merely another chamber of the billiard room in Petersburg . . .

And then, as he brooded, there came to him a new light. The redemption of the irredeemable, he now realized, came not through *man,* but through a power *outside of man.* He turned more hungrily to the Bible between whose pages he had found a note for twenty-five roubles—enough for white bread. And in its message he discovered a new and more sustaining sort of bread —the white bread of the soul . . . It is *God* who saves man, the sinner as well as the saint . . .

But if God saves the sinner, what risk is there in sin? Indeed, sin is a positive temptation, a draft upon the mercy of God, a test of His infinite goodness, just as a loan requested of a friend is a test of the friend's goodness. Those intellectuals at Petersburg who looked for a morally better world, did they not realize that there would have been no meaning to the crucifixion of Jesus if there had not been a murderer nailed beside him to a cross? "God creates the sinner—and the sinner creates God." A world of in-telligent perfection, the dream of the Petersburg intellectuals, would annihilate the creative purpose of God—"would annihilate God Himself."

And the more Dostoyevsky pondered the problem of evil, the more he realized that there was no equation between a man's crime and a man's evil, between the punishments of the courts and the will of God. "Those whom men punish, God saves." Dostoyevsky, who had taken part in revolutionary activities in the sincere hope of *saving* men, was sentenced by a sincere court to be punished alongside of murderers who *killed* men. And there emerged into his consciousness the feeling that he must search underneath the *surface* of things in order to find the true *logic* of things.

IV

AFTER four years in Siberia, he was released from hard labor. The Russian law provided, however, that the punishment was not as yet at an end. He was required to serve as a soldier in Siberia and to work his way up to an officer's rank before he would be given his freedom.

He joined a regiment in the little village of Semipalatinsk and fell in love with Maria Dmitrievna, the wife of the captain of his company. She was "a rather pretty blonde, of middle height, very thin, passionate and exaltée." Her husband was dying. But the thought had swept through Feodor, "I must never marry; I must lead a life of celibacy." For in the prison a serious illness had manifested itself at regular intervals. Epilepsy. The doctors told him that epileptics mature abnormally late in life. Here he was well into his thirties and this was the first time he had fallen passionately in love. It was a long postponed ardor, the pubescence of a grown man suddenly become a boy. Maria's husband died suddenly and Feodor, who called himself "a cured man," disregarded the advice of his doctor, and took the widow for his bride. There were nasty rumors that she spent the night before her wedding with a lover younger than Feodor. And when he finally received permission to return to Russia, it was gossiped that the lover of his wife followed one stage behind their *britshke* on the journey home.

But soon the damp winter climate brought a flush of scarlet to her face, and it was evident that she too was soon to die as her husband had died.

As time passed, she became unrecognizable. No need to be afraid of her unfaithfulness now! Feodor, still wrestling with the problem of evil, remembered far back into his childhood—the garden of the sick. The sick on the one side of the wall; the healthy on the other side . . . Well, the sick must die and the healthy must live. His passions, long held in abeyance, hungered to be let loose. And he found the object of his hunger in Apollinaria Pankratievna Souslov—a young student who marched in the Socialist demonstrations carrying a red flag and singing the *Marseillaise*. One day she had heard him at a lecture and had written him a letter that she loved him.

"She was coldly sensuous. She was a tormentor even in love . . . The Marquis de Sade could have taken lessons from her . . . A crime she would commit with *too* much indifference . . . She was as cold as the ice in winter . . . She regarded everyone dispassionately like an abbess of a medieval monastery . . . And well, there was never a woman so voluptuous as she. . . ."

As for her lover Feodor, there are now within him two men. One of these men works intensely on a problem of crime and punishment—tracing lines, notes, characters, drawing Gothic windows—struggling to fashion into words the story of the student Raskolnikov. For had he not pledged himself to search the inner world, to live and to die in the monastery of his art? . . . Such is the waking man.

The other man, swept on the wings of his feverish dream, rushes with Apollinaria all over Europe. She rebuffs him, torments him, compels him to enjoy her and hate her in turn. He kneels before her with blinding tears in his eyes, and he pleads with her night after night not to lock him out of her room.

And then news came to him that his wife had reached the final stage of her illness. He came home to her, tended her unceasingly and watched her as she coughed herself away.

V

ONE MORNING a young girl came to Dostoyevsky in answer to his call for a secretary to whom he might dictate his latest book.

She looked with awe into the face of this man who was writing *Crime and Punishment* by the side of his dying wife. When the book reached completion, Dostoyevsky grew strangely troubled. But Anna Gregorievna, his secretary, said, "Feodor Mikhailovich, two mountains may never come together, but two human beings may . . ." And she married him.

Crime and Punishment . . . The story of Raskolnikov that the whole world is reading . . . The brilliant young student who walks in a dream . . . purveyor of many intellectual theories, explorer of the depths of good and evil through a mind subject to no inhibitions. And finally in this dream, his will has melted into his intellectual abstraction of the Superman, his body has become the slave of his mind . . . All the thoughts he has written about, all his essays, all his theories have turned into a mechanical will that sweeps him along. The abstract comes to life, the living melts into the abstract. The two personalities become interchanged . . . And since his thoughts and his theories have included the existence of crime, the most horrible crime of which the human mind can conceive, he is compelled to commit a crime—automatically, driven by the power of a mind bent upon making a test of its own ideas . . . There is an old woman pawnbroker with whom he has pawned some of his belongings. He decides he must kill her. "For what purpose?" he asks himself —and then he provides the answer, "For her money, which can do the miser no good, but can finance my own career as a student . . ."

On their honeymoon Anna found Dostoyevsky lying in one of his fits, with his head dangling over the side of the bed. A second later he would have fallen off. A feeling of aura preceded his convulsions and his whole face was transformed into ecstatic bliss. She wiped the sweat from his forehead, the foam from his lips. "Bit by bit he regained consciousness. He kissed my hands, and then embraced me . . ."

Dostoyevsky went on with his novel . . . On the day appointed for the crime Raskolnikov sleeps away most of the time and indeed he oversleeps his appointment. Then he awakes and sets out for the old woman's lodgings. He detains her on a pretext and seizes an axe. Up to the last instant he has a strong feeling that it is all unreal, that no crime will ever take place . . . A fantastic dream . . . Which is the waking world, which is the sleeping world? Automatically he cleaves her head with the edge of the axe. The blood that oozes forth might be punch at a fair . . . The old woman's sister comes up the stairs. He had calculated that she would be absent. He kills her, too. He takes a few trinkets from the old woman, and her purse. For a voice within him keeps mumbling over and over, "It was for this money that you killed her . . . For this money . . . because you are poor and needy, and she is rich and aged and useless . . . and this money will advance you in your career—will further you in your studies." And then he throws away the purse without even opening it. For a new idea is now running through his mind-machine. "Weakling, do not attempt to reason, to find a milk-and-water motive. You killed this woman for the sheer fascination of the killing and for no other motive. You killed because you needed to commit a crime . . ."

Dostoyevsky went to the casino incessantly, placed his money on the red and black. The passion, the color, the risk, drew him as irresistibly as life itself. And one day he came home in the greatest despair. "He said he had lost all, and began begging me to allow him to pawn certain things. I got out my earrings and brooch . . . He fell on his knees before me and said that he must play on, that he must play on without fail . . . And then I realized that he was no ordinary gambler . . . He did not gamble to win, but because he needed to lose . . ."

. . . But the crime of Raskolnikov is not the end of the story. It is merely the beginning. One needs to commit a crime not for the sake of the crime but for the sake of the punishment that follows. "Aha, *that* is the story! Do you want to go further along the tangled maze beyond good and evil?" The murder is classified as an unsolved mystery. Surely no one in Petersburg suspects the poor student Raskolnikov with his strange theories . . . Unconsciously, automatically, in that unknown border between the real and the unreal world, Raskolnikov revisits the scene of the murder, goes to the police station to have a chat, lets fall sinister hints, places himself in the public eye, does all sorts of desperate things to call the attention of people to his guilt.

Indeed, he had committed his crime for the *sake* of its guilt . . . "Have I not been born with the burden of the sin of every one who has died and of every one who will ever live?" People are so stupid, man-made laws so coarse. Will they never recognize the intangible crimes hovering in the ether of the soul? For not only at the concrete sight of murder and blood, it seems, will men summon up a father confessor for the soul's salvation. "So one must kill in order to demand the penalty which the soul has incurred at birth." The Lord have mercy on a man who feels himself guilty of crime and whose hands are unstained by any deed of violence. He can go mad!

Raskolnikov throws himself on his knees and tells the people that with an axe, cold-bloodedly and with premeditation, he killed two old women . . . "Please, good people, do not conceive of a crime more horrible in the annals of the heart than this" . . . He is sentenced. He goes to Siberia with a song on his lips. Strange perversity. Now that he has two murders on his hands, he feels for the first time in his life entirely innocent, "like a martyred angel in an ecstasy of bliss . . ."

And Dostoyevsky whispered, "Tell me, is there a God?" And a voice that seemed to pierce the farthest veil and to lead him like Dante through the abodes of the damned, answered, "Man is saved only because the Devil exists. For only through the Devil does he earn a conscience."

VI

AND Feodor Dostoyevsky drank his tea with the young men and the young women who came to talk with him about the social destiny of man. And when they mentioned their dream of over-throwing the Czar and of setting up a republic in Russia after the model of the French and the American republics, his mind went back to the days of his political exile among the murderers who had used the axe and the gun. And he shook his head sadly. "Stay, children. What we need in order to regenerate the world is not an act of violence but a great deed, a great revolution from within." And they objected with fire in their eyes. "But how can you bring all men to the inspiration of that great deed, that revolution from within, as you call it?"

"Why do you need to summon *all* men?" Dostoyevsky would retort. "Do you not realize how powerful *one* right man might be? Let there appear one right man and all will follow him . . ."

And then his eyes grew soft as if fed with a star . . . And the life of his voice was transformed into the life of his pen. And under the magic of his pen there grew up the representation of a truly perfect and noble man, a character of Absolute Beauty—Prince Myshkin, an epileptic and an idiot released from an asylum. Ah, he is so simple-minded is Prince Myshkin, and so trustful of human nature in the face of human malice. He moves through the world of scoundrels and is beaten by them, robbed by them, wellnigh destroyed by them—and he lifts not a finger to stop them. He refuses to be "wise" to the cheapness of men. That is what angers them. They can cheat him out of everything but his faith in their goodness. When they strike him, he tends them with compassion—as if *they* were the ones that were suffering the blow and not *he*. And soon even the most dunderheaded among them begin to realize that he is merely living on a higher level of consciousness from their own.

But it is a dizzy height. All men must topple in the end. He falls in love with a woman of sin. Another lover, an earth dweller, kills her in a frenzy so that no one else may have her. And when people throng into the room, they find that the murderer has covered the corpse with oilcloth and placed jars of disinfectant around it. "They found the murderer completely unconscious and raging. The Prince was sitting by him motionless on the floor and each time that the sick man broke into a screaming or babble, he hastened to pass his own trembling hands softly over his companion's hair and cheeks as though trying to soothe and quiet him. But alas! The murderer understood nothing of what was said to him, and he recognized none of those who surrounded him . . ."

Still burrowing through veil after veil down to the innermost core of himself, Dostoyevsky presents a strange appearance during the last years of his allotted life. He goes into his garden, his head bowed down with the weight of his thoughts. What a man—this creature compounded of rubbish and flame, this angel-devil so wise in his folly, so foolish in his wisdom! And Dostoyevsky created his characters—idiots and criminals and sages and saints—and he asked of each and every one of them to give him the answer to the riddle of life. And he walked through the streets and listened to the people that he passed. Perhaps a word, a nod, a smile, the sudden illumination of a face in the ecstasy of hope, might give him the answer.

And often his thoughts carry him to a level above the consciousness of his fellow men. He wings his way through space and sees a new sun and a new earth. "The smiling emerald sea gently lapped the shores, kissing them with love, with manifest, visible, almost conscious love . . . Tall, splendid trees stood in all the glory of their bloom . . . Their innumerable leaves greeted me with a sweet, caressing sound, as though they uttered words of love. The grass was aflame with brilliant and sweet-scented colors. Flights of birds wheeled in the air, and fearlessly settled on my shoulders and my hands, joyfully tapping me with their tremulous little wings . . . It was the earth as yet unpolluted by transgression; on it lived men who had not as yet known sin . . . They showed me their trees, but I could not understand the depth of love with which they looked at them . . . I am convinced that in some way these men were in contact with the stars of heaven . . . They had no religion but they had the firm knowledge that when their earthly joy had been consummated to the limit of their earthly nature, then would begin for them . . . a yet greater expansion of their contact with the whole universe . . . They were enamored of one another, completely, universally . . . they looked at me with their dear, love-suffused eyes . . . *and I corrupted them all! How it could have been achieved—I do not know . . . I only know that the cause of the fall was I——* They learned to lie and loved lying, and knew the beauty of lies . . . Soon, very soon, the first blood was spilled . . . They began to speak different tongues. They came to know and to love sadness; they longed for suffering and said that truth could spring only out of pain . . . When they were angered, they began to talk of brotherhood and humanity . . . When they committed crimes, they invented justice and prescribed for themselves whole codes of laws to maintain it; and to maintain the codes, they set up a guillotine . . . Hardly did they remember what they had lost . . . There began to appear men who pondered how they might be united in such a way that each, without ceasing to love himself most of all, might not yet stand in the way of others . . . Whole wars were fought for this idea . . . I wept for them, pitying them. I stretched out my hands to them, accusing, cursing, and despising myself in my despair. I told them that this was all my work . . . I implored them to crucify me on the cross, I taught them how to make a cross . . . But they only laughed at me, and at last began to think me mad . . . Then I awoke . . . I lifted up my hands and called upon the eternal truth . . ."

And then at last the answer came out of the twisted gateway of human perversion and folly and pain: "He will come—the God-man whom the world has derided as the Idiot. And they shall learn to follow him when he teaches them the true meaning of Good and Evil—that the inflicter of pain and the sufferer of pain are not two different creatures but one and the same body, one and the same soul; that each man is responsible for the action of the entire human race, and the entire human race is responsible for the action of each man. He will come, this Idiot-Saviour, upon this earth where man seems real and is spectral, and God seems spectral and is real. He will come at last and teach us the one vital truth—that all men, from the highest saint to the lowest murderer, are groping by different paths toward the selfsame source of light, the light of universal *identity*, of universal *love* . . ."

Dostoyevsky sits down and holds his head. Suddenly he feels a strange moisture on his hands. They are covered with blood from his lungs.

"And life is not to be scorned. And death is not to be feared . . ."

And his weeping wife and children place candles around his body. And all the wise men of Russia send messages of comfort. And scholars specially trained by the monks chant prayers all through the night . . .

"Children, let us not long for a future life of eternity. Children, if we do not reach eternity in this world we shall never attain it. Eternity is here and now. There are moments we must reach, moments of the highest existence when time stands still and all the life of all mankind is absorbed into your life. *These* are the moments of eternity . . ."

Chanting, endless chanting. And then they laid him away. "It is toward these perfect moments out of time that the whole human race is moving." The meaning of life is not in the *transmission* of man from generation to generation, but in the *transformation* of man from the brute to the angel, from the sinner to the saint. Life is a constant reaching upward from the lower to the higher levels of consciousness—until the highest moment of the saint becomes the eternal faith of the sinner. "And all creation spreads from darkness into light."

Count Leo Tolstoy

Mother died when he was 2

Father " " " 9

Raised by Relations

Inspired Mohatma Ghandi

Martin Luther King Jr

TOLSTOY

Nonviolence

Anti death penalty

Socialist

died 7 years prior Russian Revolution

Had - 13 children

Wrote prosilific

Short Stories

Important Works by Tolstoy

Leo Tolstoy

1828–1910

Tolstoy was one of those rare individuals who, instead of *rising* from the ranks because of his superior *ambition,* voluntarily *descended* to the ranks because of his superior *compassion.* Like Buddha, that other great man who had stooped to conquer, Tolstoy came of an ancient family of princes. One of his ancestors had been a close companion of Peter the Great. Born at Yasnaya Poliana (Sunny Glen) in 1828, he lost his mother at the age of two and his father at the age of nine. Together with his two brothers and his two sisters he was put into the care of a distant relative, "Aunt" Tatiana. This woman had two outstanding virtues, "serenity and love"; and she suffered from one great vice, a weakness for associating with feeble-minded pilgrims whom she regarded as mystics and saints.

Listening to the stories of these pilgrims, Tolstoy acquired an early taste for metaphysics which he was never quite able to shake off. To the end of his life he was given to day-dreaming and mystical speculation which often clouded the vigor of one of the supreme intellects of the nineteenth century.

In school he was a very dull pupil. His teachers used to say of the three Tolstoy brothers: "Sergei is willing and able; Dmitri is willing but unable; Leo is both unwilling and unable."

But he had an unusually serious outlook upon life. At the early age of five he had come to the conclusion that "life is not an amusement but a very heavy task." At sixteen he lost faith in the Orthodox (Greek) Church. Then followed a period of philosophical wanderings through "the desert of adolescence," as he termed it. Passing from religion to agnosticism and from agnosticism to nihilism (belief in nothing), he finally came to the verge of despair. He was nineteen years old at the time.

His unhappiness was due largely to his physical unattractiveness. He had a great hunger for admiration. "I wanted to be known by all, loved by all," he wrote in his diary. Yet he believed there could be no happiness on earth for anyone who looked as unprepossessing as himself. His face was "as ugly as a gorilla's"— small sunken eyes, low forehead, heavy lips, large bulbous nose, and enormous ears. He had the mind of an Ariel in the body of a Caliban. So sensitive indeed was he of his repulsiveness that he decided to put an end to his life.

Fortunately, however, he changed his mind and sought temporary forgetfulness in dissipation instead of permanent oblivion in death.

And then, one day, he discovered Rousseau.

This discovery was just the tonic he needed at the time. It reconciled him to his own ugliness and it opened his eyes to the beauty of Nature. He had rejected the religion of the Church. He now adopted the religion of Rousseau. He worshiped him like a god. He wore a medallion portrait of him hung around his neck as though it were a holy image.

Inspired by the philosophy of Rousseau, he wrote his first novel, *A Russian Landlord*. It dealt with the problem that was to occupy Tolstoy throughout his life—the eternal conflict between the ideal of the prophet and the indifference of the public. The hero of the novel, Prince Nekhludov, has left the university in order to help his peasants. But, like most other human derelicts, Nekhludov's peasants prefer to remain in the rut of their helplessness. They can understand a tyrant who beats them, but they hardly know what to make of a master who is kind to them. They shrink from him, they ridicule him, they look upon his proffered help with suspicion, they regard him as a spy, a scoundrel, a fool—anything but a man who is simply trying to be their friend.

Nekhludov is defeated. He sits down at the piano and strikes the keys. He has no talent for music. But his imagination weaves the song that his fingers are too clumsy to play. He hears a choir, an orchestra . . . The past and the future are blended together into a triumphant fulfillment of his dream.

In his mind's eye he sees the peasants, the moujiks, not only in all their ugliness, but in all their *lovableness* as well. He forgives them for their ignorance, their idleness, their obstinacy, their hypocrisy, their distrust. For now he looks not only *at* them, but *into* them. He sees their suffering, their patience, their cheerfulness, their quiet acceptance of life, and their courageous resignation in the face of death.

"It is beautiful," he murmurs. Even though they reject his advances, he now understands them and sympathizes with them. For they are all brothers, he and his peasants, flesh of one flesh and blood of one blood—a host of helpless moujiks living and toiling and dying under the lash of the pitiless Landlord, Fate.

II

IN 1851 TOLSTOY had gambled away his money and escaped to the Caucasus in order to get rid of his creditors. He joined the army in which his brother was already an officer.

At nineteen Tolstoy had courted death. Now, at twenty-three, he was a firm believer in life. He left behind him his philosophical doubts and his overwhelming sense of sin. He became once more interested in mysticism—and in beautiful women. Like the young Faust, he accepted the world and found it a diverting toy to play with. Every experience was good if only it added to the sum of his pleasure. "Nothing is wrong," he writes in *The Cossacks*. "To amuse yourself with a pretty girl is not a sin. It is only a sign of good health."

He steeped himself in the beauty of the mountains, he fought, he gambled, he loved, and he created masterpieces of poetic realism. Tales of childhood, stories of war, novels about the Cossacks, essays, letters—a whole torrent of them came from his pen in rapid succession.

Absorbed in his literary work, he paid little attention to his military duties. He was too fond of creation to take much interest in destruction. Though still proud of his uniform, with its pretty medals and its brass buttons, he was already beginning to see war in its true colors. In *The Invasion,* written at the age of twenty-four, he uttered his first cry of protest against militarism:

"Is it impossible, then, for men to live in peace, in this world so full of beauty, under this immeasurable starry sky? How can they, in a place like this, retain their feelings of hatred and vengeance, and the lust of destroying their fellows? All there is of evil in the human heart ought to disappear at the touch of Nature, that most immediate expression of the beautiful and the good."

Thus far, in his military maneuvers, he had seen only the *image* of war. In 1853, however, he came face to face with war itself. Russia had declared hostilities against Turkey, and Tolstoy was called upon to "do his bit" for the greater glory of the Czar.

At first he was carried away by the fervor of his patriotism. Like the other young men of his nation, he became suddenly ferocious. A wave of mystical frenzy had swept over him. He slew the Turks and thanked God for His assistance in the slaughter.

Before long, however, he got over the intoxication of killing. During the Crimean War he wrote three books. The first is all a-bristle with chauvinism. In the second he speaks sadly of the mutual slaughter of human beings. In the preface to the third he condemns the rulers of the world for turning their subjects into mere pieces of "cannon-fodder."

The longer he looked at war, the more clearly he saw it in all its hideousness. From now on, he would dedicate himself to a worldwide war against war. On March 5, 1855, he wrote in his diary:

"I have been led to conceive a great idea, to whose realization I feel capable of devoting my whole life. This idea is the foundation of a new religion . . ."

The religion of non-resistance, of international brotherhood, of universal peace.

III

In 1856 TOLSTOY RESIGNED from the army and returned to St. Petersburg (Leningrad). His reputation as a soldier and a writer had preceded him. He became at once a literary lion. The leading authors and artists of the city welcomed him into their inner circle. But he found them to be an uncongenial lot of snobs. They regarded themselves as the elect, the intellectual supermen of their time, the glory and crown of creation. They wrote for the *intelligentsia,* and looked upon the rest of mankind as unworthy to share in their exalted ideas. But Tolstoy's attitude was just the opposite of this. Literature to him was a religion—a holy gospel of beauty and wisdom that must become the common possession of all. Instead, therefore, of writing to entertain the few, he wrote to educate the many.

In working for the common people, he had no illusions about their intelligence. He was quite aware of their "bestial and contemptible side." But, like Prince Nekhludov, he felt that they were instinctively groping toward the light. They were merely waiting for a leader, a teacher, a man who would show them the way. "Go to the people to learn what they want . . . Try to understand their needs, and help them to satisfy these needs."

He opened a school for the peasants at Yasnaya Poliana. In this school he tried to be not a master, but a fellow-disciple. For he maintained that all of them were nothing more than children trying to spell out the first syllables in the mysterious book of life.

The school was closed by the police, and Tolstoy was advised to leave the peasants alone in their ignorance. Then came months of sickness and despondency. Two of his brothers died of tuberculosis, and Tolstoy suspected that he himself was suffering from the same disease. He lost his "faith in goodness, in everything." Once more he began to think of suicide.

This time he was saved by his art, and by his love for the seventeen-year-old Sophia Andreyevna Behrs.

He married this child—he was exactly twice her age—and then entered upon a period of unclouded happiness that lasted almost fifty years. Gifted in her own right, Countess Tolstoy became, to use her expression, a "true author's wife." She took his dictation, she stimulated his fancy, she encouraged him, she made painstaking copies of his manuscripts, and she served as the model for some of his most charming characters.

Under the influence of his happiness, he wrote two of his greatest masterpieces—the tragedy of individual passion (*Anna Karenina*) and the epic of universal suffering (*War and Peace*). In the story of Anna, the wife of Karenin, Tolstoy develops the theme of Goethe's poem: "The heavenly powers bring us into life; they compel us to sin; and then they abandon us to our sin and our pain." For the first eight years of her married life, Anna is faithful to her husband and happy in the love of her little son, Serozha. The child adores his mother like a goddess. All would have been well but for an unfortunate visit that Anna Karenina pays to her brother Stepan in Moscow. Here, in the gay and heartless society of the Russian nobility, she meets Count Vronsky, a suave and handsome and wealthy young man who loves a good horse, a good fight, and a pretty woman. Anna Karenina and Count Vronsky fall an easy prey to a mutual attraction.

Anna is not the first of Vronsky's conquests. Indeed, at the very moment of his meeting with Anna he is involved in a love affair with Stepan's sister-in-law Kitty, a charming and popular young debutante of Moscow. Kitty has many admirers. But she prefers two above all—Vronsky, whom she loves, and Konstantin Levin, whom she admires.

Konstantin, a Moscow nobleman, is a well-to-do and serious young fellow with a skeptical turn of mind. "He is unable to believe; he is equally unable to disbelieve." With a quizzical helplessness he looks on, while the tragedy unfolds before his eyes. Anna and Vronsky, he observes, are drifting helplessly toward each other. The two victims are aware of this fact, yet they can do nothing to stop it.

Anna is desperately hungry for Vronsky's love—and desperately afraid of it. She longs for the adoration of her son and for the protection of her husband. She decides to cut short her visit to Moscow and to escape from her infatuation. She buys a return ticket to St. Petersburg. On the train she finds Vronsky.

He is determined to follow her.

They meet often in the social circles of St. Petersburg. Society looks upon their affair with a snickering approbation. It is an interesting diversion for them—and a good subject for gossip.

As for Anna's husband, he calmly points out to her the folly of her course, and then prudently shuts his eyes. He will not run the risk of a divorce scandal, and he will not endanger his life in a duel.

But things are coming to a head. There is an accident at a horse race. Count Vronsky is seriously hurt. Anna makes a public display of her anxiety. And, when Karenin upbraids her, she confesses her love for Vronsky.

Anna implores her husband to set her free. But he is determined to have his revenge. He compels her to remain under his roof.

Tortured and humiliated and crushed, Anna continues her secret relations with Vronsky. She is torn between three emotions: her love for her little Serozha, her loyalty toward Kitty from whom she has taken Vronsky, and her passion for Vronsky. Kitty finally manages to forget Vronsky and marries Konstantin Levin. And this removes one of the difficulties of Anna's position.

But the other two difficulties, her love for Serozha and her passion for Vronsky, are still present in all their bitter intensity.

And now there arises a new complication. Anna gives birth to a daughter. Karenin is magnanimous toward Vronsky's child; but Vronsky, in his humiliation, attempts suicide.

Anna's position has become intolerable. She must make a choice between Serozha and Vronsky. She decides in Vronsky's favor.

But the story is not yet ended. The author has another somber thread to weave into his plot. Anna and Vronsky go abroad. For a time they enjoy a measure of happiness in their illicit passion. Then they return to Russia and once again implore Karenin to grant Anna a divorce. But Karenin refuses.

Anna grows meditative, then morose. And finally a flaming jealousy begins to consume her. She suspects Vronsky of unfaithfulness. Her only relief is in oblivion—the death-in-life that comes through morphine.

And then—the end. Suicide under the wheels of a train.

In *Anna Karenina* Tolstoy depicts the soul-struggle of an individual. In *War and Peace,* a story about the Napoleonic invasion of Russia, he pictures the soul-struggle of the human race. The struggle from savagery to civilization, from bloodshed to harmony, from hatred to love. The solution to the individual problem is not enough. The problem must be solved for all mankind. When Prince Andrei, the hero of *War and Peace,* lay wounded at Austerlitz, he suddenly caught a glimpse of the inner peacefulness of the world. He saw "the illimitable sky which broods above the outrage and abjectness of the earth," and the sight of it filled him with an indescribable joy. This inner peacefulness, this light which now and then breaks through the darkness of life, was something which Tolstoy was anxious to transmit to his fellow men. Yet he felt that he could not do this through the medium of his art.

He began to think of a new kind of art—the art of establishing a bond of sympathy between man and man. He wanted to lead the people to the light. He had lost faith in the Orthodox Church and—outside of his temporary interest in Rousseau—he had found no faith to take its place.

In his quest for the true faith Tolstoy went back to the Church. He re-examined its dogmas and its practices. For three years he submitted to all its ceremonies. But it was useless. "I fear I am too ardent a follower of Christ to be a conventional Christian." The Russian Church, he declared, had become a business institution. The clergy were too much intent upon enforcing the commandments of the Czar and too little intent upon advancing the teachings of Jesus. "In the Russian Church," he said, "the meaning of the Christian doctrine has absolutely disappeared."

And so he "broke away from the Church and went back to God." He became the prophet of a new religion—or rather, he interpreted anew the "well-nigh forgotten" religion of Buddha, of Isaiah, of Confucius, and of Christ. This religion, of which he hoped to become the self-effacing leader, was to dispense with all rituals and churches and priests. It was to be based upon a few simple commandments: Be no man's enemy; never give way to your wrath; and never resort to violence. This was to be the negative phase of his doctrine. On its positive side, his religion was a religion of protest. He protested against the extravagance of the nobles, the bigotry of the priests, and the tyranny of the Czar. He became "a communist, a dissenter and a rebel—in short, a true disciple of Christ." He was ready to give up his fame, his position, his wealth, his very life if necessary, for the service of mankind. He dressed in a peasant's smock and associated with the lowliest on equal terms. He stooped to conquer. He descended from his aristocratic aloofness to the common level of humanity; and in so doing, he raised humanity to new heights of moral grandeur.

The world hailed Tolstoy as a prophet. But his family regarded him as a fool. His wife began to fear that he was losing his reason. His children yawned and turned away whenever he spoke about the brotherhood of man. To live a life of utter unselfishness seemed to them a sure sign of insanity. It was all very well for him to sacrifice himself, they said, but what right had he to sacrifice *his family* to his peculiar ideals? He became a stranger in his own house. "Perhaps you will not believe me," he wrote in a letter to a friend, "but you cannot imagine how isolated I am, nor in what degree my veritable *I* is despised and disregarded by all those about me."

Yet in spite of his mental torture he went right ahead with the work of interpreting Christ in the language of the nineteenth century. Christ had tried to establish the kingdom of God. Tolstoy believed in establishing the democracy of Man. He wrote a number of essays and stories to illustrate the principles of human compassion and non-resistance to evil. As a reward for this, he was excommunicated from the Orthodox Church (1901).

As Tolstoy grew old, a fantastic new note crept into his teaching. Estranged from his fellow men, from his children, and from his wife, he began to look upon all human intercourse in a peculiar, mystical, unearthly light. He became an ascetic. Earlier in life he had condemned adultery. Now—at the age of 70—he advocated complete sexual abstinence. "He who regards a woman —even his own wife—with sensuality, already commits adultery with her." There is something pathetic in the spectacle of an old man who tries to rebuild the world in the image of his own impotent desires. He even went so far as to recommend the extinction of mankind through the establishment of absolute celibacy! But his mind was already slipping at the time. His mysticism was gaining complete mastery over his intellect. In his last novel, *Resurrection,* he puts the soul of an old saint into the body of a young sinner. Nekhludov—note that the hero of Tolstoy's last novel bears the same name as the hero of his first novel—is a study in paradox. He begins as a scoundrel and ends as a martyr. Within a few years this ordinary man goes through a moral transformation that it took the very extraordinary Tolstoy a whole lifetime to achieve.

Resurrection is one of the most beautiful poems of pity in the world. But it is the work of an old man.

IV

IT WAS the tragedy of Tolstoy to outlive his own greatness. During the last ten years of his life he advocated a social, political and ethical ideal which could be possible only in a world of supermen —or of old men. As time went on, he became more and more the profound philosopher and the simple child. The very last act of his life, like almost everything that he did throughout his career, was a strange admixture of the stupid and the sublime. On October 28, 1910, at five o'clock in the morning, Tolstoy fled from the shelter of his home and went to seek peace in the wilderness. He was eighty-two years old at the time of his flight. Dressed in his peasant's blouse, his face beautified by age and furrowed by suffering, he wandered off, like Buddha, over the highways of the world. Buddha had left his home in search of life, but Tolstoy was going forth in search of death.

He wanted to die alone. Having dedicated his own life to pity, he now fled from the pity of his family. For several days he wandered from village to village, and at last fell by the wayside, never to rise again. To the physician who attended him, he said: "There are millions of human beings on earth who are suffering. Why do you think only of me?"

On Sunday, November 10, 1910, he found the peace which he had been seeking throughout his life. It was a little after six in the morning when his pain-racked body relaxed in that "final great deliverance" as he named it—"Death, blessed Brother Death."

MAUPASSANT

Important Works by Maupassant

Dramatic Pieces
Verses
The Ball of Fat
Mademoiselle Fifi
Une Vie

Yvette
A Piece of String
The Necklace
Bel-ami
Pierre and Jean
Our Heart

Guy de Maupassant

1850–1893

HE WAS BORN in the Château of Mironmesnil, Normandy. On his father's side he was descended from a line of aristocrats who had degenerated into bankruptcy; on his mother's, from a line of commoners who had risen to artistic creation. In his blood there was a curious mixture of elements—the fire of licentiousness, the sensitivity of imagination, the bitterness of disillusion, and the cold rhythmic cadence of the Norman sea.

His father was a libertine who consorted with women high and low. His mother was a dreamer who sat and warmed herself by the flame of a memory—the memory of her poet-brother whose genius had been cut off by an untimely death. Having known the perfect man in her brother, she had learned to pity the twisted fragments of a man in her husband. And she lived in the constant hope that in her son she would remold the fragments into a perfect man again.

He was brought up, this child of her hope, to understand the satyr and to worship the goddess. But whenever he grew confused at the unhappy union of moods of which he was the product, he went down to the sea. All the joy and the brutality of creation was in the face of the sea. Guy prowled around the caves along the coast with two dogs at his heels, and he bribed the fishermen to take him out on their search for mackerel in the moonlight. And he took part in all the sports of the Norman peasants in that gray mist and cold air that blew in like a life-giving breath from the sea. He danced with the peasant girls at the country festivals while the fiddles laughed under the apple trees, and he marched with the men who carried their torches like red snakes in the night. He took a nip of cheese and a quaff of cider with any friend or stranger at the inn, he made large plans with the "sea dogs" on the cliffs and he looked with them through their field glasses over the rim of the beyond. "I have in my veins the blood of the sea-rovers. I have no greater joy than on a spring morning to sail my boat into unknown ports."

His life was a cold passion of the north. But his mother, fond soul, was determined to control the winds and to shape his direction. She sent him in his early teens to the clerical seminary at Yvetot. But Guy had no intention of becoming a priest. He stove in the wine-barrels of the Father Superior's cellar and invited his schoolmates to a drinking bout at the expense of a hundred masses. A few more transgressions and he was expelled—to freedom.

He loved his practical jokes. Once he disguised himself as a young maiden and presented himself to an English spinster.

"You say you have traveled a good deal?" remarked the old maid in the course of their parlor conversation. "Where do you come from?"

"I have just come from Nouméa (a French convict settlement)."

The woman—shocked—continued uneasily, "A young girl traveling alone?"

"But, you see, I have two maids." And straightening "her" dress demurely with a faraway expression in "her" eyes, "I have also a dragoon and a cuirassier who look after me."

At these words the poor old spinster almost fainted away.

At sixteen he had his first mistress. He called himself a "glutton for life." And the little world of Normandy rapidly yielded all the delicacies it had to offer.

II

HE ENTERED the Lyceum to prepare himself for the bar and managed to receive "passable" grades in his studies. But then came 1870 and the Prussian invasion by way of Sedan. Maupassant joined the supply section of the army of France. It was not a pretty life. As the French army retreated, he read Schopenhauer and wrote love-poems and dreamed dreams of revenge against the Germans. Out of the ice of hatred and the fire of love, the young man's genius gradually came into shape.

And when the struggle was over, he went to Paris to look for work. For law was now beyond the purse of his impoverished aristocratic family. He obtained a job as government clerk in the admiralty. And none of his superiors or his fellow clerks knew that a huge lion of a man had gone into captivity. And the rest of Paris knew nothing, cared nothing about him. Much of the good in this world of a city lay hidden in the garrets, where the artists and the poets translated their visions to a heedless world.

Maupassant walked along the boulevards in the night, peered into faces under the gas lamps in search of a mark of recognition, the seal of a fellow soul, and found none.

And then there came to him the call of friendship. It was the voice of the Seine. In the dawn, in the evening, Sundays, at all forgotten hours, he quieted his great passion in rowing up and down the river. She was a bit of the sea, this River Seine. Her cold aroma drew him from the dusty office, from the wine-perfumed cafés, from the arms of dubious women. She was his mania, his mistress, his yielding, overwhelming partner of violent contrasts. "Ah, the beautiful, calm, changing, fragrant and fetid river, full of dreams and filth!" Gradually his soul was maturing, wrapped in fog, gliding among the wraiths of ship-hulks and smoke-stacks that talked in hoarse dull whistles at the crossroads of three worlds —the sky, the earth and the sea.

"I row and bathe, bathe and row. The rats and the frogs are so used to seeing the lantern on my boat at all hours of the night that they come out and say good evening. I handle my big boat as another would handle a yawl, and my boatmen friends at Bourgival are terribly surprised when I appear at midnight and ask for a glass of rum."

Night and the river—and the spirit of one great man. Through family connections he met Gustave Flaubert. The author of *Madame Bovary* was a Bohemian genius who had experimented with art after the manner in which some audacious people experiment with life. A law suit had been brought against him for his daring novel, and he lived neglected like a huge quarantined creature that nobody wanted to touch. But he was unconcerned. He bequeathed to life only the ghostly remains of himself. And he sat like a god in the exquisite temple of his art to which he alone held the key.

He had been looking for a perfect disciple. Maupassant had been looking for a perfect master. And now the two wandering half-souls met in an equality of loneliness and merged into a soul that wandered on triumphant—and alone.

For seven years on Sundays Guy brought his poems and his plays and his stories to this "broad-shouldered viking" with the large mustache and the murky eyes, and watched him run his blue-pencil through his writings. And at night they parted, each with a ribald joke to conceal an aching heart.

Gradually the pupil learned the secrets of his master's genius. It was the genius of a sharpshooter who pierced through the hypocrisies of life with arrows dipped in acid.

III

IT WAS a long time before Maupassant could get a hearing. He suffered from terrific headaches, but he refreshed himself by diving off "a tempting bridge in midwinter" and coming up in the ice-water to shout a red-hot obscenity at the people who had gathered around. He told low stories to his fellow clerks at the office; he whispered words of double meaning to the ladies whom he met at parties. "He is the most shameless young man in Paris," said everybody.

The most shameless and the most brilliant. Yet for all his brilliance—or rather *because* of his brilliance—he got himself constantly into trouble. The "reputable" Parisians shunned him when he wrote a ribald comedy and produced it at the studio of a *déclassé* painter. The police haled him into court when he composed an immoral poem and published it in the columns of a *déclassé* magazine.

And always those terrific headaches. As they grew in intensity he spent hours looking into the mirror at his eyes. Was he not suffering, perhaps, from the too ardent fatigue of his love-making? That street-girl last night, for example, the stranger who had come into his life and gone out of it again in thirty minutes?

His aches and his anxieties increased especially with the coming of the Parisian winters. To his mother—his tender love for her was the polestar of his life—he wrote: "December terrifies me . . . It is the black month, the deep sinister month, the midnight of the year. They've already given us lamps at the office, and in a month we shall be lighting the fire . . . When I'm alone at my table with my sad lamp burning in front of me, I often have such moments of dejection that I don't know where to turn."

But always in the end he turned to his stories. He picked up stray tales from the lips of fishermen, peasants, actresses, courtesans, and clerks. Once, while he was at Émile Zola's table and the company in their conversation were catching the moon in their cups, the host discussed the principles of the new literature he was writing. "Remember, we must leap into the stars from the springboard of exact observation." And one of the party suggested, "Let us each write a story about our war with the Prussians—not as historians and politicians have written about wars, but as the demons of Inferno have conceived it and as it has been carried out on earth. Let us destroy all illusions and show where true heroism lies." And Guy contributed to this volume a story of true heroism, the *Ball of Fat*.

This Ball of Fat was a "professional lady" whom men loved in haste and despised at leisure. One day during the Franco-Prussian War, she found herself traveling from Paris to Havre in the same carriage with a company of respectable people. These decent folk, as soon as they recognized her for what she was, drew their skirts about them and would have nothing to do with her. However, when they learned that she alone had had the foresight to bring along a box of lunch, they forgot their disdain and generously helped themselves to the food that she offered them.

That evening they stopped at an inn only to discover that it was being held by the German soldiers. The officer in command placed them all under arrest and declared that he would not let them go until the "fat one" spent the night with him. Indignantly she refused to yield to his command. But her fellow travelers, anxious to secure their freedom, pleaded with her and pressed upon her all sorts of arguments until finally she gave way.

The next morning the travelers resumed their trip—and once more drew disdainfully away from the woman who had made the great sacrifice in their behalf. This time they had taken along their lunches, but she had forgotten hers in the excitement. They opened their boxes and ate greedily and offered her not a morsel of their food. The tears came and glistened in the corners of her eyes.

"She weeps for shame," they murmured piously . . .

In the *Ball of Fat* the author shows his irony and his contempt for human stupidity. In several of his other stories, however, his contempt turns into compassion. Such a story—there are those who consider it the high watermark of French fiction—is *The Necklace*.

The Necklace is the tragi-comedy of Madame Loisel, a woman who was born beautiful and poor. She dreamed of princes and she was married to a clerk. She hungered for palaces and she lived in a tenement. "She possessed no perfumes, no jewels, and it was for these things that she longed, as the fleet Arabian longs for his native desert."

She did, however, possess one gift—a rich friend, a classmate from the convent. But she never visited this friend, for she suffered from the sight of the things that she could not have.

One evening her husband came home radiant. "I have an invitation for us. We are to attend a soirée given by the Minister of Public Instruction and his wife."

"But I have nothing to wear," she said.

Her husband bought her a dress, but she was still unhappy. "I have no jewels."

"Why not go to your friend, Madame Forestier, and ask her to lend you her jewels?"

She gave a cry of joy. "Yes, that is true—I had not thought of it."

She went to her friend, borrowed a beautiful diamond necklace, and was the most dazzling of all the dazzling women at the soirée. She came home radiant. She began to undress herself in front of her mirror, and then—a sudden outcry: "I have lost Madame Forestier's necklace!"

A search all over Paris—in vain. "We must manage, somehow, to replace the jewels!"

Together with her husband she went from jeweler to jeweler, until at last they found a necklace that resembled the one they had lost.

"What is the price of this?"

"Forty thousand francs. But I will sell it to you at a sacrifice— for thirty-six thousand."

Breathless visits to their friends, to the bankers, to the usurers, to the money-lenders—until at last they were able to scrape together the thirty-six thousand francs.

Madame Loisel returned the necklace—and then settled down to the slavery of paying off the debt. Day in and day out she worked, washing, scrubbing, soiling her hands, tarnishing her beauty, wasting away her health. And her husband toiled along with her, balancing the books of merchants, frequently sitting up all night to copy a document at five cents a page.

They kept this up for ten years, and finally they paid off the entire obligation—principal and interest alike.

One Sunday Madame Loisel, an old and tired woman now, was walking in the Champs Elysées. Suddenly she saw a lady, young, beautiful, charming, walking in the opposite direction. It was Madame Forestier. Madame Loisel greeted her. "Good morning, Jeanne."

Madame Forestier looked at her without recognizing her.

"Don't you know me, Jeanne? I am Mathilde Loisel."

"Oh, my poor Mathilde—how you are changed!"

"I've had lots of trouble these years—and all for you."

"For me? How?"

"I lost the necklace you lent me, but I bought another just like it. And for ten years I have been paying for it."

Touched to the heart, Madame Forestier took the poor, rough hands into her own. "Oh, my poor Mathilde! But my necklace was false. It was worth only 500 francs at most."

IV

DURING the years of their intimacy, Gustave Flaubert had given Maupassant a triple formula for literary success: "Observe," he had said, "and then observe again, and again."

And now suddenly Flaubert was dead. Guy walked into the room he had visited for seven years on Sundays, and up the stairs to where the dead man lay. Nothing was sacred to this observer. While he washed the body and prepared it for burial, his eyes and his mind were busy storing up the details for future use in his art. As he walked behind the hearse to the burial place, he noted that a cow peered above a hedge and mooed in the sunshine at something it did not understand. At the grave he observed how the clumsy diggers strained and sweated at the ropes of the coffin, how the box wedged crazily sideways in the earth and refused to enter the grave until more men came to add their strength. His heart leaped with the breathless thrill of an artist at the incongruity of things and he offered up a prayer of thanks that he was present at this moment to catch the futility and the brutality of life.

The novelist's sense, the instinct as natural as the scent of the hunting dog . . . Aye, but there was also the heart. Sometimes he laid aside his pen and waited and winced for hours until the darkness was swept away from his eyes. Frequently he inhaled ether and nodded in its fumes and dreamed away his pain. And he bought little jars of syrup drugs that ate up all the money he had set aside for a summer holiday.

But underneath the fugue of suffering there was always a clear note of pagan beauty: "I love the heavens, like a bird; the forests, like the wolf; the rocks, like the chamois; deep grass as a horse loves it to roll in; and clear waters in which to swim like a fish. I feel vibrating in me something common to every animal, some of all the instincts and all the dim desires of the lower creation. I love the world as they do and not like you men. I love it without admiring it, without poetizing it, without soaring to the empyrean. I love it with a love which is deep and bestial, which is contemptible and yet sacred . . ."

He pretended—though his stories belied his words—that he had no compassion for men. "I can split open a poet's skull merely for the curiosity of seeing what is inside." But the mysterious sufferings of dumb animals, he declared, horrified him and awakened all the tender instincts of his soul. The cry of the wolf in the trap was his cry. His genius, far above the average man's, was linked to the bodily senses of a life lower—in the scale of evolution—than the life of man. He wrote—or did he dream it in the fumes of his ether?—about a miserly old peasant woman who decided to throw her dog into a pit—a dog "that did not even bark" —so that she would not have to pay an eight-franc government tax on dogs. At first she approached a laborer to do the job. But he asked fivepence for it. "That amount seemed madly exaggerated. The neighbor's farm servant offered to do it for two-pence halfpenny, but that was still too much." So she went herself to the pit and threw the dog in by the neck. "At first she heard a dull thud; then a sharp cry, the shrill heart-rending cry of a wounded animal; next a lot of little cries of pain, one after the other; then despairing appeals, the pleadings of a dog imploring, with its head raised towards the mouth of the pit."

That night, as she lay in bed, she saw the dog in a dream. In the morning she determined to have the dog brought out of the pit. She went to a man who worked in clay-pits and asked him to help her. But he wanted four francs to get the dog out. She was taken aback. "Four francs," she screamed with anger. "Too much!" Well, at least she might appease her conscience by throwing a piece of bread into the pit for Pierrot. But in the meantime a bigger dog had been thrown into the pit with Pierrot; and when Madame cast down the piece of bread, "she could clearly distinguish the sounds of a terrible scuffle, and then the plaintive cries of Pierrot who had been bitten by the stronger dog. It was all very well for her to specify, 'This is for you, Pierrot.' It was clear that Pierrot got nothing."

And then Madame declared in a tone of self-justification, "Ah, well, I can't feed *all* the dogs that are thrown into that pit." . . . And suffocating at the thought of all those dogs living at her expense, she went away, even taking with her the rest of the bread and eating it as she departed.

The tears sprang to his eyes when he spoke of the silent suffering of the partners of his soul. And he wrote a tender and beautiful idyll on the corpse of a donkey that lay decaying in the mouths of flies just within three paces of the green fields for which it had longed—and longed in vain—during a lifetime of toiling for its master.

And what of the kingdom of man, the lesser animal? Destiny dominated mankind with the same brutality, he said, with which mankind dominated donkeys and dogs. With a few bold strokes of his plastic pen, he brought to life the entire futile struggle of the Norman peasantry. But he made contact with these poor souls not as mind to mind but as sense to sense, touch to touch, smell to smell. His sense of smell was as acute as that of the animals of the field. He scented their emotions, their ways of life, their instincts, their very thoughts. "All life in his pages . . . appears as a concert of odors."

Unsavory odors, for the most part. His vision of life was a vision of ugliness. "He fixes his attention upon some small spot of human life, usually some dreary, shabby, sordid spot, takes up the particle and squeezes it either till it grimaces or till it bleeds."

Yet even the ugliest of his stories are brightened with a sensuous gusto in the telling. He loved the electric contact of human flesh. He was the Renoir of the pen. He saw no subtle humor in the stories of life he had to tell, whether of peasants or of princes. Yet he achieved the most subtle of arts as he described the comedy of suffering, stupidity and grossness. His short stories were a revival of the fables of La Fontaine and of the witty tales of Boccaccio. The *leste conte*—licentious tale—has always appealed to the evanescent sparkle of the Latin mind.

Maupassant was the master of the short story, yet his manner of telling it was the manner of telling an epic. He wrote several novels that were short stories. And all his short stories were novels.

In all his people there is no comfort of religion, no soul. And yet he is a poet who tries to masquerade as a cynic. His pessimism, his scientific precision, his brilliant, simple, classical style are merely the dress of the young generation of men around him. Like the rest of his generation, Maupassant was a man who felt that he had been created by God but who cynically refused to trust in the parentage. He had no philosophic formula to live by. "There are as many truths as there are men . . . Each one of us forms for himself an illusion of the world, which is the illusion poetic, or sentimental, or joyous, or melancholy, or unclean, or dismal, according to his nature . . . the illusion of beauty, which is a human convention . . . the illusion of ugliness, which is a changing opinion . . . the illusion of the ignoble, which attracts so many! The great artists are those who make humanity accept their particular illusions."

The society of the Faubourg Saint-Honoré, who entertained him under their candelabra, were disconcerted. He was a lusty country bumpkin for all his fame and finery. And his eyes did not belong. They were not the eyes of a normal man. They were eyes that gave out no soul.

And Guy de Maupassant, who had become the master of laughter without jollity, looked into his eyes in the mirror and was disconcerted too. His face was growing thinner as if the eyes by a law of their own nature were feeding on the flesh. As he shaved in the morning, a mist came between him and the glass. He put his hand to his aching head. And he began to realize why he saw so deeply into the atoms of things. Did not anyone suspect? It was because his own mind was slowly breaking up into the atoms of things. Yes, each one of his thoughts was dissolving into drops of consciousness. And every atom of his thoughts beheld every fellow atom in a vision of euphoric brilliance before the final disintegration. And he was climbing the scale of art from genius to greater genius to childhood—and to the primitive man—and beyond; and he was sliding down the scale of evolution to the prehistoric man, the half-man—and below.

V

HE DID NOT UNDERSTAND why he should be dying of a venereal disease contracted in a nameless, obscure moment—an adventure with a shadow. He did not understand and he was terrified at the thought of death. "I believe in the definite annihilation of every human being that dies." When a man once jests at life, men will ever after take him for a jester. They did not realize, these million readers of his books, that the hallucinations and the ghosts that appeared in his stories were drawn from the secret hours of his own life. He buried himself in medical books, accosted doctors everywhere and questioned them about diseases. "He is collecting data for a new book, a satire on doctors, a study of abnormality," concluded the wise. And when he announced calmly to his dinner guests, "I am interested in insanity; I am going to describe the process of a man going slowly mad"—did they understand? Did his mistresses understand that he visited their boudoir because he was afraid to sleep alone?

He was suffering from autoscopia. At times he saw himself as plainly as if he had been looking in the mirror. As he entered his rooms one afternoon, he found himself seated in a chair reading a book he had laid aside when he had left the room a moment before. He wrote a tale, *La Horla,* about a man haunted by his own double. And once, while he was writing at his table, *his* double sat down noiselessly opposite him and began to dictate word for word all that he was writing. He grew livid and screamed and made a desperate movement with his hand to drive away the vision.

There was the chill of dying worlds in his blood. More than ever now he dreaded the approach of winter. He sat shivering by the fireside. In warm weather he had fires going in every room. He bought a yacht, sailed out under the Mediterranean sun, roamed the sands of Africa. But in the heat, as in the cold, he took notes with a shudder. He thought of the flies that live a few hours, the beasts that live a few days, the men that live a few years, the worlds that live a few centuries. What was the difference between the worm and the universe? A few more dawns, that was all! . . . "I now see death so near me that I want to stretch out my arms to push it back. I see it everywhere. The insects crushed on the path, the falling leaves, the white hair in a friend's head rend my heart and cry to me, 'Behold it!' It spoils for me all I do, all I see, all that I eat and drink, all that I love—the bright moonlight, the sunrise, the broad ocean, the noble rivers, and the soft summer evening air so sweet to breathe."

And now, as he listened with a seventh sense, terrible news came to him over the Mediterranean breezes. Fate had suddenly struck his younger brother, Hervé—robust, unsuspecting, serene —a mortal blow in the mind as the sun strikes a sleeping bather. As his relatives led him away to an asylum, he pointed to Guy and shrieked, "You're the crazy one, I tell you! You're the family lunatic!"

Soon Hervé was on his death bed, indifferent and quiet. But with a last effort of strength he called out to his brother, just as he used to call when they were boys together, "Come and play in the garden, Guy." And when Guy wiped away the tears, the eyes were dead.

And now, sad irony, came the period of his greatest literary creation—as if he had suddenly strayed into the keeping of unseen gods. For the toxic poisons in his blood were wringing from him the finest blossoms of his genius before destroying him. From his pen came stories of glowing silent tropics and beautiful human loves, of excursions on the Mediterranean whose waters dissolved into star planets under the creative light of the moon.

And his suffering grew apace with his beauty. Library tables, chairs, lamps became animals walking in and out of the room and down the stairs and into the street. Millions and billions of microbes were parading through his blood. When he set his heel on the ground, it jerked upwards. Once, as his servant was escorting him slowly through the fields, they came upon a giant crucifix. "Ah, François, He was thirty-three years of age when He was crucified. I am approaching forty-one."

He had become the "Grand Painter of the human grimace . . . He paints without hate and without love, without anger and without pity . . . All the grotesque souls, all the unfortunates he shows us so distinctly that we see them with our own eyes and we find them more real than reality itself. He brings to life; he does not judge . . . His indifference equals that of nature."

It is a few hours after New Year's. Maupassant presses a revolver to his head and pulls the trigger. But when he finds it empty, he slashes his throat open with a razor and stands staring with an indifferent smile. When his servant ran screaming into the room, he said calmly—"You see what I have done, François. I have slashed my throat. It is a case of sheer madness."

The naturalist had merely made one final experiment upon the human animal. And now he was ready to put aside his lessons. The doctors bandaged him and stopped the flow of blood. When the morning came up like a greyhound over the sky, they led him down to his beloved sea in the hope that the sight of his yacht, the *Bel Ami,* might bring him back to sanity. For some time he gazed at the boat. His lips moved like a child's who hasn't yet learned how to speak. He said nothing. Then he turned away. He was completely indifferent to his surroundings. "He was floating gently among the grasses and willows on that terrible tideless stream."

ZOLA

Important Works by Zola

Therese Raquin
The Fortunes of the
 Rougon Family
The Dram Shop
Nana
Doctor Pascal
Germinal
The Earth

The Dream
Rome
Lourdes
Paris
Fertility
Work
Truth
Justice
I Accuse

Émile Zola

1840–1902

ONCE A MONTH, in 1874, a group of four writers—Zola, Flaubert, Turgenev and Daudet—met for dinner at the Café Riche, in Paris. This monthly meeting—it was called *The Dinner of the Hissed Authors*—had developed into a periodic festival of grandiose ideas, spicy conversation and even spicier food. "We were all gourmands," wrote Zola, "and, speaking for myself, I had good need to be one. I had to fill a stomach that had been empty for many years."

They sat down to table at seven o'clock, and they left the restaurant at twelve. But not to go home. First they must wander through the streets till two, three, four in the morning—exchanging plots, discussing their next novels, tearing the world apart and then rebuilding it after their heart's desire.

Turgenev would be the first to break away. And after him, Daudet, Zola would then accompany "Papa Flaubert" to the latter's house on the *Rue Murillo;* Flaubert at his door would kiss Zola on both cheeks, and they would part with a final word from the master to the disciple: "All has been said before us, my son. We have nothing left except to say the same things. But we must say them in more beautiful words . . ."

Zola lived not only to say the old things in more beautiful words, but to say new things in words that were to re-echo around the world.

II

THE WORD *Zola* means *clod of earth*. Émile was true to his name; he was the son of Mother Earth, and he loved every common creature that came out of her loins.

He was a man of mixed blood—a little bit of everything that was good. His grandmother was a Greek, his mother was a Frenchwoman, and his father was an Italian.

Francesco Zola, a civil engineer who always had the right ideas but the wrong men to back them, managed at last to reach the border of success when the magistrates of Aix commissioned him to build a canal that would bring water from the mountains to the city. But he never succeeded in crossing *beyond* the border; he died (1847) before the work on the canal had begun. Madame Zola was left with her seven-year-old son, Émile, and with nothing but a disappointed dream on which to support him.

Five years of desultory schooling, interrupted by many a truant excursion on the banks of the *Torse,* and then the roughneck little vagabond was sent for a *real* education to the College of Aix.

His stay at the college was a long-drawn-out torture. He was reserved, found it hard to make friends, and suffered from an embarrassing lisp. When his classmates asked him for his name, he stammered out, *Thola*. And *Thola* became a nickname and a scourge to the stammering, awkward and sensitive little recluse.

But he didn't take his punishment lying down. He was a fighter. Though "alone against the mob," he returned blow for blow. One morning, after he had been attacked by an entire yardful of his schoolmates, he stood battered and breathless and trying very hard to keep the tears from his eyes. One of the boys who had just arrived in the yard walked up to him. "I am sorry for what has happened."

"Oh, that's all right. I can take good care of myself."

The newcomer held out his hand impulsively. "I'd like to be friends with you."

"And I with you," said Zola, taking the proffered hand. "By the way, what is your name?"

"Cézanne, Paul Cézanne."

And thus began the companionship that was to last for many years. Two determined rebels against the world.

<h2 style="text-align:center">III</h2>

AT THE College of Aix, young Zola was a good writer—at thirteen he had composed a novel and a three-act play—but a poor student. And when he left Aix for the *École Normale* in Paris, he was no better as a student. He cut his classes, he refused to "recite" when called upon, and he devoted all his time to "writing poetry and reading Rabelais, Montaigne, Hugo and Musset." At the final examination he received a zero in "literature."

His failure was a great blow to his mother. She had scrubbed floors and taken in washing in order to pay his way through college. She had wanted him to be an engineer, like his father. And now her hopes were dashed to the ground. Émile was doomed to the dreary life of a clerk, or—God forbid!—to the destitute life of a writer. Even Émile himself was in despair. "During the past week," he wrote to one of his friends, "I have been overcome by a great melancholy . . . I am twenty and have no profession . . . I have been dreaming up to now and walking on shifting sands. Who knows when I shall fall?"

Fortunately he was saved from an immediate fall through an old friend of his father's, M. Labot, who secured him a clerkship at the Napoleon Docks. Barely enough to feed his body—but nothing to feed his soul. "It is no fun at the Docks. For a month I have been living in that hellish stable; and by Jove, I feel it in my back and legs and all my other limbs. I find my desk stinking. I am disgusted and I am going to throw over this foul ware-house."

He threw it over after a few months. And then, two years in the gutter. Want, hunger, bitterness, rags, despondency—and dreams. Plans for the regeneration of man, for a new Bible that would bring heaven nearer to earth. If only he could find the strength to create that Bible! If only he could still that gnawing hunger in his stomach!

A reunion with Cézanne, who had followed him to Paris. They took rooms together, dreamed together, and starved together. The new apostle of the pen, the new apostle of the brush, in an age when nobody cared for apostles. Zola wrote poems and Cézanne painted pictures, and neither of them could find a public for their wares. And, truth to tell, neither of them as yet *deserved* to find a public. The fuel of their suffering had not as yet been touched into the flame of inspiration.

"But I *will* write that great work some day. You wait and see!"

In the meantime, further bitterness, further despondency, further want. In the winter of 1861–62 his hunger was so keen that he set traps for sparrows on the roof above his attic, and broiled them over a candle on the end of a curtain rod. There were times when he fainted from want of food.

And then, another rescue through one of his father's friends. This time it was a job as "bundle boy" at the publishing house of Hachette and Company. For several months he wrapped books in the shipping department, and spent his spare time in writing reviews of those books for his own amusement.

One day his employer caught him at this "idle amusement." He read the review. "Zola," he said, "you may be a lazy shipper, but you're not so bad at writing copy. We'll try you in the advertising department."

This promotion was a godsend to Zola. At last he had found an opportunity to earn his bread by his pen!

And now that his pen had been sharpened, he used it assiduously both day and night. When he got through with his regular office work, he went home—he now lived with his mother—and after a hearty dinner sat down to his "irregular" writing. He had now turned from poetry to fiction. "My Muse has been a pretty unfruitful jade. I shall henceforth be a prosateur." He began to send out his short stories, and had the satisfaction of seeing some of them printed in the provincial papers. And then he collected a number of these stories, *Tales for Ninon,* and took them—not to his own publisher but to another, "less conservative" firm, the house of Hetzel and Lacroix. It was the early spring of 1864. M. Lacroix looked up from his desk and saw a stocky, awkward lad with bristling hair and a belligerent pug-nose. "Sir, will you please read these stories? Only one of them, I beg you, *any* one. You will see at once that I have talent."

Amused at the lad's assurance—an assurance, however, uttered in a very timid tone—M. Lacroix promised to read the manuscript. After a delay of several weeks that to the impatient Zola appeared like several years, the publishers accepted the manuscript.

"The battle," exulted Zola, "has been short . . . I am now on the threshold of things . . . From this point it only remains for me to go forward. I shall march on!"

IV

RECOGNITION, and then romance. Zola had taken an apartment in one of the streets near the École de Médicine, on the left bank of the Seine. One evening he met Alexandrine Mesley, the daughter of the man from whom he had rented his rooms. The girl—a tall, striking brunette with eyes "like those of a child in an old Spanish portrait"—was weeping and trying to avoid him. Little by little he got her story. She had given herself to her lover, a young medical student from the provinces. The lover had gone home and abandoned her. Zola took her into his home as his mistress; and after a while he took her into his heart as his wife.

It was a union of equal tenderness on both sides. Physically there was little in common between them. "Zola was ugly as a nightmare, and Alexandrine was lovely as a dream." But if Zola adored the beauty of her body, Alexandrine adored the beauty of his soul.

And Alexandrine too, as we shall see, was to prove that she had a beautiful soul.

With an established home and a growing reputation, Zola went on with his work. He had become interested in the "realistic" type of literature—novels like Flaubert's *Madame Bovary* and plays like Goncourt's *Henriette Maréchal*—clinical studies of love, eyes that probed into the innermost secrets of life. He, too, wanted to become a seeing eye that would expose the diseases of society in order that the body of society might be healed. He wrote several realistic—he preferred to call them *naturalistic*—novels. The novels were widely read, and Zola was widely abused. "In the minds of respectable people I am lost!"

And the public continued to abuse him, and to read him, and to pour money into his purse. In the salons of the "unrespectable" intelligentsia he was becoming somewhat of a lion—or rather very much of a bear, with his hairy face and his fat paunch and his unpolished manners. He wrote a series of articles in praise of Cézanne and the other "despised new artists"—though he admitted that he hardly knew black from white—and he created a storm of controversy over his "insane" ideas. And he relished his "insanity" and his popularity. For it all paved the way toward the great project that he had in mind, the New Bible that he had planned for so many years, the complete and unadorned picture of humanity as seen through the lives of the succeeding generations of a single family. An epic of denunciation, to serve at the same time as a gospel of hope.

In writing this epic of denunciation—in ten volumes—Zola became at once a student, a critic and a teacher of his fellow men. Before he started each novel, he made a thorough survey of the scenes, the characters, the situations, the language, the hopes, the fears and the beliefs of the atoms of humanity that went into the building of the body of that novel. He read books on the subject, he visited places, he spoke to people, he observed their action, their intonation, their slang, and he took notes—volume upon volume of notes for every one of his stories. And then he took this unwieldy mass of information, re-read it, sorted it, fashioned it into an idea and a plot, traced the whole thing out slowly, methodically, painstakingly—"writing is a very difficult job for me"—and, finally, after a labor of several months, sometimes even of years, a new work of art came into life.

Let us glance briefly at one of these works of art—*L'Assomoir* —a flame that sprang out of a vast quantity of carefully-piled-up fuel. (Zola has given us a detailed account of the preparation and the writing of this novel.) This story is a picture of the sufferings of the poor—"a *frightful* picture," observes Zola in his notes, "and one which will carry its own moral." The heroine of the story, Gervaise Macquart, is a woman of the people—a prototype of the unhappy stepchildren of Mother Earth. Though barely past twenty, she is the mother of two children—Etienne and Claude—the offspring of her illicit affair with Lantier. She has thrown herself upon the protection of Lantier, at the age of thirteen, in order to escape from the cruelty of her parents. At first Lantier was kind to her, but of late he has been neglecting her. He stays away all night; and when he arrives in the morning, he can hardly stand on his feet. *L'Assomoir,* the neighborhood dram shop. And another woman, Adele. Gervaise is still attractive—but she has one physical defect, a slight limp which becomes especially pronounced when she is tired from overwork. And these days she is very tired, indeed.

One morning, as she scrubs the family clothes at a public laundry, her children rush in to report that Lantier has deserted her for Adele—and that he has taken all of Gervaise's belongings with him. Added to the children's exclamations are the gibes of Adele's strapping sister, Virginie, who has come to the laundry to enjoy the discomfiture of Adele's defeated rival. Though small and frail as compared to her tormentor, Gervaise flings herself upon her and kicks her and bites her and beats her until Virginie begs for mercy.

"But I'll never forget this!" Virginie mutters as she slinks out of the laundry.

For a time Gervaise supports herself and her children by working as a laundress. Among her acquaintances is the tinsmith, Coupeau, a young man who knows of her unhappy life with Lantier. Coupeau asks her to become his mistress, but she refuses him again and again. Finally he proposes marriage, and she accepts.

Storms and denunciations on the part of Coupeau's family, and the two settle down to an interlude of comparative happiness. Coupeau is a good tinsmith, Gervaise is an excellent laundress, and together they manage to provide a "decent" home for the two children. And for a third child, Nana, who is born four years after their marriage.

Shortly after her confinement with Nana, Gervaise returns to work in the laundry. Her one dream is some day to have a laundry of her own. Things are not so bad after all—especially if you work hard, and stay honest, and plan . . .

But one day her plans received a sudden blow. Her husband fell down from a roof that he was repairing. She refused to send him to the hospital, but insisted on caring for him at home. A long and expensive convalescence—and Coupeau emerged from it a changed man. The fall had shattered not only his body but his soul. No more ambition, no more planning, no more hope. Just one overmastering passion. *L'Assomoir*—the dram shop . . .

Destiny was playing a cat-and-mouse game with the Coupeaus. A tidbit of happiness, a plunge into despair, and then another false promise of happiness. A man who secretly loved Gervaise, the golden-bearded and golden-hearted blacksmith Goujet, prevailed upon her to accept from him a loan of five hundred francs. It was enough to open her laundry—the fulfillment of her dream.

But that tiger-cat, Destiny, was waiting for her next spring. Virginie, the sister of Adele, had become a neighbor of the

Coupeaus. She had never forgotten the drubbing she had received from Gervaise. Under a pretense of friendship, she informed Gervaise that Lantier had returned to the *Quartier*. "He has deserted Adele—and he is still in love with you."

Gervaise was terrified. But for some time her former lover made no effort to meet her. Instead, he sought out the friendship of her husband, Coupeau. The two men became inseparable companions at the dram shop; and finally Lantier invited himself to become a boarder at the Coupeaus' house.

And now, under the influence of the two degraded men, began the slow degradation of Gervaise. Obliged to support them both, as well as her children, she struggled for a time against her excessive burden—and then she succumbed. She quarreled with her husband, she neglected her business, she sought forgetfulness in the arms of Lantier. And then came the final blow: she lost Lantier and her laundry. Virginie inherited them both.

Together with her husband, she is now sucked down into the whirlpool of the *L'Assomoir*. Coupeau lapses from stupor to stupor, until he finally sinks into the nightmare of an alcoholic death. Nana, a full-grown girl, has left home to become a streetwalker. Gervaise, too, tries to walk the streets, but nobody will have her now. Starvation, liquor, despair. The edge of the abyss. The blacksmith Goujet makes one final attempt to rescue her. But it is too late. *L'Assomoir*—the world-tavern that intoxicates the poor with the bitter cup of sorrow—has taken its toll.

V

ZOLA'S NOVELS about the poor—another of Destiny's jokes—had made him very rich. And very fat. And very morose. Whatever you did, life had you by the throat. When you were poor, you *starved* to death; when you were rich, you *ate yourself* to death. Zola, a neurotic from infancy, believed that he suffered from every disease under the sun—a result, he said, of his early privation and his subsequent indulgence. Actually he was healthy as a horse. What really bothered him was not his strengthlessness but his childlessness. Without any children, he felt he was only half a man. Why had fate given him a wife who couldn't fulfill her function of motherhood? Here in his household was another woman, Jeanne Rozerot, his personal maid. Tall, healthy, gray-eyed, good-looking, fresh—what a mother *she* would make for his children! . . .

And why not? To be sure, she was scarcely twenty and he was already fifty and gray and round as a hogshead. But with the proper diet he could take thirty years off his age and thirty pounds off his weight. As for his gray hairs, they would only give him added dignity in Jeanne's eyes.

A drastic restriction in his food for several months—no fats, no pastries and no liquids with his meals—and the old professor emerged as a rejuvenated Faust. He set up an apartment for Jeanne Rozerot, and to his supreme joy became the father of two children.

But for his wife Alexandrine there was no joy. She remonstrated, she stormed, she threatened to leave—and finally she submitted to her role as first in his home, second in his heart. She went even further than that. There is a French motto—*noblesse oblige* (nobility brings obligations). In Alexandrine's case it was the other way around—obligations brought nobility. With a generosity born of her sadness, she got into communication with the mother of her husband's children, had the children legalized under Zola's name, and took a personal interest in their welfare as long as she lived.

To show his gratitude to Alexandrine, Zola dedicated to her his next book, *Le Docteur Pascal*. "To my dear Wife I inscribe this book which is the résumé and the conclusion of all my work." In one of the copies of the book, however, he wrote a different dedication: "To my darling Jeanne, who has given me the royal banquet of her youth, and who has made me the present of my Denise and my Jacques, the dear children for whom I have written this book, so that they may know . . . how much I adore their Mother."

Until the very end of his days, Émile Zola kept up his two relationships—his devotion to "my dear Wife" and his adoration for "my darling Jeanne."

VI

WHEN Zola had completed his ten-novel "epic fight for the truth," there was nothing left for him but to rest on his laurels. It was then, however, that his *real* fight began.

It concerned the trial of Captain Alfred Dreyfus.

At the beginning of the trial, Zola took but little interest in it. "Another Jew accused of unpatriotic activities." Zola had never cared much for Jews—as a young man, he had positively disliked them. As the trial went on, however, he began to sense something peculiar in the proceedings. Trained as an accurate observer in the preparation of his novels, he suspected in the charges against Dreyfus a plot to frame an innocent man. He began to study the case. His suspicion became a certainty. An act of terrible injustice was being perpetrated in his country. It was his solemn duty, as a patriotic citizen, to rectify the injustice. It was not Dreyfus, it was France, that was on trial before the world. Zola threw himself heart and soul into the business of clearing the name of Dreyfus in order that he might clear the name of France.

Dreyfus was wasting away in solitary confinement on Devil's Island. "I am innocent!" he cried again and again, believing in his despair that only the winds and the waves heard his cry.

But Zola had heard it, and he compelled the entire world to hear it. He wrote and published a pamphlet, *J'Accuse* (I Accuse), in which he carefully analyzed the entire case. In this pamphlet he not only demonstrated the innocence of Dreyfus, but he pointed his accusing finger at the men and the institutions that were guilty. "It is only today that this affair has begun, since it is only now that sides have definitely been taken: on the one hand, the culprits who want no light at all on the business; on the other, lovers of justice who would lay down their lives for it . . . I have one passion only, for light . . . My burning protest is only the cry of my soul . . . Let the culprits dare to drag me into the courts! Such an action will only hasten the explosion of truth and justice!"

There was indeed an explosion—not, however, of truth and justice, but of hatred and violence against Zola. "Down with Zola! Down with the traitor! Sold to the Jews!" His house was attacked. Stones came hurtling through the window. His books were banned. He was burned in effigy and hurled into the Seine. One of the Parisian papers, the *Libre Parole,* called for "the assassination of Zola and the sacking of his house."

Finally the turmoil came to a head. Zola was arrested for libel. A long farce of a trial—whenever Zola's attorney asked a witness for information that might bring out the facts in the case, the judge snapped, "The question will not be put!" At the end of the trial, Zola made an eloquent plea for justice—not for himself, but for Dreyfus. ". . . He is innocent, I swear it, I pledge my life, my honor upon it. At this solemn hour, before this tribunal which represents human justice, before all France, before the entire world, I swear that Dreyfus is innocent. And, by my forty years of labor, and by the authority which this toil may have given me, I swear that Dreyfus is innocent. And by all that I have won, by the name I have made for myself, by my works which have aided the spread of French letters, I swear that Dreyfus is innocent. May all of that crumble, may all of my works perish, if Dreyfus is not innocent. He *is* innocent! . . ."

As for the fate of Zola himself, "I am calm . . . I may be sentenced here. But I shall conquer. Some day France will thank me for having helped to save her honor . . ."

The jury found him guilty of libel (against the men who had accused and imprisoned Dreyfus). A fine of 30,000 francs. His fight for justice had cost him his labor, his health, his reputation, his savings of a lifetime, his friends. He was again, as he had been forty years earlier, despised and destitute and alone.

But he kept up his fight! And finally he succeeded in arousing the conscience of France. Dreyfus was retried, found innocent, and set free. Zola had conquered. He lived to see the day, as he had predicted in his trial, when his country thanked him "for having helped to save her honor."

VII

HIS ACT upon the stage of life was over. Time for Destiny to ring down the curtain. Dramatically, as befitted a protagonist of Zola's caliber. The morning of September 30, 1902. Zola's oldest friend, Cézanne, has just entered his studio at Aix. He begins to prepare his palette for his day's work. His servant, Paulin, rushes in. He is all out of breath. "Monsieur Cézanne, Monsieur Cézanne, Zola is dead!"

Cézanne's heart skips a beat. "How did it happen?"

"Accident, Monsieur Cézanne! Went to bed last night, left fire burning, fire went out, gas fumes, asphyxiation."

Zola had been working late on the night of his death. On his desk the next morning they found the unfinished page of a manuscript. A scribbled phrase—the sum and substance of his life's philosophy: "To remake through truth a higher and happier humanity."

MARK TWAIN

Important Works by Mark Twain

The Celebrated Jumping Frog
Innocents Abroad
Roughing It
The Gilded Age
The Adventures of Tom Sawyer
The Prince and the Pauper
Huckleberry Finn
A Connecticut Yankee
The American Claimant

Pudd'nhead Wilson
Joan of Arc
The Man That Corrupted
  Hadleyburg
Adam's Diary
What Is Man
Captain Stormfield's
  Visit to Heaven
The Mysterious Stranger

Samuel Langhorne Clemens
(Mark Twain)
1835—1910

Mark twain, we suspect, has not as yet received his full measure of recognition. His work has been crowned with every honor save one—an appreciative understanding. We have allowed his reputation to rest upon his second-best work. We admire him as America's greatest jester and we ignore him as one of America's profoundest philosophers. In our laughter over his jokes we forget the lash that lies hidden in many of them. Centering our attention upon his cap and bells, we have failed to see the prophet under the disguise of the clown.

To be sure, Mark Twain was a jester. But jesters of this type are men with a grin upon their faces and acid in their hearts. They laugh, as that other humorous pessimist, Voltaire, has pointed out, in order to keep from hanging themselves. Having looked deeply into the heart of things, they are overwhelmed with the pitiful stupidity of the "damned human race." And so they put on the comic mask as a means for concealing the tears that lurk behind it.

Those who have suffered most have learned to laugh best. The humorists, the satirists, the cynics—these naughty urchins of literature are the defeated rebels of life. They thumb their noses at fate because they realize, in their impotence, that there is no other gesture left to them.

Mark Twain was one of these defeated rebels. He believed that all human striving is an aimless farce—"a tale told by an idiot, full of sound and fury, signifying nothing." We scramble toward the rainbow and are drowned in the gutter. We reach for the moon and we break our bones. Our persistent aspiration in the face of our persistent defeat is a spectacle for the amusement of the gods. But we too—believed Mark Twain—can be amused if we mitigate the pangs of our defeat with the anodyne of our laughter. We can detach ourselves sufficiently to enjoy the spectacle of our own suffering. "Learn to agonize as an actor in the drama of life; but learn also, as an onlooker, to smile at your own agony."

II

SAMUEL CLEMENS was a product of his time and place. A child of the border, he met life like all pioneers—with a grim sense of humor. This type of humor, writes his biographer Albert Bigelow Paine, "grew out of a distinct condition—the battle with the frontier. The fight was so desperate, to take it seriously was to surrender. Women laughed that they might not weep; men, when they could no longer swear. *Western humor* was the result. It is the freshest, wildest humor in the world, but there is tragedy behind it."

Even as a child Samuel Clemens was acquainted with many of the tragedies of life. Brought up in a midwestern village of poor whites, he saw slaves flogged and men shot down in the streets. His parents led a migratory life of hopeless and loveless privation. They were always "on the westward wing"—trekking from the seaboard to Kentucky, from Kentucky to Tennessee and from Tennessee to Missouri. It was in Missouri that Samuel was born (November 30, 1835).

His father, a morose and discouraged derelict, hardly ever played with his children or showed them any affection. In the winter of 1847 he died; and Samuel, an unruly, ragged, under-sized, sickly and neurotic little roughneck of eleven, found him-self thrust upon the untender mercies of the world. Taken out of school, he was put to work as a "printer's devil." His employer described him as a youngster with a huge head, an ink-smudged face and an infinite capacity for laziness. He fell in with the idlers of the village and became acquainted with every phase of human aberration. And of human sorrow. In his early teens he witnessed the death of a sister and a brother. At twenty-three his hair turned gray when another of his brothers was burned to death in a steamboat explosion on the Mississippi. At thirty he was so disgusted with life that "he put a loaded pistol to his head, but found he lacked courage to pull the trigger." He decided to live and to translate his sorrow into laughter. Yet his later experiences, though they brought him many honors, afforded him but little occasion for laughter. His first child died soon after its birth. A second succumbed to pneumonia as a result of Mark Twain's absent-minded carelessness. He had been out driv-ing with the child on a snowy day and, wrapped in his own dreams, he had forgotten to cover the child sufficiently against the cold. Another of his children barely escaped death when Mark Twain heedlessly let go of the perambulator at the summit of a steep hill. "I shouldn't have been entrusted with the job," he said when the child, with bleeding head, was picked up from the stones at the bottom of the hill. "I was not qualified for any such responsibility as that. Some one should have gone who had at least the rudiments of a mind. Necessarily I would lose myself in wool-gathering." Several years later, when he returned from a triumphant lecture tour that had taken him around the world, he learned that Susy, the most gifted of his children, had died in his absence. And then came the bitterest tragedy of them all. On December 23, 1909, his daughter Jean had worked hard all day preparing for the Christmas celebration. The tree was set, the presents were neatly wrapped and addressed, and everything was ready for the holiday. Jean kissed her father good night, as usual, and went to bed. The next morning word was brought to Mark Twain that Jean was dead. She had suffered an epileptic stroke while taking a bath.

Very few men have been more famous than Mark Twain. And very few men have been more unhappy. He knew how to laugh uproariously. But there was tragedy in his laughter.

III

MARK TWAIN was a true son of the frontier—the frontier between human hope and human disappointment. Wherever he traveled—as a pilot on the Mississippi, as a mining prospector in Nevada, as a reporter in San Francisco—he became "personally and familiarly acquainted" with the struggles and the rebuffs and the renewed struggles of his "fellow-damned human brothers." Everywhere he became saturated with the life and the humor of the border. It was a boisterous life and an exuberant humor. The pioneers lived on the boundary between bitter fact and extravagant fancy. Their stories, created in the mirage of the desert, were coarse and vivid and hilarious tales of gigantic heroes and superhuman adventures. Tales of legendary American Samsons like Paul Bunyan, whose perspiration, as he toiled on the mountainside, flowed down into the valley and formed the Great Salt Lake. Sagas of American Munchausens like Jim Bridges, who lost his way in the Petrified Forest while trying to escape from the Indians, and who was himself turned into stone in midair as he leaped across a canyon, since in that forest the very law of gravity had become petrified. Fantastic extravaganzas about a grasshopper from whose rump an enormous steak had been cut to be served to all the guests in a restaurant; about a turnip whose roots reached so far down into the earth that when you pulled it up an artesian well spurted into your face and flung you into the air; about a needle which a little girl accidentally thrust into her foot and which two generations later came out through the head of her granddaughter. And—what the men of the frontier loved to hear most frequently—preposterous burlesques about the newly-made American millionaires. One of these millionaires, the owner of a silver mine in Nevada, was sleeping in the upper bunk of an inn. In the lower bunk—so ran the story—slept an ordinary workingman. In the morning the workingman awoke with excruciating aches and pains all over him. No medicine could cure him of his torture until he went to a Turkish bath—and sweated out of his pores a pile of silver dust amounting to $417.92 which he had absorbed from the millionaire who had slept above him.

Such were the folk tales that delighted the pioneers in the middle of the nineteenth century. They formed much of the early literary fare of Mark Twain.

But added to the laughter of a boisterous people overbubbling with life was the sadness of a gentle personality contending with death. Mark Twain was a pessimist. "A man who doesn't become a pessimist," he observed, "knows too little about the world." He himself knew too much about the world to regard it as anything more than a "football of the gods." The greatest gift that life can give us, he said, is death. "I have never greatly envied any one but the dead. I always envy the dead." In the first outburst of his sorrow after the drowning of Jean, he expressed his conviction that he would not bring her back to life even if he could. "In her loss I am almost bankrupt, and my life is a bitterness, but I am content; for she has been enriched with the most precious of all gifts—that gift which makes all other gifts mean and poor—death. I have never wanted any released friend of mine restored to life since I reached manhood."

With the ancient Greek philosopher, Solon, Mark Twain believed that no man ought to be accounted happy until he is dead. This epitome of human wisdom, born of human suffering, finds a continual echo in the works of Mark Twain. "Whoever has lived long enough to find out what life is," he writes in *Pudd'n-head Wilson*, "knows how deep a debt of gratitude we owe to Adam, the first great benefactor of our race. He brought death into the world." And again, "All say, how hard it is that we have to die—a strange complaint to come from the mouths of people who have had to live." In *The Mysterious Stranger* the Devil makes the following comment on human happiness: "No sane man can be happy, for to him life is real, and he sees what a fearful thing it is. Only the mad can be happy . . ."

All this was more than a mere pose on the part of Mark Twain. His words about life and death had the ring of sincerity about them. They had been minted out of his own experience. He had proved, to his own bitter satisfaction, the validity of the old Horatian advice to poets: No writer can make others weep who has not himself wept. "Words," remarks the Connecticut Yankee, "realize nothing, vivify nothing to you, unless you have suffered in your own person the thing which the words try to describe." Mark Twain, like that other great unappreciated thinker of the nineteenth century, Walt Whitman, knew whereof he spoke when he greeted "Death, blessed Death" as the gentle physician that liberates us from that most dreadful of all diseases—Life.

IV

IN ALL GREAT IRONY there is a vein of pity. Mark Twain's irony grew out of his pity—and his scorn. He had pity for the helplessness of the weak and scorn for the ruthlessness of the strong. Anatole France tells us that the entire history of the human race may be summarized in a few words—men are born, they suffer, they die. Mark Twain would have emended these words to read —men are born, *they compel one another to suffer,* they die. Although he loved human beings as harassed individuals, he detested them as a harassing pack of wolves. As a young journalist with a clear eye and a caustic pen, he was obliged to flee from San Francisco because he criticized the dishonesty of its business and the corruption of its politics. He came East, where his vision grew even clearer and his pen more caustic. The East, and New England in particular, had "an instinctive preference," to quote the apt phrase of Mr. Bernard De Voto, "for the second rate."

The "nice people" were unable to understand this redheaded anarchist from the West. But the redheaded anarchist understood the "nice people" and he found them, whether in Hartford or in Boston or in Cambridge or anywhere else, not quite so nice. Taken as a whole, he looked upon mankind—including in all fairness himself—as among the lowest of the animals. When asked whether he dared to put a man on a level with a rat, he replied in all seriousness, "I don't . . . That would be unfair to the rat." The principal difference between a man and a dog, he observed in *Pudd'nhead Wilson,* is this—"If you pick a starving dog and make him prosperous, he will not bite you." He was preoccupied with this idea for the greater part of his life. A few days before his death he wrote in that caustic-humorous vein of his: "When you reach the gate of Heaven, leave your dog outside. Heaven goes by favor. If it went by merit, you would stay out and the dog would go in."

Man is an animal, declared Mark Twain, but he is not a brute. He has not as yet reached up to the moral level of the brute. A brute kills out of hunger. A man kills out of spite. In *The Mysterious Stranger* the Devil points out to a little boy how a heretic is being tortured by his executioners. The boy, sickened by the spectacle, remarks to the Devil that it is a brutal thing. "No," replies the Devil, "it is a *human* thing."

No self-respecting animal, observed Mark Twain, would choose to live with humans if he could help it. In *A Horse's Tale* two philosophical horses, Sage-Brush and Mongrel, are discussing the ways of the gods and the wiles of men—

Sage-Brush: I've seen a good many human beings in my time. They are created as they are; they cannot help it. They are only brutal because it is their make; brutes would be brutal if it was *their* make.

Mongrel: To me, Sage-Brush, man is most strange and unaccountable. Why should he treat dumb animals cruelly? . . . (*A reflective pause, lasting some moments. And then:*) When we die, Sage-Brush, do we go to heaven and dwell with men?

Sage-Brush: My father thought not. He believed we do not have to dwell with men in heaven unless we deserve it.

V

MARK TWAIN'S INDICTMENT against the human race is not merely abstract. Time and again, even in his most playful books, he cites concrete instances of man's inhumanity to man. He holds up to ridicule every phase of oppression, of corruption, of exploitation, of bribery, of hypocrisy, of coercion, of hatred and of greed. He tries to drown injustice in a deluge of derision. He washes away the superficial gilding of the Gilded Age, and he exposes the coarse and undecorated ugliness of the politicians and the profiteers who batten upon the misfortunes of their fellows. He tears away the trappings of the dictators and the emperors, and he shows them to be nothing but "hollow artificialities" underneath. The Connecticut Yankee and King Arthur, traveling in disguise, are taken for a couple of country bumpkins and sold into slavery. The Connecticut Yankee fetches a price of nine dollars, but the king is adjudged to be worth not a cent more than seven dollars.

Kings, observes Mark Twain, are a dangerous luxury. If the world *must* have something to adore, let them enthrone a royal family of cats. "As a rule, the character of these cats would be considerably above the character of the average king . . . It would . . . be noticed that they hanged nobody, beheaded nobody, imprisoned nobody, inflicted no cruelties or injustices of any sort, and so must be worthy of a deeper love and reverence than the customary human monarch . . . The eyes of the whole harried world would soon be fixed upon this humane and gentle system, and royal butchers would presently begin to disappear."

Mark Twain had no quarrel with the *peaceful* rulers. His quarrel was merely with the royal *butchers*. These ill-behaved and dictatorial children of the human family, dissatisfied with the slice of earth that has been allotted to them, clamor for more than their share—and ever more. Mark Twain detested the spirit of military aggressiveness more than he detested anything else in the world. He had seen so much brawling as a youngster that he had become utterly cured of it for the rest of his life. When a bully wants to fight you, he once declared, take off your coat, slowly and deliberately, and look him straight in the eye. Then, still slowly and deliberately, take off your vest. Then roll up your sleeves and keep on looking him straight in the eye. And if by this time your opponent hasn't run away, you'd better run yourself.

This isn't to say that Mark Twain was either an appeaser or a coward. On the contrary, when the Civil War broke out, he enlisted in the federal army and served until he was honorably discharged. He wasn't afraid of an honest fight, but he had a horror of dishonest brigandage. And the history of the human race, he said, is full of these examples of dishonest brigandage—always under the cloak of a noble cause. "The story of mankind is little more than a summary of human bloodshed. First came a long series of unknown wars, murders and massacres . . . Next came the Assyrian wars . . . Next we had Egyptian wars, Greek wars, Roman wars, hideous drenchings of the earth with blood . . . And always we had wars, and more wars—all over Europe, all over the world. Sometimes in the private interest of royal families, sometimes to crush a weak nation; *but never a war started by an aggressor for any clean purpose*—there is no such war in the history of the race."

But the most scathing indictment against the brutality of aggression ever penned by Mark Twain, ever penned by any American writer, is his ironical *Soldier's Prayer*. This "imaginary" prayer is in reality a concrete picture of the Napoleonic—were Mark Twain alive today, he would call it the Hitlerian—type of mind:

"O Lord our God, help us to tear their soldiers to bloody shreds with our shells; help us to cover their smiling fields with the pale forms of their patriot dead; help us to drown the thunder of the guns with the cries of their wounded, writhing in pain; help us to lay waste their humble homes with a hurricane of fire; help us to wring the hearts of their unoffending widows with unavailing grief; help us to turn them out roofless with their little children to wander unfriended through wastes of their desolated land in rags and hunger and thirst, sport of the sun-flames of summer and the icy winds of winter, broken in spirit, worn with travail, imploring Thee for the refuge of the grave and denied it—for our sakes who adore Thee, Lord, blast their hopes, blight their lives, protract their bitter pilgrimage, make heavy their steps, water their way with tears, stain the white snow with the blood of their wounded feet! Grant our prayer, O Lord, and Thine shall be the praise and glory now and forever, Amen."

VI

MARK TWAIN HATED HATRED. At times this feeling within him became so intense that, as he asserted, "I have to take the pen and put my thoughts out on paper to keep them from setting me afire inside." At his best, Mark Twain belonged to the company of the prophets. Yet, by his own admission, he did not always offer his best to the world. He was too fond of luxury, and too hungry for fame, to have his full say in any of his earlier books. He tried to cover with a cloak of respectability the rebelliousness within his own soul. His one serious excursion into open rebellion—when he attempted to "clean up" the politics of San Francisco—had cleaned him out of a job and a home. Thereafter he decided that "it doesn't pay to swim against the tide." He had found that in order to be successful, you must attach yourself to those that are in power. Anson Burlingame, the American minister to China, had once said to him: "Never affiliate with inferiors; always climb." This advice, writes Albert Bigelow Paine, was to Mark Twain "a gospel which he would never forget."

For the greater part of his life, Mark Twain was chiefly interested in climbing. He didn't care to write any book "unless," to

use his own words, "there was *money* in it, and a good deal of it."
He therefore expurgated, or allowed his friends to expurgate,
much of the bitterness in those books which he wrote during his
"climbing" period. His public would neither understand, nor pay
for, serious thinking. "Irony," he wrote in *Pudd'nhead Wilson,*
"was not for those people; their mental vision was not focussed
for it." And so he gave them a series of books—*The Innocents
Abroad, Tom Sawyer, Huckleberry Finn, The Prince and the
Pauper,* and a harvest of short stories—in which there was a minimum of wormwood sweetened with a maximum of honey. His
own taste was ever so much superior to the taste of many of his
readers. He was amazed at the naive mentality that could laugh
over such an insipid story as *The Jumping Frog.* Nor was he particularly proud even of *Huckleberry Finn,* the best of his stories
which fell into this group. The appeal of these stories, he agreed
with Henry James, was "an appeal to rudimentary minds." He
wrote for a large public because he cared for his money more
than he cared for his art. He was ashamed of his enormous
public. "You have a mongrel perception of humor, nothing more;
a multitude of you possess that. This multitude see the comic side
of a thousand low-grade and trivial things—broad incongruities,
mainly; grotesqueries, absurdities, evokers of the horse-laugh."

He was ashamed of his enormous and uncritical public—and
he was ashamed of himself because he hadn't the courage to write
for a smaller and more exacting audience. "You observe," he once
remarked, "that under a cheerful exterior I have got a spirit that
is angry with me and gives me freely its contempt."

He confessed that he was carried away by the glitter of gold.
His unexpected rise to fame and prosperity was like a fairly tale
out of the Arabian Nights, and he could never quite get over the
wonder of it. A printer's apprentice, a pilot on a Mississippi
steamboat, an unsuccessful prospector in Nevada and an obscure
reporter in San Francisco, he suddenly found himself the wealthy
author of a celebrated book—he made $300,000 out of *The In-
nocents Abroad*—and the son-in-law of a millionaire coal-baron.

His head was completely turned. He began, like so many of his contemporaries, to aim at the rainbow, to reach for the moon. Literature had become a business with him. He was anxious to show his father-in-law, Mr. Rogers, that there was as much money in writing books as in selling coal. All you had to do was to give the public what the public wanted.

And so he sold laughter for gold, and the gold turned into ashes in his hands. For he was a dual personality. He had the money-grubbing body of Samuel Clemens and the freedom-loving soul of Mark Twain. It was his regular habit to write two letters when he addressed people on vital subjects. The one in which he expressed his own views he put away in his desk. The other, in which he expressed the *popular* view, he mailed. "I have a family to support," he explained, "and I can't afford to tell the whole truth."

But in spite of his indecision he was mentally—if not morally—a pioneer. It was this pioneer soul of Mark Twain that ventured forth hesitantly in *Tom Sawyer*, in *The Prince and the Pauper*, in *Captain Stormfield's Visit to Heaven*, in *Pudd'nhead Wilson*, in *A Connecticut Yankee*, in *The Man That Corrupted Hadley-burg*, in *Huckleberry Finn*. These books came like a succession of midsummer days full of a lazy sunlight and laughter but inter-rupted occasionally by the crashing of ironic thunder in the dis-tance. And it was this same pioneer soul that at last spoke out fearlessly in *The Mysterious Stranger*. In this book—at his wife's request it was not published till after his death—he finally told the truth as he saw it. He had aimed at the rainbow and had found it nothing but a passing mirage. Having made several for-tunes and lost them, having tasted the "sad satiety" of friendship and of fame, and having experienced the blessedness of loving and the bitterness of losing those that he loved, he gathered all the threads of his wisdom and his suffering and wove them into a single masterpiece—*The Mysterious Stranger*. The idea of this book had grown in his mind for several years. "I have been in-tending for a long time," he told William Dean Howells, "to write [such] a book without reserve—a book which should take account of no one's feelings, and no one's prejudices, opinions, beliefs, hopes, illusions, delusions: a book which should say my say, right out of my heart, in the plainest language and without a limitation of any sort."

The Mysterious Stranger is the only book of Mark Twain's in which he said his whole say. Artistically it may be inferior to *Huckleberry Finn*. Philosophically, however, this is his outstanding work. It is, we believe, the one book which places him on a level with the world's great satirists—Juvenal, Cervantes, Swift, Voltaire, Anatole France. *The Mysterious Stranger* is the story of Satan's visit to Eseldorf (Assville), a medieval town in Austria. Eseldorf is a miniature of the world, and its inhabitants are a cross section of the human race. Satan in this story is interested neither in helping nor in corrupting humanity. He merely watches our struggle occasionally, as an amused spectator, when he has nothing better to do. When he comes to Eseldorf, he makes himself known to three children—in the eyes of Satan we are *all* children—and for a short time he enables them to see life just as he, in his superior wisdom, sees it. He shows them what an ugly dung-heap we have made out of the beautiful garden into which we have been born. An old priest, Father Peter, is suspended from his church because he dares to assert the doctrine that God is all goodness. What will become of the fear of hell, the inhabitants of Eseldorf ask themselves, if such men are allowed to remain in the pulpit?

And the magistrates of Eseldorf are only too eager to lead the people in their persecution of Father Peter. A priest who maintains that God will not eternally torture the sinners, conclude the magistrates, must be a sinner himself. And so they accuse Father Peter of theft and lock him in a cell to await his trial.

The three boys, who love Father Peter, are aghast at the spectacle of his suffering. But Satan assures them that everything will turn out for the best.

While the priest is awaiting trial, Satan amuses two of the boys by giving them a glimpse into the heart of things. It is not a pretty spectacle. As for the third boy, Satan reserves for him a treat of another sort. He drowns him. This, he explains to the two heartbroken playmates of the dead boy, is the greatest good fortune that can happen to any living creature.

Father Peter is put on trial at last. His chances for acquittal appear to be very slim. For the magistrates have trumped up an airtight case against him. But Satan tells the boys not to worry. "Everything will turn out for the best."

And sure enough, the Devil proves to be as "good" as his word. He not only establishes the innocence of the gentle old priest, but he makes him supremely happy for the rest of his life. The manner in which he brings about Father Peter's happiness is devilishly simple. He brings to the old prisoner in his cell a false report of the verdict. "The trial is over, and you stand forever disgraced as a thief!"

The old man, hearing this, loses his mind and becomes "as happy as a bird." From now on, he imagines that he is the Emperor of the World. He enjoys all the glory, but none of the worry, of an absolute monarch. The friends of Father Peter are struck dumb with horror. But the Devil reassures them. Next to death, he explains, insanity is the greatest gift which the gods can bestow upon mankind. The only way in which they can make a human being supremely happy is to make him supremely mad.

For the world, concludes Mark Twain, is a madhouse, and life is an insane nightmare between a sleep and a sleep. "Strange," he declares, "that you should not have suspected that your universe and its content were only dreams, visions, fiction! Strange, because they are so frankly and hysterically insane—like all dreams: a God who could make good children as easily as bad, yet preferred to make bad ones; who could have made every one of them happy, yet never made a single happy one; who made them prize their bitter life, yet stingily cut it short; who gave his angels eternal happiness unearned, yet required his other children to earn it; who gave his angels painless lives, yet cursed his other children with biting miseries and maladies of mind and body; who mouths justice and invented hell—mouths mercy and invented hell—mouths Golden Rules and forgiveness multiplied by seventy times seven, and invented hell . . . who created man without invitation, then tries to shuffle the responsibility for man's acts upon man . . .

". . . It is true, that which I have revealed to you; there is no universe, no human race, no earthly life, no heaven, no hell. It is all a dream—a grotesque and foolish dream. Nothing exists but you. And you are but a *thought*—a vagrant thought, a useless thought, a homeless thought, wandering forlorn among the empty centuries!"

And then, having at last declared what he sincerely believed, the great sad satirist son of the pioneers passed beyond the frontier and into—who knows?—perhaps a fairer and truer dream.

HARDY

Important Works by Hardy

Desperate Remedies
Under the Greenwood Tree
A Pair of Blue Eyes
Far from the Madding Crowd
The Hand of Ethelberta
The Return of the Native
The Trumpet-Major
A Laodicean
Two on a Tower
The Mayor of Casterbridge

The Woodlanders
Wessex Tales
A Group of Noble Dames
Tess of the D'Urbervilles
Life's Little Ironies
Jude the Obscure
The Well-Beloved
The Dynasts (a dramatic poem)
Several volumes of
   lyric poetry

Thomas Hardy

1840–1928

"M<small>Y DEAR FELLOW</small>," Arnold Bennett is said to have once remarked to Hugh Walpole, "when you're born, you're done for!" This universal truth, spoken in jest, is well illustrated in the life of Thomas Hardy. Born with a frail body, a strong mind and a compassionate soul, Hardy was from the very first "condemned" to a literary career. As a child he loved to watch the maggots in a mud-puddle near his father's house in Dorsetshire. These helpless little creatures "were passing their time in mad carousal . . . wallowing and heaving in the tepid and stringy water of the dried pool . . ." Often he asked himself what was the meaning of all this. As he grew older, he turned his attention to the larger but equally helpless human maggots who wallowed and multiplied and died in the mud-puddle of the earth. And he decided to sit by the roadside and to spend his life in an effort to unravel the meaning of it all.

II

A<small>T HIS BIRTH</small> (June 2, 1840) he was so puny that the doctor pronounced him dead. Thanks to a vigorous slapping from the family nurse, however, he was "called back" to a life that was to last almost ninety years. His father, a building contractor, allowed his "little fellow with the face of an old man" to roam over the heath instead of going to school. "Let him drink in plenty of sunlight. He can absorb his education later on."

The child's earliest schooling, therefore, was in the outdoors. His books were "running brooks." He became familiar with living things through all the five senses. And through a sixth sense—an all-embracing sympathy. He thrilled to the faces and the voices of the animals, the birds, and the trees. "As a child," he wrote in later years, "I learned that every species of tree has its voice as well as its feature. At the passing of the breeze the fir-trees sob and moan no less distinctly than they rock; the holly whistles as it battles with itself; the ash hisses amid its quaverings; the beech rustles while its flat boughs rise and fall."

He felt at one with all nature—a "blood relationship" with the winds and the clouds, the butterflies and the bees, the sparrows and the squirrels and the lambs. In his vivid imagination he frequently tried to identify himself with these external objects and creatures. Once, as a little child, he "became" a sheep. He got down on all fours in a field and began to "eat" grass. When he looked up, he was "quite puzzled"—as he expressed it later— to see the "astonishment" in the eyes of the other sheep at the spectacle of this new addition to their fold.

When he reached his ninth year, his heart had become thoroughly attuned to the heart of Nature. And now began his formal education. His father sent him to "Mr. Last's Academy for Young Gentlemen"—a private school three miles away from the Hardy cottage. Every day, as he walked to and from school, he stopped for a "friendly chat" with his playmates—the wild creatures of Egdon Heath. But he loved especially to watch human faces. As he approached Dorchester, the town in which his school was situated, he had to cross a stone bridge. He would always stop in the middle of the bridge and study the people who passed by. "There are so many interesting stories in human faces."

At school he was the littlest fellow with the biggest head in his class. His teachers were amazed at the rapidity with which he absorbed knowledge. When he graduated at sixteen, he was thoroughly familiar with Latin, French and English literature. Especially with the plays of Shakespeare. He knew them almost by heart.

He was very anxious to go to college—this quiet, studious and sensitive little Jude the Obscure—but his father couldn't afford the luxury. It was high time for the youngster to begin to make his own living. He must be taught a profession or a trade—something easy, so it wouldn't tax his frail and puny body. Music? Tommy was a pretty good fiddler. His father had taught him to play the instrument. But there was no money in that. To be sure, father and son often played at country weddings. But what self-respecting fiddler of Dorsetshire would ever think of charging a fee for *that* friendly service? What else, then, could he try? The ministry? To this, however, there were two objections: the slenderness of his purse and the unimpressiveness of his stature. There was only one thing left, therefore—architecture. The father was a master builder; let the son become a master planner.

And so Thomas Hardy was apprenticed to John Hicks, architect, who had an office in the neighboring town of Dorchester.

But Hardy had no great love for drawing blueprints. The work was too mechanical. He was by nature an artist, not a scientist. Though faithful in his work, he spent all his leisure time in studying and in dreaming. He got up at five in the morning—sometimes even at four—and spent a couple of hours teaching himself to read Greek. Within three years he could "converse" fluently with Aeschylus and with Homer, as well as with the writers of the New Testament.

And during all this time he kept up his familiarity with his favorite language—the universal grammar of Nature. And he translated this grammar into English music. For Thomas Hardy had discovered that he was a poet. "I began to write poetry because I had to, because of orders from within."

Orders from within, but no encouragement from without. "I

sent my verse out; it invariably came back. No editors even touched it for many years." Thomas Hardy was a poor salesman. He was too unaggressive. To the end of his days he was unable to acquire the art of advertising himself. Sir James M. Barrie once remarked: "Whatever angel guards the portals of heaven, he must have had to push Thomas Hardy in." For the present, no angel that guarded the portals of the editorial sanctum was willing to *push* him in, or even to *invite* him in. Year after year he kept offering his pearls—not exactly to the swine, but to editors who took them for baubles of clay.

And, truth to tell, many of Hardy's earlier poems—even some of his later poems—had too great an admixture of clay. Hardy was not a great poet. He had everything necessary for poetic genius—music, imagination, sympathy, a feeling for the apt phrase, a conciseness of thought, a magic "that turned syllables into stars"—everything, in short, except fire. Hardy was aware of that defect in the arsenal of his talents. "I am afraid I shall never be a writer," he said. "I am doomed to the drawing of blueprints for life."

And so he went to London, a full-fledged architect and amateur poet, and secured a job as draftsman in the office of the church designer, Arthur Blomfield. Here he worked for five years —a bearded, pale and quiet little fellow, saying little and absorbing much—"a not unworthy chap, a son of very humble parentage yet a thorough artist . . . He's about six-and-twenty . . . rather untidy in his waistcoat . . . a thorough bookworm . . . knows Shakespeare to the very dregs of the footnotes . . . He will never be successful in a worldly way . . . lacks the earnestness, the energy necessary for making acquaintances, and the love for using them . . ."

This portrait which Hardy drew of Edward Spingrove (a character in *Desperate Remedies*) is a faithful portrait of himself in his later twenties. An unprepossessing and thus far unsuccessful young "country bumpkin"—in his unguarded moments he still spoke in the Dorsetshire idiom—and obscure draftsman whose future appeared far from promising.

Yet this unpromising young draftsman met and wooed and married a girl of a social station superior to his own. He was engaged in restoring the St. Juliot Church at Cornwall—a job for which he had been recommended by his employer, Mr. Blomfield. In the course of his work he had made the acquaintance of Miss Emma Gifford, the sister-in-law of the rector of St. Juliot. Miss Gifford, a descendant of "solicitors and canons and archdeacons," was an expert horsewoman, a competent singer, a fairly good painter, and an all-around snob. "What she has found in me, the son of a poor mason, I cannot tell." But somehow or other he managed to blurt out his proposal; and she, forgetting his shabby overcoat and his unkempt beard, "condescended" to say yes. And thus—"I came back from Lyonnesse (Cornwall) with magic in my eyes!"

A brief delirious honeymoon, and a long life of marital incompatibility. For they never understood each other. Socially and physically they lived at a different pace. She loved to gallop in the saddle, and he preferred to walk—he never learned to ride horseback. Throughout their days together they were unable to keep in step.

III

BUT Hardy never complained. He tried to make a comfortable home for his wife, and to provide for her at least a minimum of the "necessaries" demanded by a woman of her station. While depending upon his architecture for a living, he resorted more and more to his writing as his life's work. At the instigation of Emma, he turned from poetry to prose. "I never wanted to write prose novels at all. I was forced to manufacture them; circumstances"—a euphemism for Emma—"compelled me to turn them out."

And thus some of the greatest love stories in English literature grew out of the nagging of a woman who didn't love her husband.

The novels of Hardy are built largely upon the formula of misdirected love. This formula is humorously described by Christopher Julian in *The Hand of Ethelberta:* "I have learned of one-sided love, and reciprocal love, and all sorts, but this is my first experience of a concatenated affection. You follow me, I follow Ethelberta, and she follows—Heaven knows who!" All life is thus a comedy of errors in the realm of affection. Everybody who is loved, loves somebody else; but it is the curse of all lovers that no two of them ever love each other.

Because of this cynical attitude toward human emotion, Hardy found it difficult at first to make headway either with the publishers or with the critics. His reputation was of a slow growth. It was only after he had published several novels—some of them at his own risk—that the world awoke to the existence of a great gentleness that stemmed out of a great sadness. The two outstanding notes in his novels are irony and pity. The irony of heaven, the pity of man. Some of the critics even within recent days have failed to recognize this double aspect of Hardy's philosophy. "Hardy sees only the ugly side of the world," remarked a recent reviewer. And another reviewer, equally one-sided, observed: "One of Hardy's ancestors must have married a weeping-willow tree." But the majority of the critics today have come to recognize in Hardy a new kind of beauty, "a negative beauty of tragic tone" and at the same time "a positive beauty of tender connotation."

A new beauty, and a new philosophy. A philosophy which is neither optimism nor pessimism, but something in between. Hardy himself called it *meliorism,* an effort to better a world which is pretty bad but which has the possibility of being pretty good. "The business of men is to teach their fellow men how to breast the misery they are born to."

This melioristic theory of *compassion,* of mutual helpfulness out of mutual suffering, was a gradual development in the philosophy of Thomas Hardy. In his earlier novels he shook his fist at the Creator, the impassive and impersonal Prince of the World who cared nothing for His creatures. Later on, he shifted his blame from God to man. The fault, dear Brutus, he might have said with Shakespeare, is not in our stars but in ourselves that we are underlings. "It is not Destiny but your own weakness that is against you—your want of knowledge of a sort which brings wisdom rather than affluence." Still later, he concluded that it was neither the malevolence of God nor the stupidity of the individual man, but the cruelty of man in the mass—that is, of society—that is responsible for most of our human suffering. The older he grew, the more bitter became his quarrel with society for its organized injustice against the individual. In 1928 he wrote a Christmas epigram which summarizes all the bitterness that he felt toward the "incurable savagery" of the human herd:

> *"Peace upon earth!" was said. We sing it,*
> *And pay a million priests to bring it.*
> *After two thousand years of mass*
> *We've got as far as poison gas.*

Hardy was incensed against the murder of human bodies and the murder of human souls. Again and again he returned to this subject in his later novels. The punishment of society for individual error, he declared, was far beyond the bounds of human decency and of human fairness. This thesis, the cardinal principle of his maturer philosophy, finds its most perfect expression in *Tess of the D'Urbervilles.*

Tess is the victim of an inflexible moral law and an inexorable social code. When her father, John Durbeyfield, learns that he, a dissolute vagabond, is descended from the noble family of the D'Urbervilles, he is ready to burst with pride. His wife, Joan, begins to dream of a brilliant match for their daughter, Tess. They therefore prevail upon her to get a job as poultry girl on the farm of the vulgar old Lady D'Urberville.

Here Tess meets the old lady's son, Alec D'Urberville—a handsome and unprincipled young scoundrel. A brief romance, disillusionment, and a child. The child soon dies.

Tess returns home.

It is some time before she finds the courage to face the world again. Finally, however, she accepts a job as dairy maid on the Talbothy farm. Here she makes the acquaintance of Angel Clare. The son of an old clergyman, Angel has—to his father's regret—turned from the shepherding of souls to the cultivation of the soil.

The two young people are drawn closely together. When Angel declares his love, Tess hasn't the courage to reveal her past life. Her dream is too beautiful to be shattered by that ugly monster, the Social Code.

The wedding day approaches. In a moment of honest despair she writes a long letter of confession. She thrusts it under the door. But her hand is guided by the mysterious hand of Fate. The letter slips under the carpet. Just before the wedding she discovers it and tears it up. Her courage for punishment has proved unequal to her hunger for love.

They are married. As they depart from the church, they hear the crowing of a cock—a symbol for the disapproval of society. An ill-timed noise. A cock-crow in the afternoon. An evil omen.

Tess and Angel come to live in a picturesque old farmhouse. Here Angel confesses his one sin—a two days' dissipation with a scarlet woman. He asks for his young wife's forgiveness. This she readily grants, and then she relates the story of her own transgression. But Angel Clare is not so ready to forgive. The double standard of society. A woman must never sin.

There is a separation, and Tess returns home. Her mother takes the matter lightly; but her father's drunken D'Urberville pride is deeply hurt at what he regards as her unforgivable offense.

Tess finds summer work on the farms. A great proportion of her earnings she devotes to the support of her parents. But with the coming of winter she loses most of her work. An occasional drab and difficult and poorly paid job, and then long stretches of hunger and despair. At last she decides to make one desperate attempt to see Angel's parents. Perhaps they will give her news of him. Through the rain and the snow she trudges for many miles—but she finds the vicarage empty.

She turns back. Again there are long days of hunger and of hopeless degradation. Society must take its toll.

Once, as she passes by a barn, she hears a boisterous evangelist. The voice is familiar. She looks inside and recognizes Alec D'Urberville.

Alec pleads with her to return to him. At first she refuses. But her mother's poverty—her father is now dead—compels her finally to yield.

She gives her body to Alec. But her heart is still wandering in search of Angel Clare. And he, too, is now searching for Tess. He is unhappy and ill. His old anger has died down, leaving nothing in its place but a deep longing for his bride.

He finds her in a fashionable boarding house—a degraded woman. The relentlessness of Fate—as exemplified by the Social Code—has so tangled the threads of their lives that they can no longer reach out toward each other. Angel Clare starts on his way home.

On the outskirts of the town she overtakes him. "I have killed him . . . He called you by a foul name . . . I owed it to you . . . It was the only way I could get you back."

Hand in hand they depart from the scene of their suffering. Fate has brought them together at last, but only for a moment of tragic irony. At the dawn of the day she is arrested—note the contrast between the rising of the sun and the setting of her hope. She is tried and found guilty.

Eight strokes of the bell, and a black figure twists convulsively in the air.

Tess has paid her debt to the Social Code.

IV

Upon the publication of *Tess of the D'Urbervilles,* the critics descended upon Hardy like a flock of vultures. "It must be a vile author," was the almost unanimous verdict as summarized in the language of William James, "who could have created so vile a heroine." In the raucous chorus of condemnation it was almost impossible to hear the few small voices of honest praise. This silent minority realized that here at last was an English writer who had dared to make "a plea for charity, for a larger tolerance, for a repudiation of social hypocrisy."

As for Hardy's reaction toward his captious as well as toward his friendly reviewers, he merely shrugged his shoulders and said, "Anyhow, I have put the best of me into this book."

And he put "the best of me" into his next important novel— *Jude the Obscure*—and was repaid with an even greater avalanche of vituperation. "Thomas Hardy," wrote a reviewer in one of the American papers, "has scandalized the critics and shocked his friends . . . Mr. Hardy's mind seems to be groveling all through this story . . . He goes out of his way to be nasty . . . When I finished the story, I opened the window to let in the fresh air." An American professor branded *Jude the Obscure* as "one of the most objectionable books" he had ever read. A British magazine printed a caricature of Hardy depicted as a coarse fat giant trampling a rose into the mud and spattering all the bystanders with a shower of filth. A British lecturer burned the book in public. Mrs. Grundy—whether in petticoats or in pants—was up in arms. Hardy had dared to depict the truth. When parts of the book were published in a magazine, Hardy was compelled to mutilate the characters and the situations into unrecognizable lifelessness. From now on, he was no longer respectable. The editors either refused his stories, or else rewrote them "to suit the sensitiveness of their readers." In one of his stories, as he ruefully remarked to Mrs. Wharton, he had described an innocent walk which his hero and his heroine took on a Sunday. When he submitted the story to a Scottish editor, the scandalized gentleman promptly returned it with the demand that the walk be transferred to a weekday.

Hardy was disgusted. "I thought," he said, "that I was writing for *intelligent* readers." His prose was too strong for the nervous stomachs of the nineteenth century. He decided to return to his poetry. "Nobody will be *hurt* by my poetry, because nobody will *read* it."

He wrote and published eight volumes of lyric poetry, and a dramatic poem on the life of Napoleon—*The Dynasts*. And gradually he regained his lost respectability. Now at last nobody read him and everybody admired him. He drifted serenely into an old age marred only by the loss of his wife. It was a severe blow in spite of their marital differences. "Even a stormy life has its zestful tang."

And after the storm, the calm. He married again; and for once the autumn and the spring—he was 74 and she was 35—combined into the harmony of a perfect union. Though a poet in her own right, the second Mrs. Hardy was—to use her own expression—"content with his reflected glory."

And it was in a glorious and serene sunset that he ended the long day of his life. And he left behind him a sweet memory and a noble thought. As St. John Ervine expressed it in his tribute to Hardy, "We have learned from you that the proud heart can subdue the hardest fate. In all that you have written you have shown the spirit of man persisting through defeat."